DA CAPO PRESS SERIES IN
ARCHITECTURE
AND DECORATIVE ART

General Editor:
ADOLF K. PLACZEK
Avery Librarian, Columbia University

Volume 28

In the Nature of Materials

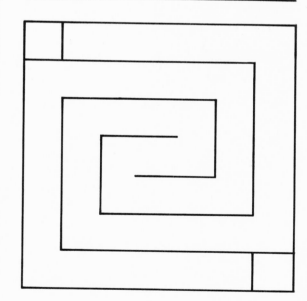

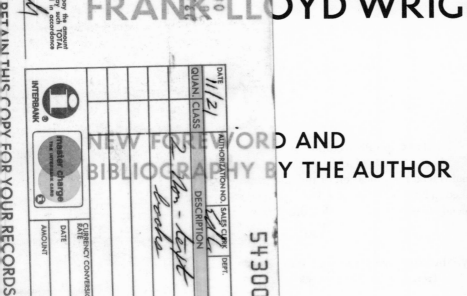

IN THE NATURE OF MATERIALS

1887 – 1941

THE BUILDINGS OF FRANK LLOYD WRIGHT

NEW FOREWORD AND BIBLIOGRAPHY BY THE AUTHOR

DA CAPO PRESS • NEW YORK • 1973

HENRY-RUSSELL HITCHCOCK

Library of Congress Cataloging in Publication Data

Hitchcock, Henry Russell, 1903-

   In the nature of materials, 1887-1941.
   (Da Capo Press series in architecture and decorative
art, v. 28)
   Bibliography: p.
   1. Wright, Frank Lloyd, 1867-1959. I. Title.
NA737.W7H5   1973   720'.92'4   72-75322
ISBN 0-306-71283-0

This Da Capo Press edition of
In the Nature of Materials
is an unabridged republication of the first edition
published in New York in 1942. It is reprinted
by special arrangement with Meredith Press.

Published by Da Capo Press, Inc.
A Subsidiary of Plenum Publishing Corporation
227 West 17th Street, New York, New York 10011

TO

WESLEYAN UNIVERSITY

first American institution

to recognize the genius of

FRANK LLOYD WRIGHT

with academic honors

Contents

TALIESIN WEST, NEAR PHOENIX, ARIZONA, 1938—

Illustrations[1]

Frontispiece: Taliesin West, near Phoenix, Arizona. 1938– . Photo. Guerrero.

---

[1] Figure numbers 227, 270, 272, 306, 319, 326 and 354 are omitted.

49. River Forest Golf Club, Bonnie Brae Ave., River Forest, Ill. [1901]. Perspective from *Ausgeführte Bauten und Entwürfe,* pl. XI.
50. River Forest Golf Club, Bonnie Brae Ave., River Forest, Ill. [1901]. Plan.
51. Edward C. Waller dining room, Auvergne Pl., River Forest, Ill. 1899. Photo. Fuermann.
52. Project: Edward C. Waller house, River Forest, Ill. 1899.
53. Warren Hickox house, 687 South Harrison Ave., Kankakee, Ill. 1900. Photo. Fuermann.
54. Warren Hickox house, 687 South Harrison Ave., Kankakee, Ill. 1900. Plans.
55. B. Harley Bradley house, 701 South Harrison Ave., Kankakee, Ill. 1900.
56. B. Harley Bradley house, 701 South Harrison Ave., Kankakee, Ill. 1900. Plan.
57. B. Harley Bradley house, 701 South Harrison Ave., Kankakee, Ill. 1900. Living room. Photo. Fuermann.
58. Project: "A Home in a Prairie Town" for Curtis Publishing Co. 1900. Perspective from *Ladies' Home Journal,* February, 1901.
59. Project: "A Home in a Prairie Town" for Curtis Publishing Co. 1900. Plans from *Ladies' Home Journal,* February, 1901.
60. Project: "A Home in a Prairie Town" for Curtis Publishing Co. 1900. Section from *Ladies' Home Journal,* February, 1901.
61. Project: "A Small House with 'Lots of Room in It' " for Curtis Publishing Co. 1900. Perspective from *Ladies' Home Journal,* June, 1901.
62. Project: "A Small House with 'Lots of Room in It' " for Curtis Publishing Co. 1900. Plans from *Ladies' Home Journal,* June, 1901.
63. Project: "A Small House with 'Lots of Room in It' " for Curtis Publishing Co. 1900. Sections from *Ladies' Home Journal,* June, 1901.
64. William G. Fricke house, 540 Fair Oaks Ave., Oak Park, Ill. 1902. Photo. Fuermann.
65. Project: "Village Bank in Cast Concrete." For *Brickbuilder,* August, 1901. Perspective from *Ausgeführte Bauten und Entwürfe,* pl. XII.
66. F. B. Henderson house, 301 South Kenilworth Ave., Elmhurst, Ill. 1901. Perspective.
67. F. B. Henderson house, 301 South Kenilworth Ave., Elmhurst, Ill. 1901. Photo. Lane.
68. F. B. Henderson house, 301 South Kenilworth Ave., Elmhurst, Ill. 1901. Plan.
69. Frank Thomas house, 210 Forest Ave., Oak Park, Ill. 1901.
70. Frank Thomas house, 210 Forest Ave., Oak Park, Ill. 1901. Plans.
71. Arthur Heurtley house, 318 Forest Ave., Oak Park, Ill. 1902.
72. Arthur Heurtley house, 318 Forest Ave., Oak Park, Ill. 1902. Plans.

123. Unity Church, Kenilworth Ave. at Lake St., Oak Park, Ill. 1906. Detail. Photo. Willard and Barbara Morgan.
124. P. A. Beachy house, 238 Forest Ave., Oak Park, Ill. 1906.
125. W. R. Heath house, 76 Soldiers Pl., Buffalo, N. Y. 1905. Living room.
126. A. W. Gridley house, North Batavia Ave., Geneva, Ill. 1906.
127. A. W. Gridley house, North Batavia Ave., Geneva, Ill. 1906. Plans.
128. Project: "A Fireproof House for $5000" for the Curtis Publishing Co. 1906. Perspective from the *Ladies' Home Journal,* April, 1907.
129. Project: "A Fireproof House for $5000" for the Curtis Publishing Co. 1906. Plans from the *Ladies' Home Journal,* April, 1907.
130. Stephen M. B. Hunt house, 345 South Seventh Ave., La Grange, Ill. 1907.
131. Project: Warren McArthur concrete apartment house, Kenwood, Chicago, Ill. 1906. Perspective from *Ausgeführte Bauten und Entwürfe,* pl. LIV.
132. Project: Warren McArthur concrete apartment house, Kenwood, Chicago, Ill. 1906. Plan.
133. Larkin Company Pavilion, Jamestown Exposition, Jamestown, Va., 1907. Perspective from *Ausgeführte Bauten und Entwürfe,* pl. XXXVI.
134. Pebbles and Balch decorating shop, 1107 Lake St., Oak Park, Ill. 1907. Photo. courtesy of Grant C. Manson.
135. Burton J. Westcott house, 1340 East High St., Springfield, Ohio, 1907. Photo. Lane.
136. L. K. Horner house, 1331 Sherwin Ave., Chicago, Ill. 1908. Photo. Fuermann.
137. F. F. Tomek house, 150 Nuttall Rd., Riverside, Ill. 1907.
138. F. F. Tomek house, 150 Nuttall Rd., Riverside, Ill. 1907. Plans.
139. Project: Harold McCormick house, Lake Forest, Ill. [1907]. Holograph plan and elevation study.
140. Project: Harold McCormick house, Lake Forest, Ill. [1907]. Perspective of lake front from *Ausgeführte Bauten und Entwürfe,* pl. LIX.
141. Project: Harold McCormick house, Lake Forest, Ill. [1907]. Bird's-eye perspective from land side from *Ausgeführte Bauten und Entwürfe,* pl. LVIII.
142. E. E. Boynton house, 16 East Blvd., Rochester, N. Y. 1908. Photo. Callisen.
143. E. E. Boynton house, 16 East Blvd., Rochester, N. Y. 1908. Plan.
144. Robert W. Evans house, 9914 Longwood Dr., Chicago, Ill. 1908. Photo. Fuermann.
145. Robert W. Evans house, 9914 Longwood Dr., Chicago, Ill. 1908. Dining room. Photo. Fuermann.
146. Robert W. Evans house, 9914 Longwood Dr., Chicago, Ill. 1908. Plan.

196. Midway Gardens, Cottage Grove Ave. at 60th St., Chicago, Ill. 1914. Interior. Photo. Fuermann.
197. Midway Gardens, Cottage Grove Ave. at 60th St., Chicago, Ill. 1914. Dining room furniture.
198. Midway Gardens, Cottage Grove Ave. at 60th St., Chicago, Ill. 1914. Wire furniture.
199. Francis W. Little house, "Northome," R.F.D. 3, Wayzata, Minn. 1913–   .
200. Francis W. Little house, "Northome," R.F.D. 3, Wayzata, Minn. 1913. Plan.
200a. Francis W. Little house, "Northome," R.F.D. 3, Wayzata, Minn. 1913–   . Photo. Hollis.
200b. Francis W. Little house, "Northome," R.F.D. 3, Wayzata, Minn. 1913–   . Living room. Photo. Hollis.
201. Emil Bach house, 7415 Sheridan Rd., Chicago, Ill. 1915. Photo. Lane.
202. Emil Bach house, 7415 Sheridan Rd., Chicago, Ill. 1915. Plans.
203. A. D. German Warehouse, Richland Center, Wis. [1915] (never completed). Photo. Lane.
204. A. D. German Warehouse, Richland Center, Wis. [1915] (never completed). Detail.
205. Project: American System Ready-Cut Duplex Flats. 1915.
206. Project: American System Ready-Cut Duplex Flats. 1915. Plans.
207. Project: American System Ready-Cut Bungalow. 1915.
208. Project: American System Ready-Cut Bungalow. 1915. Plan.
209. Joseph J. Bagley house, Lakeview and Cedar Aves., Grand Beach, Mich. 1916. Photo. Lane.
210. Joseph J. Bagley house, Lakeview and Cedar Aves., Grand Beach, Mich. 1916. Plan.
211. Ernest Vosburgh house, Crescent Rd., Grand Beach, Mich. [1916]. Perspective.
212. Ernest Vosburgh house, Crescent Rd., Grand Beach, Mich. [1916]. Photo. Lane.
213. Ernest Vosburgh house, Crescent Rd., Grand Beach, Mich. [1916]. Plan.
214. Project: Aline Barnsdall Theater, Olive Hill, Sunset Blvd., Los Angeles, Cal. [1920]. Model cut open.
215. Project: Moving picture theater, Ginza, Tokio, 1918. Model.
216. Henry J. Allen house, 255 Roosevelt Blvd., Wichita, Kan. 1917. Garden. Photo. Carlson and Bulla.
217. Henry J. Allen house, 255 Roosevelt Blvd., Wichita, Kan. 1917. Photo. Reed.
218. Henry J. Allen house, 255 Roosevelt Blvd., Wichita, Kan. 1917. Plans.
219. Imperial Hotel, Tokio, Japan, [1916]–1922. Plans.
220. Imperial Hotel, Tokio, Japan, [1916]–1922. Bird's-eye perspective.

385. Sidney Bazett house, 101 Reservoir Rd., Hillsborough, Cal. [1940]. Dining room. Photo. Born.

386. Sidney Bazett house, 101 Reservoir Rd., Hillsborough, Cal. [1940]. View from below. Photo. Born.

387. Sidney Bazett house, 101 Reservoir Rd., Hillsborough, Cal. [1940]. Living room. Photo. Born.

388. Lloyd Lewis house, Little St. Mary's Rd., Libertyville, Ill. 1940. Photo. Hedrich-Blessing.

389. Lloyd Lewis house, Little St. Mary's Rd., Libertyville, Ill. 1940. Plans.

390. Lloyd Lewis house, Little St. Mary's Rd., Libertyville, Ill. 1940. Bedroom wing. Photo. Hedrich-Blessing.

391. Lloyd Lewis house, Little St. Mary's Rd., Libertyville, Ill. 1940. Living Room. Photo. Hedrich-Blessing.

392. Rose Pauson house, Orange Rd., Phoenix, Arizona. 1940. Photo. Guerrero.

393. Rose Pauson house, Orange Rd., Phoenix, Arizona. 1940. Plans.

394. Rose Pauson house, Orange Rd., Phoenix, Arizona. 1940. Living room. Photo. Guerrero.

395. Rose Pauson house, Orange Rd., Phoenix, Arizona. 1940. Photo. Guerrero.

396. John C. Pew house, 3650 Mendota Dr., Shorewood Hills, near Madison, Wis. 1940. Photo. Teske.

397. John C. Pew house, 3650 Mendota Dr., Shorewood Hills, near Madison, Wis. 1940. Fireplace. Photo. Teske.

398. John C. Pew house, 3650 Mendota Dr., Shorewood Hills, near Madison, Wis. 1940. Plans.

399. Charles L. Manson house, 1224 Highland Blvd., Wausau, Wis. 1940. Passage. Photo. Teske.

400. Charles L. Manson house, 1224 Highland Blvd., Wausau, Wis. 1940. Study fireplace. Photo. Teske.

401. Clarence W. Sondern house, 3600 Belleview Ave., Kansas City, Mo. 1940. Photo. Ortho.

402. Clarence W. Sondern house, 3600 Belleview Ave., Kansas City, Mo. 1940. Bedroom. Photo. Ortho.

403. Theodore Baird house, Shays St., Amherst, Mass. 1940.

404. Gregor Affleck house, Bloomfield Hills, Mich. In construction, 1941. Model exhibited at Museum of Modern Art, New York, 1940. Photo. Beinert.

405. Florida Southern College, Lakeland, Fla. Project, 1938; construction, 1940–

Preface

THIS book is intended to be a sort of *ex post facto* catalogue of the exhibition of Frank Lloyd Wright's architecture at the Museum of Modern Art in New York in 1940. It is, however, no more closely linked with the exhibition than was the book, *The Architecture of H. H. Richardson and His Times,* which I prepared together with the Richardson exhibition at the Museum of Modern Art in 1936, or the book and exhibition devoted to *Rhode Island Architecture* which I arranged for the Providence Rhode Island School of Design in 1939. The Wright exhibition at the Museum included many superb models; photographs of several of them are used in this book. Many original renderings shown in the exhibition also appear here. But the plan of the book is somewhat different from that of the exhibition, although the purpose is the same: to display as fully as may be the architectural work and projects of Wright, with particular emphasis on the expression of the "Nature of Materials," the characteristic phrase Wright has selected both for the title of the exhibition and of the book.

Many things are possible in an exhibition that are not possible in a book. All who saw the exhibition will miss the models despite the few fine photographs of them which are included here. But if the pages of a book can hardly give the full value of the original drawings that were shown in the exhibition, there are compensations. The redrawn plans, mostly prepared by the members of the Taliesin Fellowship particularly for this book, should be more legible at small scale to laymen, and the more even distribution of material covering Wright's total production tells more sequentially the story of a half century's achievement.

The text is subsidiary to the plate section. Perhaps the most important part of it, or at least that into which the most work has been put, is the list of executed work and projects. There have been many earlier lists, but none has been so nearly complete or so carefully checked for factual detail, I believe. The introductory text gives a broad historical account of Wright's architecture. This is supplemented by commentary captions on many of the plates. But the generally chronological arrangement of the plates should tell the story, at least to those familiar with Wright's principles, more clearly than verbal explanation.

Had Grant C. Manson's Harvard doctoral dissertation of 1940 covering Wright's work before 1910 been available in published form I should not have given so much space to Wright's architectural background and to the stages by which he came to maturity. But in the absence of any published source in which this early development is covered, it seems important to indicate here Wright's early relation to Richardson and to analyze in some detail his better known but generally somewhat misinterpreted relation to Sullivan.

Frank Lloyd Wright on Architecture, 1941, edited by Frederick Gutheim, republishes much of Wright's prolific writing of the last fifty years. With this material now readily available, I have rarely quoted from it. No paraphrase or summary can do justice to the statements of architectural principles which Wright has continued to make through the years. All will realize that for the fullest understanding of an architect's work, and particularly the work of an architect who is also a brilliant writer, a direct knowledge of his written opinions, his formal and informal statements on his own architecture and on more general problems, is desirable. Similarly I have used only a bare minimum of biographical material.

It is impossible to discuss Wright's architecture without emotion. Those who dislike it, or certain aspects of it, usually dislike it strongly, as Wright would wish them to. Such readers will find this book lacking in objectivity. For I have made no attempt at a cold, semantic precision of statement and I even doubt whether any matter connected with the arts can be profitably discussed without warmly connotative words and phrases. The very selection of illustrative material aims frankly to present the greatness of Wright's architecture in all its variety. It is not generally worth while to study buildings in pictures except for their virtues.

I have had throughout very complete cooperation from Wright and the members of the Taliesin Fellowship, but the book is mine and not his. Doubtless it is a quite different sort of book than he would have prepared himself had he not been busy with the more important work of designing and erecting buildings. The rather complete collection of photographs and plans in whose selection Wright actively participated, together with the perspectives of many important projects, should make it widely useful. There is in existence no other book which pretends to cover the work of Wright with comparable thoroughness.

It seems unnecessary to give a formal bibliography—there is a full list of Wright's own publications in the Gutheim volume. But it may be useful to indicate the chief published sources which give for certain periods, perhaps, a more complete illustrative coverage. First, there are the magazines: the *Inland Architect* for the earliest work in the nineties, the (Boston) *Architectural Review* article of 1900, the *Architectural Record* right through, and the *Architectural Forum* of late years, particularly the first special Wright number of January, 1938, and that about to appear. I have noted in an article in *Parnassus* (December, 1940) a few of the more important European magazine publications.

The basic books on Wright are the two Wasmuth publications, the great portfolio of 1910, including much of the executed work and projects before that date in perspectives and plans, and the smaller book of 1911, with an introduction by C. R. Ashbee, covering the same period and illustrated with photographs and plans. Their confusingly similar

[xxviii]

titles are: *Ausgeführte Bauten und Entwürfe von Frank Lloyd Wright* and *Frank Lloyd Wright Ausgeführte Bauten*. After those, the other two foreign books of great importance are *The Life Work of the Architect Frank Lloyd Wright*, gathering together photographs, plans and perspectives of projects which had appeared in the early and mid-twenties in the Dutch magazine *Wendingen*, and the contemporary German book, *Frank Lloyd Wright*, by H. de Fries, 1926.

The two French books, one issued by *Cahiers d'Art* in 1928, for which I wrote a brief and perhaps rather blind foreword, the other issued by *L'Architecture Vivante* in 1930, both including material which had appeared previously in those magazines, are less important. None of these books is easy to obtain today and I have never seen the Japanese monographs. Thus far the American books, except for the little Museum of Modern Art catalogue of the exhibition of the Kaufmann house in 1938, are barely illustrated at all. But Mr. Manson's unpublished study of the early work is presumably only the first of many detailed works of scholarship which will appear in the near future.

Fortunately the rapid and full publication of Mr. Wright's work in American magazines in the last decade may assure us that in the future illustrations of his new work will generally be made available soon after their completion.

This book will not entirely take the place for the more serious student of the books and magazines that have been listed in the paragraphs above. But as they are practically unobtainable and lacking even in many large libraries, I have not hesitated to duplicate their material. Nor have I felt it worth while to include iconographic notes in the Chronological List of Executed Work and Projects to indicate where illustrations may be found of material not included in the plates. Too much is available only in the original drawings at Taliesin. In general, however, the photographers, of whom the addresses as well as the names are given in the list of acknowledgments, have many negatives of Wright's work over and above those used here, and I myself have photographs of many unpublished drawings.

The book has the advantage of a format designed in all its details by Mr. Wright.

Although this is not a publication of the Museum of Modern Art, I hope it may be worthy of the standard they have established for the books and catalogues issued in connection with other exhibitions, and fit to stand beside my Richardson book, which they published, and Hugh Morrison's *Louis Sullivan*, which they sponsored. For, as everyone knows, Wright forms the third member of the triumvirate, Richardson, Sullivan and Wright, by which American architecture is known throughout the world.

September, 1941   H.-R. H.

Foreword to the Reprint Edition

IN 1940, when the retrospective exhibition of Frank Lloyd Wright's work was held at the Museum of Modern Art in New York (an event to which the preparation of this book was closely related), Wright was still at the opening of his "second career." After the hiatus of the later 1920's and the early '30's, his architectural productivity had revived with startling results in the Kaufmann house (Figs. 320-22) and the Johnson office building (Figs. 329-38), both of 1936, and was continuing to rise through 1940 and '41 while this book was in progress. On page 130, in a footnote at the end of the list of works, it will be noted that ten houses are named as being on the design boards at Taliesin or in construction in October, 1941, a month after the date given for the completion of the book in the original preface. Thirteen works and four projects of the previous year were already included in the list, as well as one project and three more completed works from 1941.

By 1942, however, the United States—incidentally, with Mr. Wright's vociferous disapproval!—had entered World War II. Almost all architectural activity unrelated to the war ceased for three years, and even for a year or two afterwards building activity was slow to recover its prewar momentum. This necessarily caused a break in Wright's second career which began, coincidentally, just after the conclusion of the half-century's production the book had covered. Already in 1943, however, Wright was designing the initial project for the Guggenheim Museum, his only work in New York, made known in 1946 in the form of a model although actually erected much later, over the years 1956-59, in somewhat modified and expanded form.

Fortunately, although no sequential presentation of Wright's work through the last eighteen years of his life existed in print, the postwar American world was fully alive to the interest of his architecture and his personality, and much of his current work was published as soon as it was completed. Interest abroad, moreover, was rising, especially in Italy right after the war, when the Italians returned culturally to the Western World following more than a generation of Fascist isolation.

The book originally contained no formal bibliography; but in the preface, on pages xxx–xxxi, the principal earlier publications—the most important of them (other than Wright's own written works) foreign, and at the time long unavailable—were listed. By 1969, happily, all of these basic portfolios, books, and articles have been brought out anew in near-facsimile reprints. These are listed together with much equally relevant printed material —no less than eight books by Wright himself, especially, which appeared in the 1940's and '50's—in the bibliographical note that follows on pages xxxix–xlv.

Among the minor publications listed there is the article in which the correct date of Wright's birth was finally established. Thus we know that in 1942, when the book appeared, Wright was already seventy-five, even if he had not been (as he always claimed) only twenty when he built his own Oak Park house in 1889. So long a productive career for an artist— seventy years from the construction of that house to his death—is exceptional. Nor, in fact, did his death terminate the roster of his work, for such notable buildings as the Humphreys Theater in Dallas and the Marin County Government Center, among others, were completed only in subsequent years. (A brief account of Wright's later work, quoted from a 1958 text by this writer which was revised in 1968, follows on pages xxxv–xxxviii.)

But the latest work of long-lived artists such as Michelangelo, Titian, or Rembrandt, not to speak of Beethoven, to whom Wright felt a special personal affinity, has generally been recognized as different in kind—different, but not necessarily inferior or superior—to the production of the central decades of their artistic careers. If posterity should arrive at the same critical conclusion with regard to Wright, it may well be that the particular method of chronological organization and the rather even-handed coverage provided—on the whole with Wright's personal approval—in this book for the work from the late 1880's to the early 1940's would not be the most effective. I must leave to another the solution of that problem, emphasizing that no more useful service can be performed for the history of American architecture at the present time than the preparation of such a study (now, in 1972, well under way). Fortunately, *en attendant,* the bibliographical note that follows indicates the wealth of material, theoretical, narrative, and visual, in various languages from Swedish to Spanish as well as in the more usual ones, that is already available. Especially full is the coverage for the special subject of Wright's drawings, predominantly still in the possession of the Taliesin Fellowship.

The original edition of this book remained in print for nearly a quarter century. It is a great gratification to this author—and would, I trust, have been to his subject—that it will once more be available. No author can, without immodesty, suggest that one of his books is a "classic," though statistics of relative longevity may justify the claim that it has become a "standard work." But this author had recurrent evidence from the time he was invited by Mr. Wright to undertake the work that he was, to a degree, writing as a "ghost." (It should be noted that the copyright is in both our names.) I may say, therefore, without excessive pretension that this book, for which Mr. Wright personally oversaw the selection and preparation of all the visual material, passed the wording of even the shortest captions, and established all the details of the exceptional design, can stand beside his *Autobiography* (of which a new edition appeared from the same publishers, in the same series, at the same time) as a second "classic" production of the Master, providing a summary of his work, as he intended it should, by means of an illustrated sequential account, but not, of course, of his ideas and his theories. Those he had preferred to present in his own words, as he continued to do recurrently through the following years. Interested readers can find such material in gratifying quantity for the earlier periods in the third book that appeared in the early 1940's in the same series as *In the Nature of Materials* and the *Autobiography,* the *Anthology* of Wright's writings prepared by Frederick Gutheim, and for the rest of his life in his last books, from *When Democracy Builds* (1945) to *The Living City* (1958), or as excerpted most skillfully by Messrs. Kaufmann and Raeburn in *Writings and Buildings* (1960), a book which happily exists also as a paperback.

It might finally be noted that for this republication of *In the Nature of Materials* it has been possible to remake a considerable proportion of the illustrations from original photographs and redrawn plans in the author's files.

Northampton, Massachusetts   H. R. HITCHCOCK
January, 1969

The Later Work of Frank Lloyd Wright, 1942–1959*

THE Second World War interrupted Wright's career less than the First. Various projects initiated in the war years came to fruition soon after the war was over and gave evidence of the continuing vitality of his powers of invention. The second house for Herbert Jacobs at Middleton in the country west of Madison, Wis., was very different from the Usonian one of 1937. Ever since an unexecuted house project of 1938 Wright had been fascinated by the possibilities of using the circle in planning. While he had tried out the form in the Florida Southern Library before the war, the Jacobs house of 1948 was the first of a series of houses that he built with curved plans. Its two-storey living area bends around a circular sunken garden court with the bedrooms opening off a balcony above. On the other side the house is half buried in the hill-top, above which rise its walls of coursed rubble. A tower-like circular core near one end of the convex side provides a strong vertical accent.

Another house of the post-war years, also based on the circle, is quite different in character. The Sol Friedman house in Pleasantville, N. Y., is roofed with mushroom-like concrete slabs; the two intersecting closed circles of the actual dwelling are balanced at the end of a straight terrace parapet by the open circle of the carport. This was completed in 1949 with battered walls of almost Richardsonian random ashlar masonry below a strip of metal-framed windows. A still later 'house of circles' for his son David J. Wright was built near Phoenix, Ariz., in 1952. This is of concrete blocks and raised off the ground, with the approach up a gently sloping helical ramp to the various curved rooms on the first storey. The circle and the helix appear also in an urban building of these years, the shop for V. C. Morris in Maiden Lane, San Francisco, completed in 1949. Here the street facade is a sheer plane of yellow brick broken only by the entrance, which is a Sullivanian—or Richardsonian—arch like that of the Heurtley house of 1902. Inside, a helical ramp rises around the central circular area beneath a ceiling made of bubble-like elements executed in plastics.

*Reprinted with permission from Henry-Russell Hitchcock, *Architecture: Nineteenth and Twentieth Centuries,* 3d ed. (Harmondsworth, England: Penguin Books Ltd., 1968), pp. 330–332. Copyright © 1958, 1968 Henry-Russell Hitchcock.

A major work of these years, the extension of the Johnson Administration Building in Racine, Wis., also completed in 1949, makes much use of circles also. North of the existing office building Wright surrounded a square court with open carports whose outer walls of solid brickwork shut out the surrounding city; inside these walls are ranged short concrete columns with lily-pad tops like those in the section that he built ten years earlier. In the centre of the 'piazza' thus defined rises a laboratory tower of tree-like structure. The upper floors of this, alternately square with rounded corners and circular, are all cantilevered out from a central cylindrical core which contains the lift and the vertical canalizations. Alternate bands of brickwork and Pyrex tubing, such as were used on the original building, enclose the tower except at ground level; there the space of the court continues under the cantilevered floors above as far as the solid central core.

This relatively modest tower prepared the way for Wright's skyscraper in Bartlesville, Okla., of 1953-5 . . . . Actually this Price Tower, which is partly occupied by offices and partly by flats, is the final realization of a project originally prepared in 1929 for a block of flats for St. Mark's Church in New York. This he had elaborated in the intervening years in projects for blocks of flats in Chicago and for a hotel in Washington.

While Wright was continuing to employ in his houses of the late forties and early fifties a variety of modes of design that go back to the thirties, and also developing at Florida Southern and in Bartlesville ideas dating from his inactive period in the late twenties, he continued to strike out in other directions too. The Neils house at 2801 Burnham Boulevard on Cedar Lake in Minneapolis, Minn., completed in 1951, is all of coloured marble rubble provided by the client; the Walker house at Carmel, Cal., completed in 1952, is a glazed polygonal pavilion overhanging the sea. Where the Prairie Houses of the first decade of Wright's mature career may all seem in retrospect to have come out of the same, or nearly identical, moulds, the many houses designed in his seventies and eighties are notable for the great variety of their siting, their materials, and the geometrical themes of their planning.

Nor was the domestic field anything like the sole area of his activity. In addition to the college buildings, the shop, the skyscraper, and the laboratory that have been mentioned, Wright built during the years 1947-52 a Unitarian church in Madison, Wis., of very original character. The products of his multifarious activity in these years include, moreover, many projects for all sorts of structures, some of which have been completed—notably the Solomon R. Guggenheim Museum in New York. A decade and more of designing and re-designing preceded the initiation of this remarkable helical concrete building in 1956. Of three other late projects, those for an opera-house in Baghdad and for an Arizona state capitol in Phoenix, dating from 1957, are unlikely to be built; but the county buildings for Marin County, Cal., are now well advanced.

In spite of so much late activity, greater than that of his early maturity, in spite (or perhaps, in part, because) of its kaleidoscopic variety, Wright's actual influence was less significant than forty years before; at least it was of a very different order. He still outpaced his juniors both of the next generation and the one after; but few if any were able to follow with any success along the intensely personal paths he opened. Like Perret to the end of his life, Wright continued at ninety to offer an inspiration to all architects, but there has risen no school of imitators to vulgarize his manner as there was long a school of imitators of Perret in France.

Selected Bibliography, 1942–1968 and 1969–1972

1942–1968

Special Numbers of Magazines

Architectural Forum, Vol. 88, No. 1 (January 1948), pp. 65–156; Vol. 94, No. 1 (January 1951), pp. 73–108.

House Beautiful, Vol. 97, No. 11 (November 1955), pp. 233–380 (with bibliography by Bernard Karpel).

Metron, Nos. 41–42 (May–August 1951), pp. 20–108.

Prairie School Review, Vol. 1, No. 3 (1964), pp. 5–7; Vol. 2, No. 3 (1965), pp. 5–19, 23; Vol. 3, No. 3 (1966), pp. 5–23; Vol. 4, No. 3 (1967), pp. 5–29.

Reprints

Ausgeführte Bauten und Entwürfe von Frank Lloyd Wright ("The Wasmuth Portfolio"). Berlin: Wasmuth, 1910. Reprinted as *Buildings Plans and Designs of Frank Lloyd Wright.* New York: Horizon Press, 1963.

Frank Lloyd Wright Ausgeführte Bauten ("The Smaller Wasmuth Book"). Berlin: Wasmuth, 1911. Reprinted as *Frank Lloyd Wright: The Early Work.* New York: Horizon Press, 1968.

"The Life-Work of the American Architect Frank Lloyd Wright, With Contributions by Frank Lloyd Wright. . . ." *Wendingen,* Nos. 3–9 (1925), pp. 1–163. Reprinted as *The Work of Frank Lloyd Wright.* New York: Horizon Press, 1965.

R. C. Spencer, Jr., "The Work of Frank Lloyd Wright." *Architectural Review,* N.S. Vol. II, No. 6 (June 1900), pp. 61–72. Reprinted as *The Work of Frank Lloyd Wright from 1893–1900.* Park Forest, Illinois: Prairie School Press, n.d.

Writings and Buildings [with list of executed works], ed. by Edgar Kaufmann, Jr., and Ben Raeburn. New York: Horizon Press, 1960; paperback, New York: Meridian Books, 1960.

Writings by Frank Lloyd Wright
An American Architecture. New York: Horizon Press, 1955.
An Autobiography. New York: Duell, Sloan & Pearce, 1943.
The Future of Architecture. New York: Horizon Press, 1953; paperback, New York: New American Library, 1963.
Genius and the Mobocracy. New York: Duell, Sloan & Pearce, 1949.
The Living City. New York: Horizon Press, 1958; paperback, New York: New American Library, 1963.
The Natural House. New York: Horizon Press, 1954.
The Story of the Tower. New York: Horizon Press, 1956.
A Testament. New York: Horizon Press, 1957.
When Democracy Builds. Chicago: University of Chicago Press, 1945.

Books on Drawings
Drawings for a Living Architecture. New York: Horizon Press, 1959.
Arthur Drexler, ed., *The Drawings of Frank Lloyd Wright.* New York: Horizon Press, 1962.
Taliesin Drawings: Recent Architecture of Frank Lloyd Wright Selected from his Drawings. New York: Wittenborn, Schultz, 1952.

Studies of Individual Buildings and Projects
Mortimer J. Cohen, *Beth Sholom Synagogue: A Description and Interpretation.* Elkins Park, Pennsylvania: Beth Sholom Synagogue, 1960.
George R. Collins, "Broadacre City: Wright's Utopia Reconsidered." In *Four Great Makers of Modern Architecture.* New York: Columbia University, 1963; reprinted, New York: Da Capo Press, 1970.
Dallas Theater Center. 1959.
[Falling Water] *La "Casa sulla Cascata" 25 anni dopo.* Milan: Etas Kompass, 1962.
"The Frank Lloyd Wright Campus." *Florida Southern College Bulletin,* April 1953.
Grady Gammage Memorial Auditorium. Tempe, Arizona: State University of Arizona, 1964.
Peter Blake, "The Guggenheim: Museum or Monument?" *Architectural Forum,* Vol. 111, No. 6 (December 1959), pp. 86–93, 180, 184.

The Solomon R. Guggenheim Museum. New York: The Solomon R. Guggenheim Foundation and Horizon Press, 1960.

Marin County Civic Center. 1962.

The Midway Gardens, 1914–1929; An Exhibition of the Building. Chicago: University of Chicago Press, 1961.

Historic American Buildings Survey. *The Robie House, Frank Lloyd Wright.* Palos Park, Illinois: Prairie School Press, 1968.

R. F. Johonnot, *The New Edifice of Unity Church* [1906]. Oak Park, Illinois: Unity Church, 1961.

G. Nelson, "Wright's Houses: Two Residences Built by a Great Architect for Himself." *Fortune,* Vol. 34 (August 1946), pp. 116–125.

Biographical Studies

Piero Bargellini, *Libello contra l'architettura organica.* Florence: Vallecchi, 1946.

Peter Blake, *Frank Lloyd Wright, Architecture and Space.* Baltimore: Penguin Books, 1964.

H. Allen Brooks, "Frank Lloyd Wright and the Wasmuth Drawings." *Art Bulletin,* Vol. XLVIII, No. 2 (June 1966), pp. 193–202.

H. Allen Brooks, "Wright, Frank Lloyd. Architect." *Encyclopedia of World Art,* Vol. XIV, cols. 857–869. New York: McGraw-Hill, 1967.

Barry Byrne, "On Frank Lloyd Wright and his Atelier." *Journal of the American Institute of Architects,* Vol. 39, No. 6 (June 1963), pp. 109–112.

Finis Farr, *Frank Lloyd Wright, A Biography.* New York: Charles Scribner's Sons, 1961.

James Marston Fitch, *Architecture and the Esthetics of Plenty.* New York: Columbia University Press, 1961.

James Marston Fitch, "Wright and the Spirit of Democracy." In *Four Great Makers of Modern Architecture.* New York: Columbia University, 1963; reprinted, New York: Da Capo Press, 1970.

Arlesa Forsee, *Frank Lloyd Wright, Rebel in Concrete.* Philadelphia: Macrae-Smith, 1959.

Thomas S. Hines, Jr., "Frank Lloyd Wright—the Madison Years." *Journal of the*

Society of Architectural Historians, Vol. 26, No. 4 (December 1967), pp. 227-233 [reprinted from *The Wisconsin Magazine of History*].

H. R. Hitchcock, "Frank Lloyd Wright, 1867–1967." *Zodiac,* No. 17 (1967); revised version, *Prairie School Review,* Vol. IV, No. 4 (1967), pp. 5–9.

H. R. Hitchcock, "Frank Lloyd Wright and the Academic Tradition of the Early Eighteen-Nineties." *Journal of the Warburg and Courtauld Institutes,* Vol. 7, Nos. 1 and 2 (January–June 1944), pp. 46–63.

H. A. Jacobs, *Frank Lloyd Wright, America's Greatest Architect.* New York: Harcourt, Brace & World, 1965.

Edgar Kaufmann, Jr., "The Fine Arts and Frank Lloyd Wright." In *Four Great Makers of Modern Architecture.* New York: Columbia University, 1963; reprinted, New York, Da Capo Press: 1970.

Grant C. Manson, "Frank Lloyd Wright and the Tall Building." In *Four Great Makers of Modern Architecture.* New York: Columbia University, 1963; reprinted, New York, Da Capo Press: 1970.

Grant C. Manson, *Frank Lloyd Wright to 1910* [with bibliography]. New York: Reinhold Publishing Corporation, 1958.

Doris Ransohoff, *Frank Lloyd Wright, Living Architecture.* New York: Brittania Books, 1962.

Eduardo Sacriste, *"Usonia" Aspectos de la obra de Wright.* Buenos Aires: Ediciones infinito, 1960.

Vincent J. Scully, *Frank Lloyd Wright.* New York: Braziller, 1960.

Vincent J. Scully, "The Heritage of Wright." *Zodiac,* No. 8 (1961), pp. 8–13.

Vincent J. Scully, "Wright vs. the International Style." *Art News,* Vol. 53, No. 1 (March 1954), pp. 32–35; 64–66.

Norris K. Smith, "The Domestic Architecture of Frank Lloyd Wright." In *Four Great Makers of Modern Architecture.* New York: Columbia University, 1963; reprinted, New York: Da Capo Press, 1970.

Norris K. Smith, *Frank Lloyd Wright, A Study in Architectural Content.* Englewood Cliffs, New Jersey: Prentice-Hall, 1966.

C. B. Tröldsson, *Two Standpoints Towards Modern Architecture: Wright and Le Corbusier.* Göteborg, Sweden: Elanders Boktryckeri, 1951.

Dimitri Tselos, "Exotic Influences on Frank Lloyd Wright." *Magazine of Art,* Vol. 47, No. 4 (April 1953), pp. 160–169.

R. C. Twombly, "Frank Lloyd Wright in Spring Green, 1911–1932." *Wisconsin Magazine of History,* Vol. 51, No. 3 (Spring 1968), pp. 200–217.

Bruno Zevi, *Frank Lloyd Wright.* Milan: Il Balcone, 1947; 2nd ed., 1954.

Bruno Zevi, "Frank Lloyd Wright and the Conquest of Space." *Magazine of Art,* Vol. 43, No. 5 (May 1950), pp. 186–191.

Bruno Zevi, *Verso un architettura organica.* Turin: Einaudi, 1945.

Books by Relatives

Maginel Wright Barney, *The Valley of the Godalmighty Joneses.* New York: Appleton-Century-Crofts, 1965.

Iovanna Lloyd Wright, *Architecture: Man in Possession of the Earth.* Garden City, New York: Doubleday & Company, 1962.

John Lloyd Wright, *My Father Who Is on Earth.* New York: G. P. Putnam's Sons, 1946.

Olgivanna Lloyd Wright, *Frank Lloyd Wright: His Life, His Work, His Words* [with complete list of works]. New York: Horizon Press, 1966.

Olgivanna Lloyd Wright, *Our House.* New York: Horizon Press, 1959.

Olgivanna Lloyd Wright, *The Roots of Life.* New York: Horizon Press, 1963.

Olgivanna Lloyd Wright, *The Shining Brow: Frank Lloyd Wright.* New York: Horizon Press, 1960.

Guides

Buildings of Frank Lloyd Wright in Six Middle Western States. Chicago: Art Institute of Chicago, 1954.

Buildings of Frank Lloyd Wright in Seven Middle Western States. Chicago: Art Institute of Chicago, 1963.

A Guide to the Architecture of Frank Lloyd Wright in Oak Park and River Forest, Illinois. Oak Park, Illinois: Oak Park Public Library, 1966.

Architectural guidebooks to cities, states, and regions generally call attention to Frank Lloyd Wright's works.

1969–1972 (Prepared by William G. Foulks, Avery Library)

Special Numbers of Magazines

L'Architettura: cronache e storia, Vol. 15, No. 7 (November 1969), pp. 422–484.

Reprints

Four Great Makers of Modern Architecture: Gropius, Le Corbusier, Mies van der Rohe, Wright. New York: Columbia University, 1963; reprinted, New York: Da Capo Press, 1970.

Frank Lloyd Wright, *Genius and the Mobocracy.* New York: Duell, Sloan & Pearce, 1949; enlarged edition, New York: Horizon Press, 1971.

Frank Lloyd Wright, *An Organic Architecture: the Architecture of Democracy.* London: Lund Humphries, 1939; reprinted, Cambridge, Massachusetts: M.I.T. Press, 1970.

Studies of Individual Buildings and Projects

Carlo Cresti, *Wright: il Museo Guggenheim.* Florence: Sadea/Sansoni, 1970[?].

Frank Lloyd Wright: Kaufmann House, "Fallingwater," Bear Run, Pennsylvania, 1936. Edited and photographed by Yukio Futagawa. Text by Paul Rudolph. Tokyo: A.D.A. Edita, 1970.

Cary James, *The Imperial Hotel: Frank Lloyd Wright and the Architecture of Unity.* Rutland, Vermont: C. E. Tuttle, 1968.

"Pope-Leighey House." *Historic Preservation,* Vol. 21, Nos. 2–3 (April–September 1969), pp. 2–120.

Henry Wright, "Unity Temple Revisited." *Architectural Forum,* Vol. 130, No. 5 (June 1969), pp. 28–37.

Biographical Studies

Reyner Banham, "The Wilderness Years of Frank Lloyd Wright." *Journal of the Royal Institute of British Architects,* Vol. 76, No. 12 (December 1969), pp. 512–519.

Wolfgang Braatz, ed., *Frank Lloyd Wright, humane Architektur.* Gütersloh: Bertelsmann, 1969.

H. Allen Brooks, "Chicago Architecture: Its Debt to the Arts and Crafts." *Journal of the Society of Architectural Historians,* Vol. 30, No. 4 (December 1971), pp. 312–317.

[xliv]

H. Allen Brooks, *The Prairie School: Frank Lloyd Wright and His Midwest Contemporaries*. Toronto: University of Toronto Press, 1972.

Alan Crawford, "Ten Letters from Frank Lloyd Wright to Charles Robert Ashbee." *Architectural History,* Vol. 13 (1970), pp. 64–76.

Leonard K. Eaton, *Two Chicago Architects and Their Clients: Frank Lloyd Wright and Howard Van Doren Shaw*. Cambridge, Massachusetts: M.I.T. Press, 1969.

Wilbert R. Hasbrouck, "The Earliest Work of Frank Lloyd Wright." *Prairie School Review,* Vol. 7, No. 4 (1970), pp. 14–16.

Donald Hoffman, "Frank Lloyd Wright and Viollet-le-Duc." *Journal of the Society of Architectural Historians,* Vol. 28, No. 3 (October 1969), pp. 173–183.

Edgar Kaufmann, Jr., "Frank Lloyd Wright: the Eleventh Decade." *Architectural Forum,* Vol. 130, No. 5 (June 1969), pp. 38–41.

Eileen Michels, "The Early Drawings of Frank Lloyd Wright Reconsidered." *Journal of the Society of Architectural Historians,* Vol. 30, No. 4 (December 1971), pp. 294–303.

James F. O'Gorman, "Henry Hobson Richardson and Frank Lloyd Wright." *Art Quarterly,* Vol. 32, No. 3 (Autumn, 1969), pp. 292–315.

Dimitri Tselos, "Frank Lloyd Wright and World Architecture." *Journal of the Society of Architectural Historans,* Vol. 28, No. 1 (March 1969), pp. 58–72.

Acknowledgments

THIS study of Frank Lloyd Wright's work began with a careful examination of the material sent from Taliesin for the exhibition at the Museum of Modern Art which was made available to me and with a detailed revision of the list of Wright's work prepared at the Museum by Henrietta Calloway. For this major assistance as well as for other continued favours I must first of all thank John McAndrew, then Curator of Architecture at the Museum of Modern Art, and Janet Henrich, Assistant, and now Acting, Curator.

Grant C. Manson of Columbia University very kindly put at my disposal his erudition on the early work of Wright through 1910 in conferences and correspondence. I owe to him also many facts included in the List of Work which come from his Harvard doctoral dissertation deposited in the Widener Library in Cambridge.

Two librarians, Ruth V. Cook of the Harvard Architectural School in Cambridge and Marion Rawls Herzog of the Burnham Library of the Art Institute in Chicago, gave me continuous and important assistance. Indeed, the thorough study of Wright and of his Chicago architectural environment is impossible without using the resources of the Burnham Library.

Much important information on Wright's California work was collected for me by Richard J. Neutra of Los Angeles and Woodbridge Dickinson, Jr., of Pasadena. Joseph Brewer, president of Olivet College in Michigan, tracked down for me many Michigan houses. John F. Kienitz of the University of Wisconsin, has done as much in Wisconsin. I cannot hope to itemize all the others who have kindly replied to my letters about points of detail. For at one time or another I have written to almost all the Wright clients and present owners of Wright houses built since 1911 and the greater number of them, as well as many others, have assisted me with information and in some cases with photographs as well. I hope they will accept this general expression of gratitude.

Credit for photographs is given briefly in the List of Illustrations. A very large number of photographs of the early work come from Henry Fuermann and Sons, 410 N. Michigan Ave., Chicago. Another important group of photographs was taken by Gilman Lane, 825 North Ridgeland Ave., Oak Park, Ill., who has been photographing Wright's work for many years, and who has taken many new photographs particularly for this book. In addition to these two sources, a great many old prints used in the book come from Wright's own files. Unfortunately these often lack the names of the photographers and so it is impossible to give the proper credits. For the further benefit of those who may care to build up their own collections of Wright photographs I list here the full names and addresses of other photographers whose prints have been used.

Art Institute, Chicago, Ill.
Barnum & Barnum, Chicago, Ill.
Jay W. Baxtresser, Albright Art Gallery, Buffalo, N. Y.
John D. Beinert Architectural Forum, New York, N. Y.
Esther Born, 720 Montgomery St., San Francisco, Cal.
S. A. Callisen, University of Rochester, Rochester, N. Y.
Carlson & Bulla, Wichita, Kan.
Chicago Architectural Photographic Company, Chicago, Ill.
Samuel H. Gottscho, 150–35 86th Ave., Jamaica, N. Y.
P. E. Guerrero, 37 N. Mesa Drive, Mesa, Arizona.
Hedrich-Blessing, 723 N. Michigan Ave., Chicago, Ill.
G. E. Kidder Smith, 133 East 62nd St., New York, N. Y.
Thorkel Korling, Racine, Wis.
Leavenworth's, 1315 West Michigan Ave., Lansing, Michigan.
University of Minnesota Photographic Laboratory, Minneapolis, Minn.
W. Albert Martin, 963 E. Colorado St., Pasadena, Cal.
Willard and Barbara Morgan, 100 East 42nd St., New York, N. Y.
Museum of Modern Art, New York, N. Y.
Ortho Photographic Co., 1326 Oak St., Kansas City, Mo.
Roy E. Peterson, Racine, Wis.
Fred H. Reed, Wichita, Kan.
M. D. Ross, Tulane University, New Orleans, La.
Roger Sturtevant, 720 Montgomery St., San Francisco, Cal.
Edmund Teske, 1519 E. 85th St., Chicago, Ill.
Harvey A. Weber, 8827 187th Pl., Hollis, L. I., N. Y.
L. S. Willis, 115 N. 34th St., Philadelphia, Penna.
Bureau of Visual Instruction, University of Wisconsin, Madison, Wis.

Large sections of the text were read in manuscript by Natalie Hoyt and by Professor Hugh Morrison of Dartmouth, who also loaned me many Sullivan photographs. Their comments and suggestions were of great assistance. Nor can I neglect to mention Frances B. von Groschwitz, Ruth B. Hanson and Priscilla Hedge who typed the various drafts of the manuscript.

Many of the illustrations other than photographs come from the Taliesin files, but the greater part of the plans and several of the perspectives were especially redrawn by members of the Taliesin Fellowship for use in this book. The plans of the Blossom and Harlan houses were redrawn by Sebastian J. Passanesi. It is impossible to itemize further the various sorts of cooperation of Mr. Wright and the Taliesin Fellowship. It will be obvious that without their continuous assistance this book would not have been possible. Indeed Mr. Wright's position in relation to the book should be considered almost as much that of co-author as of subject.

PART ONE

1887–1893

I. Chicago Architecture in the Eighties and J. L. Silsbee

FRANK LLOYD WRIGHT left the University of Wisconsin to come to Chicago in the spring of 1887, just as Middle Western leadership in commercial building was being established. Yet it was not the Chicago of the "Commercial Style," of functional masonry buildings and of the new metal skeleton skyscrapers, with which he first had contact.[1]

Since the completion of Trinity Church in Boston in 1877 the leading force in American architecture had been the influence of Richardson. In 1887, the year following Richardson's death, Chicago saw the completion of his masterpiece, the Marshall Field Wholesale Store. At the same time he had been building two houses, the MacVeagh house on the North Side and the Glessner house on the South Side, the latter undoubtedly his finest and most mature masonry mansion. Richardson had no real contact with the remarkable structural and functional developments which were taking place around him, although in a sense the Marshall Field Store was the finest of all Chicago's "elevator buildings." But he set a standard, hitherto unknown in Chicago, of completely mature and integrated fusion of structure and design.

Wright was to be at first, both by innate calling and by force of circumstances, chiefly a domestic architect. Hence his early relation to the widespread influence of Richardson upon American architecture was in the domestic field.

Various and confusing were the architectural enthusiasms of the eighties in domestic design, yet there was generally a real identity of manner behind the nominal eclecticism. Nor was the childish passion for the quaint, the picturesque and the whimsical, whatever its source, necessarily inconsistent with the achievement of much real coherence of design. The best houses were in plan freely functional, if rather cut up; plastic in mass, with richly sensuous surfaces of cobblestones and shingles; and often quite restrained in their use of ornament. Such houses derived their major inspiration from the country and suburban houses of Richardson and it is not unjust to call them Suburban Richardsonian.[2]

In Chicago architectural design had reached a nadir in the early eighties. The commercial architects were technicians first, and little interested in design as such. Yet, because they were using structural innovations for which there existed no apparent architectural

---

[1] The latest and best accounts of these are in Sigfried Giedion, *Space, Time and Architecture,* Cambridge, 1941, Pt. V, and Thomas S. Tallmadge, *Architecture in Old Chicago,* Chicago [c1941] Ch. IV.

[2] For further discussion, see my *Architecture of H. H. Richardson and His Times,* New York, 1936, Ch. XI-XV.

precedent, they soon found their way to a somewhat barren but expressive functionalism. In domestic architecture, however, the same men had neither functional nor structural reasons for refusing to ape Eastern modes. The fussy Queen Anne of New York, and the François Premier, with which Hunt had launched the social career of the Vanderbilts,[3] were the ideal of South Side and North Side alike. The first imitations of Richardson's supposed Romanesque were quite as bad and most domestic work mingled elements from all three sources.

A new day opened when Richardson himself arrived to build two houses as well as the Field Store. But Richardson built no wooden houses in Chicago and his Glessner and MacVeagh houses were in no sense suburban. The more mature and less incoherent picturesque manner, which may be called Suburban Richardsonian, came independently in the mid-eighties and was probably chiefly established in Chicago and its environs by J. L. Silsbee.

Silsbee came of a well-known Salem, Massachusetts, family. Before he settled in Chicago he had practiced in Syracuse, N. Y. His New York State work, in no sense exceptional, is of a confused Queen Anne like that of his Chicago contemporaries. As Silsbee was a Unitarian, it may well have been the commission to build All Souls Church for Jenkin Lloyd Jones, its vigorous pastor and Wright's uncle, which brought him to Chicago about 1885. Curiously enough, All Souls did not follow, even at second or third hand like most churches of the eighties, the model of Richardson's Trinity. Perhaps because Jenkin Lloyd Jones was already developing his ideal of an institutional church, finally realized on the same site in Abraham Lincoln Center almost twenty years later, All Souls had the look of a suburban mansion, varied in mass and materials, domestic in ornamentation, and related more to Richardson's wooden houses than to his masonry monuments.

In 1886, when All Souls was completed, Silsbee also built Unity Chapel in the Helena Valley near Spring Green, Wisconsin, for Jenkin Lloyd Jones and his family. This was a simple shingled edifice, quite unornamented, and with a clarity of form and functionalism of parts far more like Richardson's best late work than All Souls.

At the same time in suburban Edgewater, where he lived himself, he was building many similar houses for J. L. Cochran almost equally free from the elaborate picturesqueness of composition and detail of All Souls. Very soon definitely Colonial elements appear in his work, gambrel roofs, and even the slender white Tuscan columns of his native Salem.

When Wright came to Chicago in the spring of 1887, it was with Silsbee that he first found work, anonymously and without dependence on his family connection, since it was

---

[3] Hunt himself built the François Premier Borden house in Chicago in 1887.

[4]

against his Uncle Jenkin's will that he had left the University of Wisconsin. Wright was already a draftsman of exquisite delicacy and precision. He had then had only two years of professional training in the Engineering School under Dean Conover. As he was also employed in Conover's private office, however, these two years had given him well-rounded introduction to the practice of building. At this time Conover was supervising the Science Building at the University, by H. C. Koch of Milwaukee, and also building the Chemistry Building. The former was a clumsy, though not undignified, monument of red brick and stone of rather rudimentary Richardsonian character; the latter was a structure of the barest functional design in the local yellow brick.

Other aspects of Wright's earlier education may seem now more important. Wide reading in general literature had been encouraged by the Transcendental background of both his parents. His mother had surrounded him in childhood with pictures of great buildings; while his father had nourished his passion for great music. His contact with the artistic content of the Froebel kindergarten method had come well beyond kindergarten age and was, therefore, more formative. Finally, intelligent study of such great nineteenth century architectural books as Ruskin's *Stones of Venice*, and Viollet-le-Duc's *Dictionnaire*, had given him a critical background. Such broad culture was perhaps of little interest to prospective employers.

Not surprisingly the earliest executed work by Wright, the house for his aunts, the Misses Lloyd Jones, at Hillside, Spring Green, Wisconsin, is wholly in Silsbee's manner (Fig. 2). Indeed, it is slightly less advanced and more picturesque than certain Silsbee house projects published in 1887 and 1888 which were drawn but not designed by Wright. It may not be entirely fanciful to see in the wide windows of the house, and even more in certain aspects of a project for a Unitarian Chapel, also published in 1887, early hints of a more personal taste (Fig. 1). But in the house he was probably responding to the family demand for a broader outlook on surrounding nature. And as regards the chapel the polygonal ends may be either a first expression of his later characteristic liking for the octagon, or a mere merging of the ecclesiastical apse with the domestic bay window. Interest in the very first designs of Wright is chiefly historical impertinence. Were we not concerned with his later career, the signature of Silsbee's young draftsman would be effectively anonymous on the designs of 1887, except for the drawing of the plants, at once so exquisite and so vigorous.

Wright's stay with Silsbee was not entirely without consequence, as a relation to Silsbee's work can be traced down through the Bagley house of 1894 (Fig. 30). Justified assurance of ability, however, set Wright seeking new opportunities after a few months. When he was refused a raise in pay by Silsbee, he went to Beers, Clay and Dutton, but soon returned to

[5]

Silsbee, receiving his raise. It was then he settled in suburban Oak Park, the Universalist "Saints' Rest," which he was, in the score of years he lived there, to make an international center of pilgrimage, an Ile-de-France of modern architecture.

But, before the end of the year, he heard of an opening with Adler and Sullivan. With the construction of the Auditorium Building well under way, they were seeking a draftsman capable of detailing its rich interiors. Wright sold himself to Sullivan with the drawings he brought with him. There were drawings in the Silsbee manner and others in the historic styles, based on Owen Jones' *Grammar of Ornament;* there were drawings in Sullivan's own manner, already known as the most individual in Chicago, and even some in a manner "perhaps original." Now Wright's generic apprenticeship could end; henceforth he was for six years, and even longer, the disciple of the "Lieber Meister," as he called Sullivan.

II. Sullivan's Maturity and Wright's Work with Sullivan

AS we mention the great triumvirate of American architects, Richardson, Sullivan, and Wright, we think we understand the links between them, but we often forget certain aspects of the sequence which are implicit in mere chronology. The relation between Sullivan and Richardson is a peculiar one. Sullivan, unlike his Chicago contemporaries, was hardly influenced at all until after Richardson's death, and then in a very limited way. Moreover the influence was soon so completely digested as to be unrecognizable and hence ultimately irrelevant. If we join in imagination Sullivan's earliest work of 1880–1884 with his latest great work of 1898–1899, the line clearly need not have passed through the definitely Richardsonian phase of 1886–1889 at all. Wright's relation to Richardson was at least as close as Sullivan's and more lasting. While Wright's relation to Sullivan was particularly close and also very personal. And Sullivan's influence on Wright even appears to have increased rather than decreased after they separated, at least for a few years.

This influence was probably also mutual. Wright's rapid metamorphosis in five years from the Silsbee imitator who designed the Lloyd Jones house to the authentic and original architect of the Charnley and Harlan houses was undoubtedly due to his association with the "Lieber Meister" in Sullivan's great years after 1887. It is not enough to say merely that Wright went to school to Sullivan with the same assiduity that he had gone to school to Silsbee. The Harlan house (Fig. 21), which he did on his own, and even the Charnley house (Fig. 9), which he did as lieutenant of Sullivan, represent something rather more than a domestic adaptation of Sullivan's skyscraper manner.

Recalling the drawings that Wright had shown Sullivan, a relation to Silsbee is still evident in most of Wright's wooden houses of 1889–1894. Historic detail, based on Owen Jones, or other similar sources, also appears. The drawings in the manner of Sullivan, of course, prepared the way for Wright to become a sort of *alter ego* of the master. But there were also drawings which were "perhaps original"; and original elements are very evidently present in Wright's independent work of these years. His originality should also be traceable in work done for Adler and Sullivan and, as a matter of fact, Wright's hand is generally recognized by students of Sullivan in the houses of which Wright had charge for the firm.[1] I believe it can also be recognized in more important work.

---

[1] See Hugh Morrison, *Louis Sullivan*, New York [c1935], pp. 132–133.

It is not often that a question of counter-influence upon the master arises so early in the career of a disciple, actually some ten years before Wright's own characteristic maturity was achieved. It is not like the question whether one angel's head in a Verrocchio Baptism may be by Leonardo, but more like the problem, lately investigated by Fiske Kimball, as to who in the office force of J. H. Mansart was responsible for the major innovations in French architecture around 1700. If my conclusions are correct, it is possible that Sullivan would never have freed himself entirely from the partly irrelevant influence of Richardson, nor carried the "Commercial Style" to its latest apotheosis in the Carson, Pirie, Scott Building, but for the young Wright's association with him nearly a decade earlier. Such conclusions should in no way reduce our conception of the true genius of Sullivan. For the supreme quality of the Carson, Pirie and Scott Building, erected long after Wright's departure from the office, is, of course, due to Sullivan alone.

The early commercial buildings of Adler and Sullivan were generally smaller and less monumental than those of other leading Chicago architects, but they were much more open in design. In construction, they were Adler's, easily rivalling his contemporaries in bold functionalism, if not in scale. But they were also distinguished, as were the houses designed by the firm in the same years, by the conspicuous ornament, coarse in scale, quite without historic precedent and of a vital if crude originality. To contemporaries, this was Sullivan's great and unique contribution.

Up to 1886 and the designing of the Auditorium Building, Adler and Sullivan's work shows not only less influence from Richardson than the work of other Chicago architects, such as Beman or Burnham and Root, but practically none at all. The other Chicago architects swung gradually through various stages of only partial comprehension into the Richardsonian orbit. But Sullivan was bowled over quite suddenly by the Marshall Field Wholesale Store as it rose in 1886. He grasped by the response of genius to genius much of the secret of Richardson's most mature style all at once.

The Auditorium Building is in its exterior design the child of the Field Store, but it is not its inevitable child. The shift to light-coloured stone and to smooth surfaces above the base was a protest, related to the contemporary Eastern protest, against the antediluvian gloom of the Brown Decades. The light granite of Richardson's Chicago houses and the smooth buff sandstone of his contemporary Warder house in Washington suggest that Richardson himself was ready for such a change. The thinning of the piers, particularly at the corners, the grouping of more storeys under the arches and the greater sharpness of the reveals indicate how far Sullivan had already come toward thinking in terms of isolated piers, how ready he was to design in terms of a sheathed skeleton and not in terms of solid masonry. This can also be paralleled in the Pray Building in Boston, Richardson's last commercial design.

Though the relation of the tower to the main mass is awkward, the tower itself rises above any direct relation to the Marshall Field Store into a new age. Over against the earlier buildings which have technical claims to being the first skyscraper, this tower, though not of skeleton construction, has a claim to be considered the first successful skyscraper design. Doubtless it was the last portion of the exterior to be designed in its present form. The reveals are shallower than below. The small grouped windows of the shaft suggest a continuous pierced screen. The framed colonnade above, behind which were Adler & Sullivan's own offices, provides a more unified horizontal motif than the triplet windows above each bay of the main building. The broad fascia of the terminal band concludes the upward thrust of the tower more harmoniously than the conventional cornice of the main block below. The masonry has the air of a smooth envelope covering a hollow volume. The screen-like window penetrations and the long gallery suggest an interflow of exterior and interior space.

A similar development took place in the handling of the sumptuous decoration of the interior. The somewhat clumsy, coarse quality of the earlier ornament gives way to an almost Byzantine or Southern Romanesque suavity. Above all, the new patterns are more organic, more sensuous, more musical, as if the stiff stalks and circles of the earlier ornament had flowered. Into the dead foliage of the past a new and rather Wagnerian life entered to produce a sort of *Zukunftsschmuck,* premonitory of the European Art Nouveau of the nineties.

The rapid process of creative absorption by which Sullivan learned and passed beyond the lesson of the Field Store must have been effectively complete by the time Wright entered the office. Wright was taken on to assist in the detailing of the interior, not for the large scale tasks of draftsmanship for which others already in the office were more suited. Though Wright was chiefly responsible as draftsman for certain features of the interior, it is unlikely that he made any original artistic contribution. At this time he was, as he has put it, only "the good pencil in the master's hand."

The Walker Warehouse, designed in 1888, confirms and records, less confusingly than the Auditorium, Sullivan's rapid absorption and adaptation of Richardsonian design. The three city houses for Victor Falkenau, of which the published rendering of this year was signed by Wright, indicate how much slower and less creative this absorption was in domestic design. These houses need neither be blamed nor credited to Wright. But in the Pueblo Opera House of 1890 the clean cutting of the windows in the rock-faced masonry and the broad eaves above the top floor gallery seem somewhat unrelated to the course of Sullivan's development. These elements suggest another hand, presumably Wright's. The studiously Romanesque character of the detail is also unlikely from Sullivan's own hand at this date.

For this was the year the Wainwright Building, generally considered Sullivan's masterpiece and certainly his first skyscraper, was designed. This building and the contemporary remodelling of McVicker's Theatre, Sullivan's masterpiece in the field of the ornamented interior, must be wholly his own.

If our eyes are adjusted to the openness of Adler & Sullivan's commercial buildings of the early eighties, to Holabird & Roche's Tacoma Building of 1887, and to Jenney & Mundie's Leiter Building of 1889, we will be surprised, as certain European critics have been, at the definite sacrifices of Adler's sense of function in the Wainwright Building to Sullivan's sense of form. It is hard to understand how this building can so long have been considered the prime illustration of Sullivan's slogan, "form follows function." The Wainwright Building is manifestly, if ambiguously, of skeleton construction and is not at all Richardsonian in design. But it is most remarkable for the quality of "style." Possibly Saint Louis, mellowed beyond the rugged commercial functionalism of its mid-century cast iron, was readier for such work than Chicago, where clients did not as yet expect or want "architecture" in their tall buildings, except as a subsidiary embellishment.

The main divisions of the Wainwright design mark off a base, shaft and cap. The heavy slab cornice represses any tower-like aspirations. The pilaster-like verticals that sheathe the supports are not differentiated from those that are in structural function mere window mullions. These repeated verticals, the continued thickening of the corner members, and the careful restriction of the architecturally scaled ornament to the sunken spandrels, the broad frieze and the capital-like tops of the vertical members, all respect universal traditions of architectural design. "Chicago construction" and the immediate traditions of the Chicago "Commercial Style" were subordinated to a crystalline expression of formal absolutes infinitely more rigid and coherent than in McKim, Mead & White's buildings of this time. Here Sullivan set an architectural standard as high as Richardson's. For Wright, the privilege was to be close to Sullivan as this masterpiece took shape. But there was no chance for delegation, as there may have been with some of the ornamental work on the Auditorium, or with a minor commission like the Pueblo Opera House. To work on the Wainwright drawings was to participate; and by that participation some transfusion of the creative blood stream took place. Henceforth there were two great designers in Adler & Sullivan's office, and we are here interested in the younger one.

Sullivan, within two years of entering the office of D. Adler & Co., was Adler's designing partner. Wright had risen in the office almost as rapidly, but Sullivan needed no designing partner. From 1890 on until Wright left the office there was, however, a division of designing labour. Moreover, the complete freedom which Sullivan gave Wright in domestic commissions—including even his own houses—bore immediate fruit. From 1889, when Wright built his own house in Oak Park, through 1893, when he left Adler & Sullivan's, there are three kinds of products of Wright's architectural brain: the work he did on his own out of office hours—in his terms the "bootlegged" houses; certain commissions of Adler & Sullivan, chiefly houses, in which Sullivan was not interested; and finally a few hotels, sky-scrapers and loft buildings, which Sullivan might well have designed himself, but which were left largely in Wright's hands while Sullivan spent more time in Mississippi. Wright was more intentionally and completely the *alter ego* of Sullivan in such work than in the houses. But at times indications of the creative and individual force of his developing genius seem to cry for a recognition that Wright himself largely withholds.

Wright's own house in Oak Park precedes any commissions with which he was entrusted by Sullivan. But this house properly opens the cycle of his independent work. It will be better to discuss first the Adler & Sullivan commissions, even though these two types of work went on concurrently.

The first houses which fell to Wright's lot to design for Adler and Sullivan were Sulli-van's own summer house at Ocean Springs, Mississippi, with its servants' cottage and stable, and the nearby house and cottage of the James Charnleys who had introduced Sullivan to this distant region. The plan of the Sullivan house as published in the *Architectural Record* in June, 1905, does not correspond with the early photographs that remain. It is hazardous, therefore, to draw many conclusions as to the original form from the present state of these buildings. The authenticity of the stable, demolished only this year, was evident, however. Generically, this is still Suburban Richardsonian, a single storey shingled structure with high roofs and out-curved eaves (Fig. 3). The octagon form of the ends of the Sioux City chapel project appears in the two bays of this stable, the ends of the main house and the picturesque water tower and dovecote (Fig. 4). There was little or no detail on either house or stable, except for the great and inappropriate Richardsonian arch of the stable entrance and its curious cross-shaped windows.

Doubtless the work was unsupervised either by Sullivan or by Wright. The simplicity was partly out of respect to the rustic environment, partly out of regard to the limitations of the local carpenter. We are reminded chiefly of the seaside houses of Richardson and his followers in New England and certainly of no earlier work, domestic or otherwise, from the offices of Adler & Sullivan. The high roof, though not unknown in Sullivan's work of this time, is rare; whereas it is frequent on the early independent houses of Wright. Moreover, the whole air of carefully restrained picturesqueness and domesticity is as foreign to the designer of the Wainwright Building as it would be natural to a graduate of Silsbee's office. It is a pity we cannot speak with more assurance of the plans, but there is no doubt as to the blunt T-shape of the stable and apparently of the house as well, the favorite plan type of most of Wright's early independent houses.

The James Charnley house in Chicago of 1891 is of a very different order than the Ocean Springs cottages. Here there is no trace of Silsbee's left, nor indeed of Richardson, but rather a remarkable parallel to the "style," in the generic sense, of the Wainwright Building. Even in these years, when the example of McKim, Mead & White's reaction against Richardsonian and Queen Anne picturesqueness was leading many American architects to seek severe formality and urbane dignity in city residences, there are few to compare with this. Moreover, there can be no question that although the general direction was Sullivan's, the designing hand here was Wright's (Fig. 9). The thin Roman brick is more elegantly used than it was even by McKim, Mead & White, who introduced it to this country. The light stonework of smooth-cut random ashlar is skilfully treated as a base to the composition, as a link between the projecting end bays, and as an articulated frame for the entrance beneath the delicate balcony. The small attic windows beneath the flat Sullivanian cornice adapt the monumental frieze windows of the skyscrapers to domestic scale. But the large, boldly cut windows below resemble in their shape and their uncompromising directness those of the Pueblo Opera House. The ornamental detail inside and out is Sullivanian, but the refinement of scale is as unerringly that of an urban palazzo as if it were by Peruzzi.

The living room is at one end, the dining room balances it at the other; while the hall in the middle is entered from a stepped entry between two reception nooks and has the main stair in one flight along the rear wall. Such a plan is the most classical refinement of a standard type long in general use for corner houses on narrow city lots. Beside it, Richardson's Trinity Rectory in Boston, technically similar, appears confused and even perverse in its avoidance of the symmetry implicit in the parti.

Unlike the Lloyd Jones house of 1887 (Fig. 2), which is wholly Silsbee without being very good Silsbee though of Wright's technically independent design, the Charnley house because of its high quality must dispute with his own house in Oak Park of 1889 (Fig. 11), and even more with the contemporary Harlan house (Fig. 21), the honor of being Wright's first serious work. His independent practice began two years later with the Winslow house, but the heights which he was destined to attain, if not all his ultimate originality, were already implicit in these houses.

In the next year, however, the house built for Albert Sullivan and occupied immediately by Louis is no great credit to either Wright or Sullivan. But the Victoria Hotel of 1892 (Fig. 10), essentially office work, has markedly Wrightian elements in the clean-cut windows, the projecting ornamental frieze of the top-storey and the panelled treatment of the tower.

The Schiller Building of 1891, an important work of whose drawings Wright certainly had charge, is more essentially Sullivanian. Yet the return to arched bays and the very richly arcaded eaves gallery, both elements omitted in the Wainwright Building, may well be the design of a Wright for the moment *plus royaliste que le roi*. Elements hitherto unknown in Sullivan's work are the coupled windows set flat in the wall screen of the rear section; the crisply panelled bay windows of the side wings; and above all, the motif at the top of the side wing, the little inset balcony subdivided by a central colonette, the germ of a horizontal instead of a vertical sort of skyscraper design (Fig. 5). These are probably Wright's original contribution.

The little balcony motif is of far more consequence than any hypothetically Wrightian elements in the famous Transportation Building at the Fair. In the next year this motif became the essential unit of design in the Meyer Building, of which Wright had general charge of the drawings (Fig. 6). This seven-storey loft building, perhaps hardly a skyscraper despite its skeleton construction, is the first work from the Adler & Sullivan office since 1887 of predominantly horizontal and not vertical design. Its relative unimportance make it plausible that Wright should have had a more completely free hand in its design—a hand freed as much from his own conscientious delight in being "a good pencil in the master's hand," as from any external supervision—than in the Schiller Building. It is in function and in expression far more in the line of the "elevator buildings" and the first skyscrapers by other Chicago architects. And, like even the best of their work, and unlike everything which is authentically Sullivan's, it is also a little dull.

The Stock Exchange Building, designed before Wright left Sullivan but not executed until 1894, is neither so dull nor so sound, but possibly historically even more important (Fig. 7). Despite the vertical lines of its bay windows (themselves very likely a Wrightian motif, as has been suggested for the earlier ones on the side wings of the Schiller Building) this is also a tentatively horizontal expression of skeleton construction.[2] The wide unmullioned window openings are cut crisply in the wall screen, like those on the rear of the Schiller Building, and filled with great fixed center panes with opening ends, the "Chicago Windows" that all the commercial architects were using in the nineties. But there is something about

---

[2] Wright's project of 1896 for an apartment house for Robert Perkins follows the Stock Exchange design very closely, with very similar bay windows.

this building which is unintegrated, as if two personalities who were arriving at a break had worked on it.

What seems significant is that Sullivan's next skyscraper, the Guaranty Building of 1894–5, in Buffalo, perhaps intrinsically a finer work than the Wainwright, grows directly out of the Wainwright and owes nothing to those elements in the Schiller, Meyer and Stock Exchange Buildings which suggest the hand of Wright. On the other hand Wright's Luxfer Prism skyscraper project, designed after he left Sullivan, has a mature type of horizontal screen-wall design toward which those three Adler & Sullivan buildings were leading the way (Fig. 8).

Sullivan's two late masterpieces, the Gage Building of 1898 and even more the Carson, Pirie & Scott Building, begun in 1899[3], seem also the natural sequel to the Schiller, Meyer and Stock Exchange Buildings, rather than to the line that runs from the Auditorium through the Wainwright to the Guaranty. On the other hand, they have an equally obvious relationship to Sullivan's work of the early eighties and of course also to the contemporary work of other Chicago skyscraper architects. Indeed the Gage Building was actually built by Holabird & Roche with only the façade by Sullivan. The contrast of the Gage façade with those to the south, designed at the same time by Holabird & Roche, illustrates beautifully how Sullivan's architectural genius rose out of and soared above the merely competent functionalism of his contemporaries.

---

[3] The original commission for remodelling an earlier building on the site goes back to 1891. There is no way of telling whether there were projects of the intervening years leading up to the executed building. The possibility of an earlier design before 1894 somewhat strengthens my argument.

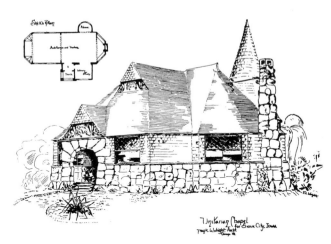

1. PROJECT: UNITARIAN CHAPEL, SIOUX CITY, IOWA. FROM *Inland Architect*, JUNE, 1887.

2. MISSES LLOYD JONES HOUSE, HILLSIDE, SPRING GREEN, WIS. [1887].

Wright's first executed building; designed in the manner of Silsbee.

4. LOUIS SULLIVAN HOUSE, OCEAN SPRINGS, MISS. 1890. (Adler and Sullivan.)

3. LOUIS SULLIVAN STABLE, OCEAN SPRINGS, MISS. 1890. (Adler and Sullivan.)

The first published project, for a chapel, is definitely Suburban Richardsonian in character. This character is still maintained four years later in the Mississippi group designed for Sullivan, but the manner is simpler, more formal and hence more personal.

6. MEYER BUILDING, 307 WEST VAN BUREN ST., CHICAGO, ILL. 1893. (Adler and Sullivan.)

5. SCHILLER BUILDING, 64 WEST RANDOLPH ST., CHICAGO, ILL. 1891–92. (Adler and Sullivan.)

7. STOCK EXCHANGE BUILDING, 30 NORTH LA SALLE ST., CHICAGO, ILL. 1893–94. (Adler and Sullivan.)

On the opposite page are grouped three skyscrapers designed in the Adler and Sullivan office while Wright was there. Supervision of the drawings of the Schiller Building and of the Meyer Building was in Wright's hands. Despite the extremely Sullivanian character of the Schiller Building as a whole, the clean-cutting of the windows in the rear wing and the little horizontal motif above the bay windows on the front appear due to Wright's hand. The horizontal motif with the central colonette becomes the consistent theme of the Meyer Building, whose quality is somewhat denatured by the loss of its heavy but simple ogee cornice. The horizontality of the Meyer Building is partially maintained in the clean-cut "Chicago windows" of the Stock Exchange Building between the projecting bay windows which recall those of the Schiller Building. Designed before Wright left Sullivan, but not executed until 1894, the treatment leads directly to the Luxfer project by Wright where frank expression is given to the cage of the steel skeleton. The Exchange and the Luxfer project also lead to Sullivan's late masterpiece, the Carson, Pirie and Scott Building of 1899.

8. PROJECT: LUXFER PRISM SKYSCRAPER. [1895.]

9. JAMES CHARNLEY HOUSE, 1365 ASTOR ST., CHICAGO, ILL. 1891. (Adler and Sullivan.)

Long recognized to have been designed by Wright. The Charnley house early set a standard of mature achievement.

10. VICTORIA HOTEL, CHICAGO HEIGHTS, ILL. 1892–93. (Adler and Sullivan.)

PART TWO

1889–1900

III. Wright's Independent Work Before 1893

IT is something of a disappointment at first to turn from the exciting question of Wright's possible influence upon his master, or even from the superb urbanity of the Charnley house, which he certainly designed for Sullivan, to the work done by Wright on his own during the years he was with Adler & Sullivan. We are back once more in the world of Silsbee, a suburban world whose physical and economic scale is very different from that of the world of Adler & Sullivan. Something of domestic simplicity and restraint we have noted in the Ocean Springs houses. But it is interesting to see how first in his own house and later in somewhat larger houses, Wright began to move away from the picturesque toward ordered symmetry and even toward academic formality.

The Oak Park neighbors used to ask if Wright's house of 1889 were "Seaside" or "Colonial." In the terms of the time it was both (Fig. 11).

The greater simplicity, clarity and symmetry of the design accord well, for example, with that of McKim, Mead & White's W. G. Low house in Bristol, R. I., of 1887 (designed *after* their academic Colonial H. A. C. Taylor house in Newport). The two bay windows of the front, in one of which is the entrance, are balanced. The wide overhanging gable sweeps down over these bay windows. The extremely compact T-shaped mass is broken only by a simple cross gable at the rear. Such an orderly composition would have appealed more at the time to advanced taste in the East than in Chicago. A long group of windows, with a hint of Palladio in the central lunette, ran across the broad shingled gable. This motif can be matched on James Brown Lord's house of 1886 for Pierre Lorillard at Tuxedo Park, N. Y. Which, of course, is not to say that Wright imitated it from that source, any more than to claim that he emulated consciously other specific Eastern Seaside Colonial houses. The point is that Wright at this point shared in the current development of the Suburban Richardsonian toward clearer and more orderly design, so soon to be obscured in the East by preoccupation with particular historic "forms."

But if Wright's Oak Park house of 1889 can thus in retrospect be floated in the general current of the time, it has also elements which are quite personal to Wright. The extensive terrace at the front, forming in Wright's own image a stylobate, and the almost unbroken roof, with the gable coming forward to crown the bay windows below, provide a sort of domestic analogy to the base, shaft and cap treatment of the Wainwright Building. This terrace is also the earliest instance of Wright's mature practice of relating his houses closely to the earth. The unified roof, subsuming subordinate elements beneath, is the first step toward those hovering planes parallel with the flat prairie which are the hallmark of his best-known later houses.

The widened doorways in the interior appear to be of the type ubiquitous throughout the eighties, but there is a marked and, indeed, a crucial change in their expression (Fig. 13, 14). The door openings have no surrounding architraves. Instead a string course, continued around the room below the cornice and related to the pattern of articulated plaster beams and panels on the ceiling, defines their top; and the walls beneath this string are pulled back, as it were, to form the openings. Because of this device the interior space is really sensed as a unity, as it only appears to be in the ordinary houses of the day when studied in plan.

Otherwise the plan is not extraordinary (Fig. 12). As in many Eastern houses even of the next decade, there is a Queen Anne hall which is a small room, not a mere entry, but filled with rather elaborate stairs. This opens into a larger living room, which in turn opens into a dining room behind, while pantry and kitchen fill out the square. The chimney at the center of the house provides both for the kitchen stove and for a living room fireplace. This fireplace is set in an inglenook in the Queen Anne tradition. But the inglenook is here not so much an atavism as an early hint of the way Wright was going to break up the cubic form of his main rooms in the next decade. Similar plans were used by Wright in the nineties for many houses, even after he left Sullivan, wherever economy demanded compactness.

The increasing use of polygonal forms in the Ocean Springs houses of 1890 as well as a further dramatization of the roof by steepening the pitch and curving out the eaves to emphasize the plane parallel with the earth have been noted (Fig. 3, 4). In the contemporary MacHarg house the most important new element is the continuous line at the second storey sills marked by a change from shingles to clapboards. This line, echoing the horizontals of the stylobate and the eaves and also serving to tie together the second storey windows, was to be almost universally used by Wright from the Winslow house of 1893 onward.

The houses for Thomas H. Gale and R. P. Parker in Oak Park and that for Robert G. Emmond in La Grange, all of 1892, are practically identical in plan, although the Emmond house is much the most elaborate in detail. These houses are unbalanced and quaint as seen from the street, with a single corner tower and high hipped roof, like cottages in a fairy story (Fig. 17). But seen from the side, the composition is symmetrical with the octagonal corner bays rising two full storeys. The separate tower roofs of these bays flank the high main roof which rises from the top of the lower storey. In plan, these houses have three minuscule living rooms on one side, with the usual Queen Anne hall and elaborate stair on the other side in front, and kitchen and pantry at the rear. Such planning is fussy and *retardataire* compared to the fewer and larger rooms of the architect's own Oak Park house (Fig. 18), but the commissions were, in a sense, mere pot-boilers.

These little houses are also, if not fussy, at least rather precious in exterior and interior treatment. Narrow Middle Western clapboards, a sort of wooden equivalent of the elegant Roman brick of the Charnley house, replace the more homely shingles of the Suburban Richardsonian tradition. Whimsical screen-work, rather like that on Stanford White's Newport Casino, decorates the Emmond porch; and there is much intricate leaded glass in the front door and windows.

The Gale and Parker houses are more restrained in detail. But the windows of their octagonal bays form more continuous horizontal bands, intersected only by the corner studs, than on the Emmond house (Fig. 17). These window bands, of course, like the long studio window on his own house, are an early step in Wright's development toward a new and more open expression of wooden construction.

Two other domestic commissions of 1892 are more important. The Warren McArthur house and the George Blossom house stand side by side in Kenwood, one of the South Side suburban villages which, on account of his uncle's church in Oakwood and his wife's family in Hyde Park, were almost as much Wright's home territory in these years as Oak Park. Yet, while the three houses described above are all but identical, it would hardly appear possible that these could be the work of the same architect and certainly not that they were built within the same year. The McArthur house is very similar to the later work of Silsbee as represented by the Arthur Orr house in Evanston of 1888. The Colonial gambrel roof and the front porch with corner arch orders of academic character now seem in retrospect conventional enough, though they were novel in Chicago in the early nineties. There are, however, a few more individual touches to note. The bay windows at the corners, nearly full octagons like those on the Emmond, Gale and Parker houses, are kept under the eaves and the gable as on Wright's own house. The variety of material is interesting, brick to the window sills and plaster above. The heavily moulded arch of the entrance door on the side continues the string at the top of the brick work, a motif elaborated on the Williams house of 1895. This gives a hint of the more individual decoration within and contrasts sharply with the academic detail of the porch.

It is only this porch in all of Wright's work up to this time that prepares us for the character of the Blossom house. The McArthur house repeats on the whole an early stage in the general modulation of the Suburban Richardsonian toward the Colonial Revival. But the Blossom house is an example of the fully academic phase of the Colonial Revival which

[19]

hardly became widespread in the Middle West, or even for that matter in the East, until about 1900 (Fig. 19).

There could be on Wright's part at this time, as never again, an actual choice between possible "styles," motivated by the desire to avoid in his private work the manner associated with Sullivan. It is not necessary to query whether the choice here was the client's, as in the case of the Moore house three years later, or the architect's. In this year 1892, as all Chicago was enthusiastically aware, the majority of the buildings for the World's Fair were being designed in various types of Classical academic style. And, although there were almost no other examples in existence, except McKim, Mead & White's H. A. C. Taylor house in Newport, R. I., earlier than certain of the state buildings at the Fair, such academic formality in domestic design was one possible end point to the later development of the Suburban Richardsonian.

The front and the two sides of this house are coldly symmetrical and more papery in the measured precision of their elegant, narrow clapboarding and thin detail than the H. A. C. Taylor house. But other things are more significant. The conventional low hip roof is now for the first time in Wright's work a single sheltering unit, without cross gables, towers or gambrel breaks, but with wide projecting eaves. Such roofs were to be increasingly Wright's favorites. The refinement and stylization of the Ionic order is quite personal. And by the consistent use of the Palladian motif, in excess of any Colonial precedent, the windows could be grouped in banks of three in every room, in contrast to the single windows of the Charnley house.

In the plan the formality is at its most arbitrary in the front third of the house (Fig. 20). The identical square reception room and library flanking the entrance vestibule have thickened partitions to give depth to the archivolts of the door arches. These arches link the tiny, semi-independent rooms axially together in the Beaux Arts manner. The middle third of the house, however, combines a very large living room (in the modern sense) with a Queen Anne living hall. An elaborate spatial composition of stairs rises in several flights at one end. A wide and rather deep inglenook terminates the axis from the entrance; while a minor cross axis from the library passes through two arches to the dining room at the rear.

This dining room is the finest thing in the house. Its projecting polygonal bay, boldly breaking the symmetry of the rear of the house, reminds us of that of the dining room in Richardson's Glessner house of five years before and leads directly to that of the dining room of Wright's "first" house built for the Winslows in River Forest in the following year (Fig. 26, 28). Moreover, the continuous bank of leaded casements in this bay, by its greater length and the greater number of angles which it crosses, is a more striking example of a horizontal window band than those on the octagons of the little Oak Park houses. It is also closer to the splendid bays in the English work of Norman Shaw's followers in these years.

The arbitrary formal plan of this house does not become an archaeological strait jacket like the revived Colonial plan with central hallway and four roughly equal rooms which McKim, Mead & White had used in the H. A. C. Taylor house. It is hardly more than a geometrical frame which brings order out of the irregular quaintness of the Suburban Richardsonian tradition, and initiates the organic development toward the cross-shaped plans of Wright's Prairie houses after 1900.

The academic design of the exterior is related closely to Wright's only other Classical design, that submitted in competition for the Milwaukee Library and Museum in 1893. That Wright on leaving Sullivan should apparently have gone over to the opposing camp of the World's Fair Classicists is more to be explained by expediency than by conversion. The great colonnaded false façades of the Fair had been received with general acclaim. The Chicago Public Library and the Art Institute, then building by the newly converted heirs of Richardson, the firm of Shepley, Rutan & Coolidge, were both of academic Classical design. Possibly also, there was a style restriction in the programme. For such reasons Wright may well have felt that only an academic Classical design could hope to win. But the extraordinary thing about the façade design of this project—the plans are unfortunately lost—as about the external design of the Blossom house, is that Wright at the first try should have shot so far ahead of his Eastern contemporaries along their chosen line. The general parti is that of Perrault's front of the Louvre, a long colonnade above a plain base, broken with a pedimented pavilion in the center. This is a much more rigid and authentically Classical scheme than the academic Eastern architects were to use for some years yet.

Modern architects, like modern painters, need not regret that among their early works are buildings and projects which are remarkably successful exercises in traditional design. They answer the malicious criticism that the avoidance of conventional modes is due to inability to manipulate them.

The one work of integrated excellence among what Wright has called his "bootlegged" houses—and significantly the one which Wright remembers as having caused the break with Sullivan—is the Allison W. Harlan house in Kenwood (Fig. 21). This we can look at not merely with the analytical eye of historical criticism, but in sincere appreciation of a finished and remarkably perfect work of architecture. Here all traces of the Suburban Richardsonian or the Colonial Revival are gone and the academic virtues of order and balance are directly adapted to functional convenience.

The plan, for all its excellence, is the chief thing that dates the house—there are still too many separate rooms (Fig. 22). But the open vestibule is now pushed to one side, so that the living room, with its range of french doors opening on the raised front terrace, extends almost all the way across the front. The central stair hall, though ample, with the stair at the left leading to a gallery above, is cut off at the right to provide a small library enlarged by a projecting bay window. The dining room and breakfast room extend across the rear in front of the kitchen wing. This plan is formal in its avoidance of loose ends or casual protuberances and in its sense of axes, but free in its adaptation to actual living, without wasting space on areas introduced purely for balance.

In the exterior design there is a similar organic sense of order. The range of piers articulating the front wall, with the open vestibule in the end bay and the french doors of the living room in the others, produces regularity rather than forced symmetry (Fig. 21). Pilaster-like members tie the storeys together at the corners and unify the subdivision of the wall into Roman brickwork below and plaster above, as on the McArthur house. But these pilasters are not the arbitrary coin of academic style, as on the Blossom house. They are quite as organic units of design as the piers between the ground floor windows.

The ground plane of the terrace below is repeated firmly in the broad eaves of the hip roof which now extends well beyond the wall line in a continuous sweep. Under the eave across the front hung—it is now largely destroyed—a light and ornamental balcony. The delicate cusped members of the balcony alone suggest the historic past, and that so distantly and in such an American spirit as to recall more the Carpenter's Gothic "gingerbread" of the mid-century than Late Mediaeval work. It is true that the railings and soffits of this balcony and of the smaller balcony in the middle of the side have patterns, like those on the Charnley balcony, of somewhat Sullivanian character; but their jigsaw quality hardly suggests Sullivan's terra cotta or metal. What is striking about the balconies is the suspended tenuity of their traceried supports, the character of which is repeated in the open screens above the low dormers of the roof. The handling of these balconies foreshadows the way minor breaks in plan, and especially second-storey projections, were to be brought under continuous roof planes in the Prairie houses.

If it seems that the quality of this house is higher than that of the Charnley house (Fig. 9), it may be because Wright was freer here. Certainly of all the almost precisely contemporary works of 1891–92 this is the most mature. Few apprentices can ever have displayed their own mastery so completely before setting up for themselves as Wright does in this house.

IV. The Maturing of Wright

IN the years between 1893, when Wright left Sullivan, and 1900, when in almost all respects his maturity is complete, there are a great number of executed works and projects. They need not all be discussed with the same detail as those in the last section. Most of the wooden houses are unimportant, as well as the various remodellings, now that larger commissions were coming his way. Many projects and several executed works suggest alternative developments which were not to be pursued now that the lines leading toward the mature Prairie houses began to converge. The commissions of this period fall into two groups. Those of the mid-nineties are already relatively more coherent in character than what preceded. In those from 1897 on, the speed of development increases, until a "style" finally appears by 1900 as sure, as complete, as original, as that of Sullivan in the Wainwright Building, yet with a far greater breadth of immanent possibilities.

The Winslow house has often seemed very Sullivanian. But in the light of the work of Wright done in Sullivan's office and on his own in the preceding years it should be evident that it is not, except in certain very minor details of foliage ornament. The plan is much more academic than that of the Harlan house or even the Blossom house (Fig. 26). Indeed, with its central chimney, it bears a certain resemblance to the early Colonial "five-room" plan and yet it already offers a hint of the later articulated T and X-shaped plans. The number of rooms is reduced, despite the relatively great size and cost of the house. Although the entrance hall seems unnecessarily ample, the stair is no longer a conspicuous and space-consuming feature as in the earlier houses. The living room is enlarged to fill one end of the block, quite as so many Eastern architects were to do in adapting the late Colonial plan in this decade and the next. The dining room, essentially a repetition of that of the Blossom house, is moved to the center of the rear, so that in plan a main axis of extension is strongly felt. The covered porch is brought within the main block of the house. In the project, though not in execution, it is also connected by a covered gallery with a free-standing octagonal pavilion. This pavilion was to balance the axially placed port-cochère on the other side.

In this almost country location on a part of Edward C. Waller's large River Forest estate, there is less of a base than at the Harlan house, but the double entrance path in front with its central panel establishes a formal plane upon which the house rests. The broadly extended hip roof, like that of the Harlan house, hovers over the whole front and the horizontal line is repeated once more at the sill of the second-storey windows (Fig. 25). The composition of the ground storey is quite like that of the Charnley house, with the broad windows cleanly cut in the Roman brickwork and the entrance motif in stone broadened to enclose two small windows on either side of the door. This stone framework is unified by a band of ornament around the whole motif, which then passes across the bottom and up over the door exactly as on Adler and Sullivan's Wainwright Tomb.[1] On the upper storey the projecting moulded frieze in which the windows are set repeats almost identically, though with more refined execution, that of the Victoria Hotel of the previous year (Fig. 10).

There are no elements of academic detail here. But when Daniel Burnham, shortly after the completion of the Winslow house, with the Blossom house and the Milwaukee Library and Museum project in mind, met Wright at the Wallers' across the way, he tried to persuade the younger man to go to the Beaux Arts in Paris at his expense and return to be his designing partner. The gesture was not a fantastic one. Burnham correctly realized that at this moment Wright was the best, if not the only, academic designer in Chicago. If anyone in Chicago were to develop brilliantly and solidly the new academic classicism, to which the World's Fair had given a tremendous impetus, it might have been Wright, as the designing partner of Burnham. But Burnham had to go his way with the assistance of decreasingly talented designers. Wright also went his way, because he already knew that architecture could not be split between designers and "practical men." Indeed, he must have seen even at Adler & Sullivan's, so much less of a "plan factory" than Burnham's office, the dangers of a division in architectural responsibility. Up to this time, and working in close relation to the virtuoso Sullivan, Wright had been more precocious as a designer than as a constructor, but henceforth he was determined to be both. His earliest training, after all, was as an engineer.

The rear of the Winslow house could never be mistaken for an academic design. There the picturesque still rules. But despite a certain fussiness in details, such as the leaded bays let into the tower, the asymmetry is compactly organized into an abstract composition of voids and solids, verticals and horizontals, oblongs and polygons. This is extraordinarily full of implications altogether richer and more creative than the dignified serenity of the front (Fig. 28).

Among the later wooden houses the Frederick Bagley house in Hinsdale, built just after the Winslow house, deserves mention. It is one of the last of Wright's essays in the Suburban Richardsonian and the best. Yet it is not for its gambrel roof and stylized Ionic columns that it is notable; but for the compact asymmetry of the plan, with its fine inglenook richly lined

---

[1] For the composition of the Tomb Wright was responsible, although its ornament, so different from the discreet lozenge pattern here, is a particular triumph of Sullivan's virtuosity.

with polished slabs of red marble, and the charm of the detached octagonal library with its band of high windows, an enclosed version of the projected octagonal pavilion of the Winslow house. Here for the last time is a house by Wright which might have seemed to Eastern contemporaries conventionally up-to-date, neither exotic in its originality, nor *retardataire* in its refusal to use a "correct" sort of detail (Fig. 30).

The excellence of the Roloson row houses of 1894 was of a sort better understood in the nineties than today (Fig. 23). Such superb brickwork has almost been forgotten; and the high gables and the grouping of the mullioned windows suggest at first glance an intention of Late Gothic style, actually very subtly avoided. Although such city house commissions have rarely been sympathetic to Wright or even come his way, he handled these four, both as regards ingenuity of planning and quiet dignity of façade design, with a suavity urban-minded Easterners like McKim, Mead and White rarely achieved, even with all the academic past to draw on (Fig. 24). In addition to the splendidly articulated stone framework of the grouped windows, so much more abstract than Late Gothic in character, the rich panels of rather Flamboyant foliate ornament should be noticed. It is as if once he left Sullivan Wright felt freer to develop his own considerable virtuosity at Sullivanian ornament.

The Roloson houses are not really at all Late Gothic, but at the specific insistence of the client, the half-timbered Moore house in Oak Park of 1895 was (Fig. 32). The remarkable thing, however, as in the case of the Blossom house, is not that Wright was willing to depart from the line of what his uncle Jenkin Lloyd Jones called his "Oscar Wilde houses," but that having done so, the result should be on its own terms so excellent. In solid structural scale, in the avoidance of confused picturesqueness, in the regularity of the fenestration, and in the sense of craftsmanship, the exterior of this house is closer to actual Tudor work than the more pictorially archaeological half-timbered houses built in the East in the nineties. Yet the large piazza Americanizes the type clearly and frankly.

Also of 1895 are Wright's first multiple dwellings, the Francis Apartments on Forestville Avenue on the South Side and Francisco Terrace to the west of the Loop. The Francis Apartments have always been considered very Sullivanian (Fig. 31). But the bay windows in Adler & Sullivan's work were very possibly, as has been said, of Wright's design; and the suave, urbane use of grey Roman brick and terra cotta was by this time more characteristic of Wright than of Sullivan. Terra cotta has never been a favorite material of Wright's because of its lack of an organic form-giving character. But it was superbly suited to Sullivan's sensuous ornament, and it is not surprising that the ornament here, though more restrained within a geometrical grid, is very much like Sullivan's.

These medium-sized apartments are sensibly but not very originally planned. The lower-cost flats at Francisco Terrace and in the contiguous block on Walnut Street are more ingenious (Fig. 35, 36). The court of the Terrace is closed off from the street, unlike most of such terraces in Chicago, with open stairs in the corners and outside entrances to the second-storey flats from a continuous balcony (Fig. 34). So shabby has this become, in a neighborhood blighted by semi-industrial zoning, that it is hard to imagine it with planting in the court and flower boxes along the balcony, as Spencer described it in 1900 when it was known as "Honymoon Terrace" (Fig. 33).

The problem of the desirable amenities of low-cost housing will not be solved by architectural means alone; planting and upkeep are more important than at higher economic levels and lie perhaps beyond the power of the architect to control. But this early low-cost project by one who has been accused of having no "sociological" interests foreshadows certain aspects of the best Dutch public housing after the last war.

The Williams house of 1895 is in certain respects *retardataire*, reminding us of the high-roofed houses of the opening nineties, but it is the perfection of its type (Fig. 29). The high roof has sharply projecting eaves with slots over some of the windows to let the light through. The half octagons of the dining room and library are completely integrated into the general plastic mass, while the original dormers repeated firmly the horizontal line of base, brick dado and eave, against the dominating vertical of the superb chimney. The plan is freer than that of the other houses of the mid-nineties, and the large living room extends most of the way across the back, opening on a garden terrace.

The Roman brick below the window sills is extended to the rear with pierced patterns to form an open terrace parapet. The band of plaster above is broken by the delicately leaded windows which surround the semi-octagonal bays. The entrance repeats the McArthur house motif of an arch rising out of the dado string-course. The artfully naturalistic arrangement of the boulders at the base ties the more finished materials of the architecture in with the rougher stone of the entrance terrace. This use of rough stone suggests for the first time the influence of Japanese art.

The Ho Ho Den, the Japanese Pavilion at the World's Fair, had had, contrary to generally accepted theory, almost no immediate effect on Wright. But the subtle and functionally expressive asymmetry, the particular sort of naturalism of Oriental art, as he imbibed it from Japanese wood-block prints, was to have almost as powerful an effect over the years on Wright as it had had on the European painting of the Impressionists and the Post-Impressionists since the sixties.

Wright's own studio, contiguous to his Oak Park house, breaks wholly and all but finally with the picturesque tradition of the Williams house (Fig. 39, 40). The functional asymmetry is now much more formal. The interplay of planes, building up from parapet and terrace to the different levels of the articulated mass, expresses a new and wholly personal sort of order. This can be read more clearly in the plans and drawings than in the actual building which is of necessity rather jammed in between the street and the pre-existing house (Fig. 38, 41).

Ceiling grilles for overhead light, still somewhat Sullivan-like in their curved though geometrical tracery, had first appeared in the dining room and the playroom added to the house just before this (Fig. 15, 16). But in the large octagon and square grille which forms practically the entire ceiling of the drafting room, itself an octagon rising out of a square in three dimensions, we see for the first time the mature results of that training in pattern-making with geometrical elements which Wright had received from the Froebel kindergarten method fifteen years and more earlier.

Henceforth—and this differentiates Wright as much from Sullivan as from the later "international" functionalists—there is for Wright *no* dichotomy between architecture and ornament, between structure and design, between the whole and its parts. A large-scale project of 1895 for an amusement park illustrates even more vividly than the studio, particularly in its present remodelled form, the integration that was taking place. This large-scale plan is not asymmetrical, like that of the studio, but wholly in the brilliant academic tradition of Root's World's Fair plan, which Wright so much admired (Fig. 37). In the parts, particularly the tall finials with their banners, there is an extraordinarily festive spirit. Throughout the separate edifices a profusion of cross-shaped hip roofs and cantilevered balconies make of the total design a large-scale plastic architectural pattern. The temporary release from the restrictions of designing medium-sized houses for prairie towns, to which he was soon to return with final mature force, seems to have set free his imagination.

The McAfee project of the mid-nineties is in some ways more interesting than any executed house of these years. The use of polygonal forms is more integral. The organization of the rooms is articulated in a plan one room thick. A cross arm appears in the stair wing. The interior space was considered as a whole and only partially broken between the main rooms by columns, wall-spurs, and screens. Such new elements were gradually realized in the executed works of 1896–99, the George Furbeck house, the Heller house and the Husser house (Fig. 46). The Aline Devin project, for a lakeside house with its living quarters raised off the ground, also led the way to the Husser house.

The Heller house of 1897 has superb grey and buff Roman brickwork and an unusually lush moulded frieze in which the nudes of Richard Bock particularize surprisingly the generic Sullivanian sensuality (Fig. 43). But the important thing to observe is the plan. Though restricted by the deep narrow lot, the cross-shaped main rooms reach out toward one another

(Fig. 44). Neat enclosure and interlocking of parts within a predetermined oblong or L or T-shape had been at its most compact in the small Peter Goan house of 1894 and the Goodrich house of 1896. Now there is an expansion from within. The space of the rooms seems to break out of the long oblong mass into a cross axis at the dining room bay and into a similar subordinate mass, echoing the main mass, at the front living room bay. Henceforth the new plan schemes, based on a new relation of interior volumes, and the exterior mass compositions are the inevitable counterpart of one another.

Similar ideas appear in rather less happy form in the Rollin Furbeck house of 1898. The most remarkable feature is the way a cross-shaped mass seems, more definitely than at the Heller house, to rise in the third storey out of the oblong mass below. And this plastic articulation is carried much further in the Waller project of 1899, particularly in the open pavilion (Fig. 52).

The one-room-thick plan of the Heller house is in the Husser house of 1899 extended to a cross shape. A staircase wing like that in the McAfee plan projects on the land side. The dining room bay, like that of the Blossom house, projects on the other side toward the lake. All the reception rooms of the raised main floor open into one another with only the slightest subdivision by columns and screens (Fig. 46).

The moulded ornament of the Husser eaves galleries is the last example of such sensuous ornament which Wright was to use and surprisingly like that at the top of the Schiller Building of six years earlier. But the gold mosaic panel surrounding the fireplace with its lovely flat patterns of rather naturalistic hollyhocks, copied five years later in the Martin house, breathes a new and more Japanese spirit. (Fig. 45).

The interiors of this house are apparently gone beyond recall, but good photographs exist of the dining room added by Wright in 1899 to the Edward C. Waller house in River Forest. Here the great picture window at the far end, rising above the characteristic wooden string course which defines the line of the door tops, and the articulation of the other windows in groups illustrate in surprisingly developed form Wright's new conception of interior space. The room is no more enclosed within a single box, with holes cut through its walls. Rather it exists within a complex of intersecting lines at right angles in three dimensions, its space spreading out through the interstices of this framework into subsidiary areas and even into the out-of-doors. The room is, as it were, plaided with intersecting, overlapping and crossing volumes. A horizontal column of space, determined by the area of the great end window, may be conceived as beginning out-of-doors and extending down the long axis of the room. This column of space interpenetrates the wider main space of the room, lying below the horizontal string course, and also rises above it to the full height of the ceiling.

A cluster of bands of space seem to shoot across between the mullions of the grouped side windows and below the string course at one end of the room; while at the other a broad cross space, like a transept, terminates the movement in that direction (Fig. 51).

Such space composition is not immaterial, purely geometrical, abstracted in terms of line and plane in three dimensions, like the space compositions of the "international" architects of the twenties. It is material and kinaesthetic. Indeed, if you are tall enough, the difference between a high space and a low space may be materialized for you in a bump on the brow. And throughout the linear elements are thickened and solidified so that they have structural significance.

The executed houses of the late nineties, the related projects, and the Waller interiors, were expensive. But two buildings of these years show how the stimulus of economy led to structural innovation; and how structural innovation led to new types of expression, elemental in their means, yet rich in plastic interest, without the conventional luxury of "fine" materials or of moulded ornament. These buildings were the windmill and water tower built for his aunts at Hillside in 1896 and the River Forest Golf Club of 1898.

In the water tower Wright was primarily an engineer, offering his solution in opposition to a conventional open metal tower. Time has established his claim that his tower would last longer, thus far about twice as long, as the supposedly "practical" commercial product. He seemed to understand empirically the nature of wood. The bracing floors every ten feet within the lozenge were like the braced articulation of a hollow plant stem, so that the tower was in a real sense like a product of nature (Fig. 42). In the clutch of lozenge and octagon, symbolically that of Romeo and Juliet, he found structural justification for his favorite plan forms. The tower remains for Wright, as for most visitors to Taliesin, a beacon pointing toward that ultimate marriage of engineering and architecture which we find in Wright's major works of the twentieth century, from the Larkin Building to the Johnson Building, from the Imperial Hotel to the Kaufmann house.

The original covering of the water tower was of shingles in the Suburban Richardsonian tradition, but with the shingles banded to give bolder scale and more rugged character. On the River Forest Golf Club shingles give place to siding with projecting horizontal battens. Such a treatment was sturdier and more integral to the structure than a covering of shingles nailed to the surface. The siding exploited both economically and artistically the intrinsic qualities—the fibrous texture, the long lengths, the particular thickness—of wood as processed by the sawmill.

The front wing of the Golf Club was erected first. Subsequently the whole was completed and then exhibited and published in 1900. Further additions, amounting to a

[29]

complete rebuilding of the rear and larger portion, were carried out later. All the essential innovations appear in the first version as published in 1900, and most of them in the original front wing, presumably of 1898. The original plan can best be described as a sort of basilica of which the front wing constituted the "nave," with the "transepts" providing separate dressing accommodations for men and women, and a large "apse" at the rear containing the half circular dining room. The cross plan is thus much further developed than in the contemporary Husser house (Fig. 47, 48).

Since the arms of the cross are of different heights, the Golf Club also provides the equivalent in exterior mass composition of the plaiding of interior space in the Waller dining room. But to speak of mass is false. For this exterior is more a composition of inter-penetrating spaces. The open porches at the front and at the wing ends extend the interior space out into nature. The continuous bands of windows in the upper wall permit exterior and interior space to flow through the wall. The continuous modular stud-skeleton of the light wooden construction is revealed in the window mullions, while the sturdy structural lines of the horizontal siding and its battens cross in front of the vertical lines of the stud-mullions (Fig. 49, 50).

Above, the low hipped roof with its continuous eaves protects the rows of windows and the porches with equal thoroughness. At once hovering and sheltering, the roof defines the shape of the total covered space, which is larger and differently shaped from the interior space actually enclosed by the walls. The chimney is neither obscured and apologized for, as on the Charnley house, nor yet given picturesque emphasis, as in the case of the fine chimney on the Williams house. It provides a solid core of masonry to anchor the building to the ground and also the pivot of the whole composition at the crossing of the axes. It is the point of absolute mass about which are organized all the varieties of more or less open interior and exterior space.

In a more vital sense than the Winslow house of 1893 the River Forest Golf Club represents the beginning of a new architecture. It is not a mere Opus 1, but a First Symphony. If the essential character of its construction and design, so closely integrated as to be inseparable, can be understood, almost all the work of the first decade of Wright's maturity will fall into place.

The work of 1900 leads directly into what has been considered Wright's classic period, the period of the "Prairie" houses, as christened by Wright in this year. But the houses of 1900, and even a few works of the next year or two, still have transitional elements and this moment of crystallization merits separate consideration. The houses and house projects of 1900 group themselves into three pairs: the Bradley and Hickox houses in Kankakee; the

Pitkin and Wallis summer camps; and the two designs prepared for the Curtis Publishing Company and published in the *Ladies' Home Journal* in February and June, 1901.

Publication thus made available at once the first fruits of Wright's maturity to a wide general public, had they cared to profit from the opportunity. At the same time Robert C. Spencer's appreciative and well-illustrated article in the *Architectural Review* of 1900 made clear the stages by which this maturity had been reached.

Before analyzing the work of 1900, it may be well to indicate how the Chicago architectural scene had developed since the eighties. The commercial architects had continued on the whole in the way they had started. But by 1900 the Chicago chapter in the history of the skyscraper was almost over, the New York chapter hardly yet properly begun. The last great monuments were Sullivan's Gage Building and his Carson, Pirie, Scott Building of 1898 and 1899, his swan-song and the swan-song of an era. After this Sullivan fades gradually from the picture, his bolt shot after a decade of intense if not profuse creative activity.

Of the old lights of the late eighties, the young men of promise when Wright had come to Chicago, only Pond continued on his fitful and ambiguous way. But a new group was appearing, many of them sharers of Wright's new quarters in Steinway Hall. Of them for a few years much was to be heard. This new "Chicago School," quite different from that of the eighties, owes its impetus partly to Wright and partly to the tradition of Sullivan. It produced few strong personalities and its best work has a certain anonymity. Eventually its members either left architecture altogether or turned to a tasteful traditionalism. Foreign visitors like the English Ashbee and the Dutch Berlage and the German Kuno Francke saw before 1910 that Chicago architecture had come to its full fruition in the mature work of Wright, and in the years after 1900 in that work almost alone.

The small Hickox house was built, together with the larger but less mature Bradley house, at the south end of Harrison Avenue on the river at Kankakee, Illinois. The plan of the house is a blunt T set sideways to the street like the Emmond and Gale houses (Fig. 18). But the suggestion of four arms forming a cross is very strong because of the terrace projecting in front of the living room and the central gable above. As in the little houses of 1892 the garden front is quite formally symmetrical, but the other sides of the house are functionally asymmetrical. The house is slightly more commodious than the Emmond and Gale houses, with larger rooms and a little reception nook, in Wright's phrase of these years, a "social office." But the chief difference is the way in which the three little boxes of the 1892 houses have been expanded and opened up into a square central living room and two large half-octagonal bays. Subdivision is barely suggested, the whole forming one apartment which occupies most of the ground floor of the house. The living room opens on the terrace through full-length glass doors, while high bands of windows are carried around the bayed ends of the dining room and the music room (Fig. 54). As in the River Forest Golf Club the chimney with its fireplace forms the vertical core of the house, though the cross axis here passes to the front of it. The upstairs plan is compact and avoids as far as possible the awkwardness of walls cut by slanting roofs. It is in the plan that there is the least change between this house and its wholly mature twin, the Henderson house of the next year (Fig. 68).

The use of materials at first sight may seem less expressive than in the Golf Club. But this is not altogether the case. We have only to compare it with any of the wooden houses of the previous decade to see how successfully the light wooden stripping of the exterior plaster covering ties the windows into the composition. By suggesting the studs beneath, this treatment negates any feeling that the windows are mere holes in a solid wall. This is surely a most valid expression of American wooden construction, despite the resemblances to half timber which some critics see. A more probable relation is to the flat panels of Japanese architecture (Fig. 53). The emphasis on the gabled roofs, with their tapered points modifying the perspective, gives a curious suggestion of the oriental isometric and may well also be Japanese in inspiration.

The asymmetrical façade toward the street is as perfectly organized, as formal and anti-picturesque, as the symmetrical façade toward the garden. This indicates how little value these terms, symmetrical versus asymmetrical, formal versus picturesque, have in relation to Wright's mature work. He had now learned from Japanese prints—rather than from Japanese architecture—the secret of occult balance which had meant so much to the great European painters Degas and Toulouse-Lautrec.

The larger Bradley house next door is less developed in plan than the Hickox house. The living room opens out into subsidiary spaces, lower than the main portion, but the dining room is more or less separate (Fig. 56). However, a covered porch on one end and a porte-cochère on the other extend the side arms of the cross plan. A two-storey bay in the middle of the front gable not only brings plentiful light into the living room and the main bedroom above, but forms a strong vertical accent in the center (Fig. 55). The construction and the design motifs are similar to those of the Hickox house, but there is more geometrical virtuosity in the design of the leaded glass. All the furniture of the interior was especially designed to harmonize with and complete the house (Fig. 57).

These houses are not quite masterpieces, like their immediate successors, but they come very close, closer by far than the summer cottages in the woods for the Pitkins in Ontario and the Goodsmiths in Wisconsin. Discussion of the way in which the general formula of the

Golf Club was directly adapted to domestic use, first in summer camps and then in suburban houses, can well await more mature examples.

That the Curtis Publishing Company should have commissioned from Wright three houses, two in 1900 and a third in 1906, indicates how the architectural division between the East and the Middle and Far West at the opening of the century has been exaggerated in retrospect. The Eastern lay public, if not the ringleaders of the profession, amid their enthusiasms for Colonial furniture and foreign knickknacks, still had an eye out for novelties. This the American version of the English *Studio* and Stickley's *Craftsman* make plain, as well as the immense amount of Stickley's "Mission" furniture absorbed in these years even in the East. The *House Beautiful* was published in these years in Chicago by friends of Wright and several times illustrated his work among the Chippendale chairs and the Art Nouveau bric-a-brac. We know that little except the ephemera of this interest in creative innovation took root. *But Wright's work was not unknown in the East in the early years of the twentieth century;* and Messrs. Curtis and Bok may well have expected as widespread and visible results from their sponsorship of Wright's domestic architecture as from their famous later and more concerted campaign for traditional "taste." Among the bungaloid types we vaguely dismiss as "Craftsman," from their most enthusiastic and energetic purveyor, there are traces in the East, as well as in the Middle and the Far West, of the influence of Wright in these years, spread probably via the *Ladies' Home Journal*.

The first *Ladies' Home Journal* house, "A Home in a Prairie Town" designed in 1900, is in conception not unlike the Hickox house. But in the more thoroughgoing development of that conception, rather than because of the name under which it was published, it may be considered the first Prairie house. No house of equal maturity was, however, executed until the following year. In plan both elements of the T are prolonged (Fig. 59). Furthermore, the covered porch in front of the living room extends the T into a cross. The eaves run through along the side of the house at the top of the first storey. The T of the second-storey plan rises above, its cross bar lengthened by the cantilevered oblong bays at the ends. These bays are almost as open as the porte-cochère and porch at the ends of the stem of the T in the storey below. Beneath the eaves of the first and second storey the windows are grouped as in the Golf Club, though not quite so continuously (Fig. 58). And as in the Golf Club the chimney rising above the low-hipped roof forms the solid core and anchor of the whole composition. Even more remarkable, because not prefigured in the Golf Club and not actually carried out till near the end of the decade, is the way in which the central portion of the living space is carried up for two full storeys, thus receiving light above the porch roof. Communication is maintained by a gallery at the second-storey level across the chimney breast (Fig. 60). Thus the interior space flowed vertically as well as horizontally. But the published plans also suggest the more economical alternative of placing two bedrooms in this central portion of the second storey.

The external treatment of the plastered walls is somewhat less "Japanese" and more masonry-like than in the Hickox and Bradley houses. But the description of the interior recommends and the sections illustrate the stained sand plaster and the flat stripping of natural soft wood which are henceforth to provide the characteristic treatment of interiors. The image of the Prairie house was now essentially complete and all its varieties of the next ten years may be seen to derive from this. No executed Prairie house is identical, but almost all have points of plan, of mass composition and of exterior treatment in common.

Wright's first general planning scheme, the "Quadruple Block Plan," for a new type of block subdivision neither romantically confused in the tradition of Olmsted's naturalism, nor a mere imposition of equal narrow lots on the helpless soil of the prairie was published with the first *Ladies' Home Journal* house. The house, in other words, was not just one house, it was a unit in a middle-class suburban scheme. As in the case of the low-cost housing of Francisco Terrace, so soon to be amplified in the Lexington Terrace project of 1901 and later years, Wright's interest went wherever possible beyond the unit of the individual building. It was not his lack of interest, but society's lack of response that restricted his early development as a "sociological" architect.

The second *Ladies' Home Journal* house also designed in 1900, "A Small House with 'Lots of Room in It'," is intended for clients with less money. It is somewhat looser, though possibly more strikingly novel in its asymmetrical cross plan. It is also closer to the slightly "Japanese" expression of the Kankakee houses in its low projecting gables and wood-stripped exterior walls (Fig. 61). The way in which the chief rooms are connected at the interior corner of the cross, both having fireplaces in the same central chimney stack, was a more widely acceptable, and possibly more practical arrangement than the radical running together of the rooms in a single apartment in the Hickox house and the first *Ladies' Home Journal* house (Fig. 62, 63). It was, moreover, rather more frequently used in the next decade, even in houses which in appearance seem closer to the other model. To the eyes of the mid-twentieth century the open terraces of this project, like those at Wright's own Oak Park house and at the Harlan house, seem to provide freer access to the grounds, if less complete spatial extension of the interior, than do covered porches. But the latter were more practical in the Middle West, for they could be and usually are screened—alas, with a considerable loss of their value as voids in the composition.

In the case of this house, as of the first for the *Ladies' Home Journal,* we may feel assured that had it been built the following year, with the slight changes that adaptation to a specific family and a specific site that execution would have entailed, it would have entered as surely into the canon of early masterworks as any that exist. But there are several works and projects of the next year or two which in one way or another still seem "early" in character, for instance, the Fricke house, of which the building permit is dated 1902. Its height and its lack of the new clarity of cross-shaped plan and mass recall the last stage before the Prairie houses as illustrated in the Eckart-Waller projects of 1899. The solid masonry-like treatment of the plaster walls and the Sullivanian framing and columnar mullions of the triple windows are also surprising in 1902. Yet this house has often been published as if it were a characteristic example of the new Prairie type. Such things help to explain certain aspects of Wright's influence in Europe (Fig. 64).

The "Village Bank" in cast concrete, published in the *Brickbuilder* in August, 1901, may have been designed a year or two earlier (Fig. 65). But the relatively rich and naturalistic ornamentation can be matched on the elevation drawings for Lexington Terrace in its first form, which are dated 1901. Its chief significance is as an indication of Wright's early interest in a new material, of which his Unity Church of 1906 was to be the first American masterpiece.

The elaboration of the Fred B. Jones house at Delavan Lake and the markedly Japanese character of the boathouse, even in the drawings dated 1901, is partly due to the early date. For at least the house itself was certainly designed somewhat earlier. But the exceptional and uncanonical character of the executed work is more due to the fact that it was unsupervised. It is not worthwhile puzzling over the *retardataire* ambiguities of the Hills remodelled house in Oak Park, designed in 1900, but possibly not carried out for several years. So great is the profusion of riches of the years 1901-1910 that the problem is how to group them so that in stressing the existence of types and classes no single masterpiece is neglected.

PART THREE

1901–1910

V. The Prairie Houses

WE think properly of Prairie houses and not of a Prairie style, not only because the concept of closed style is false to the first principles of Wright's approach to architecture, but because there is no necessary relationship to the prairie in the Hillside Home School of 1902, the Larkin Building of 1904, or even in the Unity Church of 1906 and the City National Bank of 1909, to mention some of the chief examples of non-domestic work of this decade.

The Prairie houses might be grouped in various ways, by plan, by size and cost, by location, by materials, or even by roof types. But basic to Wright's architecture are his feeling for the nature of materials and his relation to the natural environment. Had he worked at first in the East or in the Far West instead of on the prairie his first mature houses would have been not Prairie houses, but "Seaside" houses, or "Desert" houses. Even in this period his "Forest" houses, some of them built in the wooded suburbs of the North Shore as well as on the lakes of Wisconsin and Michigan, rival those of the more strictly Prairie type.

We may, therefore, consider first the masonry houses, almost all on prairie sites of more or less open character, and then the wooden houses of two sorts, the typical suburban ones with plaster surfaces and the more rustic ones covered with wood siding. The brick houses are mostly large, and several of the finest of them such as the Heurtley house are unique.

The brick Heurtley house of 1902, on suburban Forest Avenue in Oak Park, is of about the same size as the best houses and projects of the late nineties. As in some of them the living floor is raised above a high basement. The plan is roughly a square which is defined by the plane of the eaves of the hip roof above (Fig. 72). But as the upper storey porch off the living room introduces a large void within the solid cube, while several small triangular bays break out of the square to the edge of the eaves, there is no feeling of restriction. In the interior the living room and dining room form a continuous L-shaped space, barely broken by a screen of columns and flowing as well into the hall.

The great entrance arch with its long voussoirs and the projecting bands of the rich orange brickwork have a solid and even Richardsonian air (Fig. 71). Projecting piers flank the playroom windows below the living room. The entrance terrace, with its triangular end and open slots in the brick parapet, lightens and loosens, however, the solidity of the basement storey. And the screen-like treatment of the walls above, with their windows separated

[39]

only by heavy wooden mullions, is even more open. The terms symmetry and asymmetry, have ceased to have any real meaning at this stage of Wright's work, but it is worth pointing out that the general form of this house is both abstract and formal, while the way the interior is subdivided and the plastic accents of the exterior are placed is unusually free and functional.

The marvelous placing of the Japanese cherry by the entrance, and the great old oaks, which gave Oak Park and Forest Avenue their names, provide all the landscape effect. For grass and trees are now the chief ingredients of Wright's settings. The herbaceous border which obscures the base line in the renderings of the *Ladies' Home Journal* houses has been given up. The only additional planting would have been flowers and hanging plants, particularly the latter, in the superb vases at the entrance and in the flower boxes at the top of the piers and along the porch parapet. This architecture was to be seen in relation to natural surroundings of its own scale, the grass of the prairie plain, and the towering forest trees or strategically placed exotic ones. But flowers and small-scale plants were to be used on the exterior as inside the rooms, in vases and boxes, a minor, almost feminine, touch replacing the rich plastic ornamentation on the houses of the late nineties.

The only rival among the masonry houses to the early Heurtley house is also unique, the Robie house of 1909. Here the living quarters are also raised off the ground, but the living room and dining room now lie in a continuous line, like the public rooms of an ocean liner, partially separated by the chimney and stairs, and opening at the ends and all along the side onto continuous balconies like nautical decks (Fig. 164, 165). In the third storey above; a cross element appears leading back to a service wing at the rear of the narrow corner lot. This house, with its hovering lines of balconies and hipped roofs is almost as suggestive of an airplane as the more dramatically located Gilmore house in Madison of the previous year, which is called the "Airplane House" (Fig. 157). Thus, it is more exciting than the Heurtley house, though perhaps intrinsically no finer.

The brick work is smoother, more like machine work, the lines are crisper, and the dependence upon the setting is less. There is also more provision made for plants in long boxes on the outside of the structure, as if the house were a great ship carrying the world of nature, as well as the world of abstract space, into the urban commonplaceness of Hyde Park.

The interiors have all Wright's original furniture and even his minor fittings, and retain, with the piety of a museum, the full character of his interiors of these years. Doubtless the wood has darkened, and the walls have lost some of their freshness of texture and color, but in no other early house is the ensemble more complete (Fig. 166).

In the Dana house in Springfield, Illinois, of 1903, Wright was somewhat restricted in plan by the necessity of building around an earlier house. There were several rooms, however, which, for the first time in Wright's executed work, rose two full storeys (Fig. 86). The slanting planes of the gable roofs bring out a main cross form and tie together the many subsidiary parts (Fig. 88). A patterned wall below the eaves, a more mature variant of the Winslow house frieze, fills in the considerable blank spaces between the upper windows above the marked line of the second-storey sills. Pier-like projections flank the wing ends under the gables (Fig. 85). But the house is empty and neglected now and it is hard to respond to what it must once have been when the gaiety of its unusually rich decorative accessories was supported externally and internally by a profusion of flowers and plants (Fig. 87).

The empty Martin house in Buffalo of 1904, on the other hand, is obscured today by too lush a growth of planting riotously rising out of the bands of masonry prepared for more discreet foliage and flowers. With the darkening of the interior woodwork and walls, and above all of the ceilings and eave soffits, the interiors have become rather dreary. The glint of the gold mosaic around the living room fireplace and of the decorative leaded patterns in the windows gives a hint of the brilliance and richness that was once there (Fig. 104). Of the interiors only the kitchen with its lighter woodwork and its profusion of white tile retains to the full its original quality.

This is the largest and most ambitious expression of the T plan. The long axis parallel with Jewett Parkway begins with the open porte-cochère at one end and terminates with the open porch outside the living room at the other. The cross axis at the porch end rises two storeys, as does most of the shank of the T (Fig. 101, 102). Beneath the lower eaves and again beneath the upper eaves on front and rear are almost continuous rows of windows separated by masonry mullions. At the ends of the cross wing a bay below and a balcony above project as far as the edge of the eaves overhead. The rhythms are stopped at the corners rather more subtly than on the Dana house by pairs of piers at right angles. The hip roof is broken by two broad low chimneys suggesting the direction of the two main axes. The adjuncts to this house, the gallery at the rear leading to the conservatory, the conservatory itself, and the large garage with living accommodations above, as well as the little Barton house to the rear, are all interesting (Fig. 103).

The Martin house represents externally a magnificent extension and confirmation of the compositional possibilities of the Prairie house, but in so large a house, the type of planning originated for a rather different scale of life was not at its best (Fig. 100). Eventually in the Harold McCormick project and the Coonley house Wright worked out a pavilioned sort of plan more suitable to such large houses. But three smaller masonry houses of 1903, 1904, and 1905, the Little house in Peoria (Fig. 89), the Cheney house in Oak Park (Fig. 105) and the Heath house in Buffalo represent more effectively the more normal Prairie house in masonry. The Little house and the Heath house, set on rather narrow corner lots, extend their plans chiefly in a single axis, although the later Clarke addition to the Little house developed somewhat the cross axis (Fig. 91). But the disposition and interrelation of the rooms is a clear adaptation of the T and cross plan about a central chimney (Fig. 92). This elongated plan type is found also in such wood and plaster versions as the Mary M. W. Adams house or the superb Boynton house (Fig. 143).

The Cheney house is square in plan and raised over a high basement (Fig. 107). The basement provides a well-lighted suite of rooms at the rear and also dark cellars under the raised terrace at the front. The extension of the base by this terrace and by the approaches on either side makes a splendid stylobate. The calm unbroken square of the wide-eaved hip roof leading up to the central chimney shelters a plan in which the continuous flow of the main living area across the front is backed by rooms which fill out the square behind an interior passage. The resultant classic serenity is of almost temple-like character, surprising in a house of medium size (Fig. 105, 106).

Masonry plays some part in several other houses and projects. The large and elaborately formal Shaw project for Westmount, Montreal, for example, is interesting in section, as it rises against the hillside, and also distinguished in its elegant use of random ashlar. But it is too complex in its axial treatment, so that the scheme came to more satisfactory development in the Tokio Embassy project of 1914, whose public character and larger size better justified the almost French monumentality. In the Beachy house in Oak Park of 1906, brick piers are used as supports for a generally projecting upper storey of wood and plaster (Fig. 124). The Beachy plan is somewhat effected, like that of the Dana house, by the incorporation of an earlier house. In general such combinations of masonry elements with wood and plaster, although suggested in several projects, and somewhat more broadly used on the Irving house of 1910, did not really come to fruition until the building of Taliesin in 1911.

The fullest range of Wright's genius in these years is undoubtedly to be found in the plastered wooden houses. The Henderson house of 1901 is the first great example, perhaps; but in this the modification of the expression of the Hickox house by greater horizontality of treatment, particularly in the substitution of hip roofs for the gables, is so obvious as to require no discussion (Fig. 66, 67, 68). And despite the excellence of its L-shaped plan the Thomas house, also of 1901, looks backward more than forward (Fig. 69, 70).

The masterpieces begin with 1902, the year of the Heurtley house. The brick houses stand chiefly in rather closely built suburban settings, but the Willitts house has a site in a grove at Highland Park, Illinois. The grove has been thinned enough to let light into the house, and a smooth lawn marks the ground plane instead of the rough forest floor, otherwise the natural setting is unchanged. Particularly delightful is the pattern of the vertical tree trunks against the long horizontal lines of the house and of the lawn (Fig. 73).

The plan is a broadly articulated cross, a superb development of the possibilities of the Bradley house (Fig. 74). The space of the rooms connects at the center of the cross, as was first suggested in the second *Ladies' Home Journal* house (Fig. 62) and executed in the plan of the Thomas house (Fig. 70). The long low hip roof extends from the porte-cochère at the right, penetrating the two-storey central wing, across the front of the dining room to the left to hover over the porch at that end. A two-storey cross-shaped block, its eaves set back a little from the line of the eaves below, rises above this long sweep. The porte-cochère leads through the somewhat exiguous front doorway into the entrance hall and reception nook. The interior space, partially broken by screens at the fireplace, flows on into the living room extending at right angles toward the street (Fig. 75). Then, continuing straight across in front of the fireplace, but once more cut by a screen, the interior space flows on into the dining room, beyond which lies the covered porch at the end of the further wing. The ample services occupy the rear wing and thus connect with the entrance hall as well as with the dining room. Upstairs the rooms are efficiently organized in a smaller cross.

The plaster surfaces are very evidently a continuous skin over an articulated structure, without suggestion of masonry solidity. The restrained wooden stripping no longer recalls half-timber. But it serves to tie the windows into the composition. And their size and grouping, with wooden mullions which are manifestly a mere sheathing of structural studs, expresses as clearly as in the best Late Gothic half-timber design, but with a purely American lightness and tensility, the underlying wooden skeleton. Similar sand-finished plaster, stained with colour, and similar plain wooden stripping relate the interiors closely to the exterior expression. The delicate ornaments of nature, hanging plants and flowers, grow out of the podium of the house itself or hang down from window boxes or urns.

A whole group of cross-shaped houses are clearly the progeny of the Willitts house, although they vary in the disposition of the rooms within the cross, in their adaptation to different sites and above all in size and complexity. The Evans house of 1908 makes a particularly vivid impression because of the way it crowns a gently rising slope with urn-topped pylons to terminate the side wings (Fig. 144, 145, 146). But the complimentary masterpiece is the small Isabel Roberts house, also of 1908. In this the living room at the front rises two storeys, with the interior balcony proposed for the first *Ladies' Home Journal* house, and a superb two-storey bay nearly the width of the front wing (Fig. 154, 155, 156). Even the later substitution of brick veneer for plaster has hardly damaged the perfection of the house. The similar but less delicate Steffens house of 1909, now sadly blighted, suggests how effectively this type could crown a rise, like the ampler Evans house. The perspective, published in the Wasmuth portfolio as of the Roberts house, but actually of the Melson project for Iowa City, shows the unexpected drama of these supposedly quintessentially Prairie houses when their two-storey bays rise above a ravine.

Other more dramatic possibilities of steep sites above water for these wingèd—and indeed almost wingèd—houses are to be found in the Johnson house at Delavan Lake and the Scudder project for one of the islands at the Sault—although both are of wood siding. But the masterpiece is the Hardy house of 1905 in Racine. Here the main wing with the dining room below and two-storey living room above projects out and also cascades down toward the lake. Yet it is also tied to the steep slope by anchoring terrace walls and pylons on either side (Fig. 112, 113, 114).

Some mention has been made of the wood and plaster houses designed like the Little and Heath houses for narrow sites or at least upon oblong rather than more articulated plans. Of these the Sutton house of 1907, among others, is balanced in design. The Boynton house of 1908 is not. But its unusually large window areas and forceful vertical accents, like the two storey stair window bay on one side, are more interesting and quite as perfectly integrated (Fig. 142, 143).

Three other types deserve particular mention. The fundamentally square houses have virtues of compactness and ingenuity, even though they are sometimes rather dull and formal, like the Hoyt and Hunt houses. Then there are those which might be called T or L-shaped except that they are more significantly like crosses—Latin crosses, placed with their long sides toward the street. Finally, certain large and even palatial houses, like the Harold McCormick project and the Coonley house, have plans of linked pavilion type.

It is perhaps inaccurate to call the Gridley house of 1906 square (Fig. 127). A very long projecting one-storey porch, with the usual hip roof and parapet, balances a narrow two-storey wing at the rear on the other side. But the thickness of the main block, the continuous band of mullioned windows brought out to the eave edge in front, and the cantilevered slab in the center of the lower storey, emphasize the cubic form. This sort of composition was also very happily used in this year for the third *Ladies' Home Journal* house project. As this was to be of cast concrete there were technical advantages in the square plan, in that the same wooden forms could be used for all sides. The roof, of course, was a flat slab (Fig. 128).

The Ingalls house of 1909 is of a much more formal type and more definitely square (Fig. 163). Here the projecting porches and balconies suggest a cross within the square. The more delicately detailed woodwork was always intended to be painted. Perhaps because of its crystalline compactness and lack of true Prairie extension—which is so artfully introduced into the Gridley house—this was more frequently imitated around Chicago than any of the other types. European imitators also often followed this least genial of Wright's house types of these years.

The Gale house of 1909 is also more or less square (Fig. 160). But like the completely different Isabel Roberts house it is a small masterpiece. It is also closer to what the Europeans who were most creatively inspired by Wright's were to come in the early twenties. Most of the other wood and plaster houses had hip roofs and hence a very slightly weighted emphasis on the hovering eaves plane. But this has the more abstract and less traditional slab roof, first proposed for the Yahara Boat Club project of 1902 (Fig. 79). The slab is used in a very different way than any of Wright roofs up to this, since it does not unify or harmonize irregularities below but rather gives variety to the cube of the house by its own broken form. The planes and the vertical elements of this composition have a definite structural thickness and are not like sheets of paper hung in the air, as in so many European projects of the twenties, but the handling of the elements is more abstract than in any earlier work by Wright. The front toward the street consists of three horizontal elements, the usual podium-like terrace parapet below, a lightly less extended cantilevered parapetted balcony above, and finally the roof slab, which projects further in front than on the sides. The line of the "wall" is marked less by the completely open screen of glass doors below and windows above than by the flanking pylons which rise to the balcony top at either side at this point in plan. On the left side a projection of the height of these pylons contains the entrance hall. This lies outside the main square of the plan and is further accented by a cantilevered slab which repeats the floor plane of the front balcony. Above this projection a slab roof extending at right angles to the main roof over the front of the house is stopped, as are all the eaves, against the chimney. The chimney, forming the vertical pivot of the whole composition, is half sunk in the main mass of the house, but also rises half free above the entrance wing.

Curiously enough the plan which this revolutionary plastic invention clothes is not very extraordinary (Fig. 161). The L-shaped living-room-dining-room is a smaller and more unified version of those elements in the square Heurtley house, quite similar to those in several smaller square houses of which the third *Ladies' Home Journal* house is the best example.

The Baker house in Wilmette of 1909 is of a very different order. It presents to the street a long low façade with continuous rows of windows above and below (Fig. 158). At one end this façade is stopped against a projecting cross arm. This cross arm contains the living room, which is two storeys high like that of the Isabel Roberts house (Fig. 159). Beyond this cross arm the roof of a projecting porch continues the lower eave of the main façade.

[45]

The rear of the house is somewhat less schematic. The mass composition of the Baker house is thus somewhat like that of the brick Martin house, but the scale is more domestic and less monumental; and the great living room bay provides a stronger vertical accent to balance the long horizontal lines. The clear pattern of the wooden window mullions, the plaster of the unpierced lower walls and the delicate lattice of the diamond panes offer a particularly happy and expressive chord of materials. As in the River Forest Club the mullions reveal the underlying wooden skeleton of studs; the plaster forms a sheathing plane carried in front of the studs; the diamond panes provide a penetrable screen at the point where interior and exterior space meet. The whole is, perhaps, the most logical and consistent of all the wood and plaster houses.

Somewhat smaller and less crystalline in composition is the Davidson house, also of 1909, in Buffalo, in which the living room bay also rises the full height of the house. But the whole effect, today, is lost in vines and shrubs, while the Baker house has little planting except for the great trees which arch above it.

On quite a large group of houses in this decade Wright substituted, at least in the lower walls, the horizontal battened sheathing of the River Forest Golf Club for the plaster of the houses described above. Most of them are summer houses in the woods beside Delavan Lake in Wisconsin and White Lake in Michigan. But a few are in the more wooded suburbs north of Chicago and there is one in Montecito, California.

The first to be built were the Goodsmith house at Delavan Lake and the Pitkin house near the Sault, both of 1900. But as with the wood and plaster and the masonry houses the type came to maturity two years later. The fine little Walter Gerts cottage at White Lake is almost identical with the front wing of the Golf Club. The Ross house at Delavan Lake is slightly larger with a very compact cross-shaped plan improved from that of the nearby Goodsmith house (Fig. 78). The upper storey, which rises above the cross arm, has plaster between the windows instead of the vertical board and batten treatment which gives a somewhat immature air to the Goodsmith house (Fig. 77). Although unsupervised and quite small, this house ranks in quality with the Willitts house and the Heurtley house of the same year. The adaptation of the cross plan to a rather steeply sloping site, with the entrance on the side and the porch projecting out toward the Lake, reveals once more how readily Wright adapted his houses to varied site conditions. As at the Willitts house, the woods are slightly thinned and the forest floor grassed to provide a setting. The house, for all its somewhat rustic materials, is not merged with the natural surroundings. It stands clean and crisp among the trees, harmonious in texture and tone, and yet clearly man-made.

The Millard house in a thick grove at Highland Park is not especially remarkable in plan or composition. Among the suburban wooden houses the Glasner house of 1905, at the crest of a steep ravine in Glencoe, is the most interesting. Like the Usonian houses of the thirties this has no separate dining room, and the whole plan is drawn out very long and thin, like some of the projects of the nineties (Fig. 111). It even has octagonal pavilions like several of the houses of the nineties, but these are tied into the general composition by the square roof projections above. The striking contrast between the very low façade on one side and the deep base extending down into the ravine on the other and the dramatic interest of the attached octagons make this house unique (Fig. 110). The particular articulation of the plan, which cannot be defined as cross, T or L-shaped like most of the houses of this decade, quite as much as the unification of the living space, foreshadowed later developments in Wright's domestic work and prepares, despite its small size, for the two largest house designs of this period.

Neither the project for a house for Harold McCormick at Lake Forest, which was never built, nor the Coonley house, which many consider the culmination of Wright's early domestic work, fit into the earlier plan categories. The McCormick house, rising above Lake Michigan, would have been almost like a Persian palace (Fig. 140). Pavilions, completely surrounded by windows, are joined by a gallery, in front of which an open terrace projects toward the Lake. Behind the gallery is a court with a very elaborate master's wing on one side, connected by a bridge with the living room pavilion, and a service wing on the other side (Fig. 139). Generally low, though the pavilions rise out of the cliff on high bases, loosely linked about gardens and ornamental pools, formally as well as organically arranged, this private palace might suggest a group of exposition buildings as much as an ordinary dwelling. And yet except for the size, there are none of the vulgar palatial luxuries. Structure and expression are simple; the scale of the parts, despite their extent, remains domestic; yet the fullest advantage is taken both of the charms of the natural site and the possibilities of rich planting in the courts. Among all the many magnificent unexecuted projects, this is one whose loss is particularly to be regretted, even though many of the same qualities are present in the Coonley house.

The Coonley house has nowhere near so fine a site. But the estate was large and, with the river at the edge, as potentially attractive as the western suburbs of Chicago could offer. To make up for the flatness, all the living quarters are raised as in the Heurtley house. The pavilion treatment of the McCormick house is repeated, particularly the isolation of the service and master's wings, with the entrance to the court passing under a bridge (Fig. 147). But the living room pavilion dominates the chief façade; the dining room faces in a different direction, and the flanking galleries, in which are the stairs, are less open than in the McCormick project.

Two of the most striking things about this house are the terrace and pool arrangement in front of the main pavilion, and the ornamental frieze on the upper storey (Fig. 148). The pylons, eventually linked with a pergola, extend the architectural composition out toward the pool in which the playroom doors below and the band of windows of the living room above are reflected. Now with the addition of the plane of the water, and above all the pattern of reflections in it, a schematic analysis of the space composition such as was possible for the work of the opening of the decade or even for the Gale house, would become unintelligible without diagrams (Fig. 49). Inside, with the ceilings now following the external pitch of the living room roof and the flanking galleries and the stair wells open to the storey below, Wright's orchestration of space has also become very much richer (Fig. 152). One may even prefer the relatively simpler organization of plane and void and line in the less elaborate houses of this decade. But the increasing complexity points the way forward to later periods (Fig. 150, 153).

In the frieze on the exterior of this house small coloured tiles inlaid in a tooled pattern of straight lines in the plaster form a crisp geometrical pattern which contrasts sharply with the Sullivanian friezes of the nineties (Fig. 151). Such ornamental work at architectural scale had not been wholly unknown on the houses since 1900. The Dana house of 1903 has a somewhat similar frieze, but of a less geometrical character. But in general the ornament—if one can ever properly make it a separate category in Wright's work—had been restricted in the Prairie houses to the leaded glass in the windows and the wooden ceiling grilles and the marking strips on the ceilings. In this ornamental frieze, introducing bright permanent colour in a discreet pattern which enlivens the whole wall surface of which it is a physical part, we have a foretaste of the more elaborate structural ornament and the richly textured surfaces of much of Wright's work in the next twenty years.

VI. Non-Domestic Work

THE Prairie houses may be, as they have generally been considered, the greatest achievement of Wright in the first decade of this century. But despite the predominance of domestic commissions the general range of his architectural work is extraordinary. Few other architects of this period, and surely none who were chiefly famous for their houses, also built factories, shops and churches, schools, exposition pavilions, and office buildings, and in addition made projects for various large-scale housing schemes and even for whole towns.

The clubs Wright built, the two River Forest Tennis Clubs of 1905 and 1906, which succeeded the River Forest Golf Club, and the unsupervised Como Orchards central clubhouse in Montana of the end of the decade, are so similar to the domestic work that they hardly require discussion. The project of 1902 for the Yahara Boat Club is, however, important. Although not large, this project initiates a new sort of design which, in the light of what was to follow, it is not absurd to call monumental. It is, however, the boldly cantilevered slab roofs, providing long before the Gale house a premonition of the more abstract plane composition of much of Wright's later work and the work of the young Europeans in the twenties, which gives the Boat Club its particular significance (Fig. 79). One wonders if this motif may not have been introduced the previous year in the Universal Portland Cement pavilion at the Pan-American exposition in Buffalo. Of this no trace in photograph or drawing seems to be extant.

The true heirs of this project in the next few years are the Larkin Building and Unity Church. But before coming to them a very important executed building of 1902 should be discussed. The Hillside Home School was built beside Wright's first house of 1887 for his Lloyd Jones aunts. Although it has a close relation to the domestic work of the time, the school is more monumental in construction and design. The plan is simply an H, one storey high in the rear wing, two storeys high on the front, and with the cross bar a bridge under which passes the drive (Fig. 82). At either end of the front wing are two pavilions marking the two large rooms of the interior, the rest of which is subdivided into small class rooms, opening on a corridor at the rear. These two pavilions balance one another, but they are not identical, since the rooms within are quite differently disposed. The composition is thus formal but asymmetrical, the asymmetry beautifully related to the diagonal slopes of the site (Fig. 81).

The construction is unusually solid for this period of Wright's work, comparing thus with the contemporary Heurtley house. The lower walls are of native rock-faced random ashlar, superbly laid and reminding one of the finest of Richardson's masonry. But the stone was light and flesh-coloured and has remained so in this country environment, so that the effect is not grim or even severe. The marked batter of the pavilion walls serves to centralize and to concentrate their design. This batter was used on the Imperial Hotel fifteen years later. It also appears once more in the rough stone and concrete bases of Taliesin West, 1938, and the Pauson house, 1940, near Phoenix, Arizona.

Above this masonry substructure, made more solid by the rough surfaces and the batter, the upper portion of the school is as open as the Prairie houses. On the pavilions the tall windows descend between corner pylons, like those on the Dana and Martin houses, deep into the masonry, opening on a plant-filled terrace. The simple wooden mullions which separate the windows are unusually sturdy, well scaled to the monumental vigor of the whole design.

The interiors have mostly been modified in remodelling the school since 1933 for the uses of the Taliesin Fellowship, but in the living room inside the larger pavilion the original treatment is still entirely extant. The chief feature is an enormous stone fireplace with a large flat lintel in the rock-faced random ashlar of the solid wall. On this is a finely cut inscription. The bold and rough-surfaced woodwork harmonizes with the stone and is stained, inside as well as out, a rich dark brown. A balcony in the form of an open square is set diagonally to the cross-shape of the room itself (Fig. 84).

The use of native stone from the hills nearby, the adaptation to the hillside site, and the absence of all compromise with suburban domestic ideals already suggest the later domestic manner of Wright's own Taliesin built on the next hill in 1911.

Superficially there could hardly be a greater contrast between two buildings than between the Hillside House School and the Larkin Administration Building in Buffalo. This was designed just as the School was being completed and begun in 1904. They are both large in size and both of masonry, but there, unless we understand how the inner consistency of Wright's principles necessarily demands in edifices of different purpose and environment a different expression, the similarity seems to end. Yet this tall brick structure, rising out of a grim industrial backwater of Buffalo, dominates and even harmonizes with its environment, in much the same way as does the school with the Wisconsin countryside. Here nothing is rustic, everything has the finish and perfection of an industrial product from the hard, smooth brick of the walls rising almost blank at the front to the amazing plate glass entrance doors set in their flat metal frames (Fig. 97).

[50]

In some ways the structural expression of this building may suggest brick masonry less than poured concrete and there is reason to believe Wright would have preferred to use the newer industrial material had his clients been willing. For the construction makes no use of the arch and by means of reinforced beams and lintels achieves almost as open an effect, internally and in the greater part of the side walls, as if it were of steel or concrete skeleton construction. But it is open at the sides merely to let in light, not so that space may flow freely between the inside and the outside. For the outside environment is instead shut out. Indeed, the building was perhaps the first to be truly sealed, its interior climate controlled by an early form of air-conditioning (Fig. 94).

Too much was made by European admirers of the industrial severity approaching grimness of the exterior of this building (Fig. 92, 96). They rarely realized its great scale or its relation to the cliff-like old-fashioned factory buildings across the street. Misunderstanding it, they merely imitated at small scale its stern forms. But Wright intended rather to humanize and soften this severity, particularly on the entrance front, by the simple, if rigidly geometrical grille, the carved fountain and above all by the planting which has unfortunately not been maintained. The sculptured groups, generally disapproved by critics of the twenties, are now gone. Set against the attic at the top of the piers of the front façade, they had an important part to play. The figures considered purely as sculpture were not altogether happy, since no sculptor available as a collaborator seemed to know how to translate into another art the architectural innovations of Wright. But the great globes contrasted effectively with the right angles of the architecture and perhaps by their evident solidity helped to suggest that the blank corner towers were hollow.

However, it is the interior of the Larkin Building which came first to Wright as a builder and as a designer. The lighting and the space distribution of the great covered central court, rising the full height of the building, and of the galleries opening into the court between the vertical piers constitute its chief distinction (Fig. 93, 95). The central court has really monumental scale and even grandeur, not unlike the finest interior courts of certain commercial buildings of the seventies and eighties, yet this grandeur is in no way unsuited to the purposes of the building. There is little embellishment beyond the abstract carving at the tops of the piers, so much more suited to this architecture than the human figures on the exterior. But as always there were troughs along the parapets and other fittings for growing plants and flowers.

The gallery offices are masterpieces of detail with which the later development of an industrial vocabulary of design has hardly caught up a generation later. The banks of built-in metal filing cases below the high windows, the specially designed metal desks and chairs, the first metal office furniture, already displayed to the full the possibilities and limitations of mass-produced fittings of this sort. Today they seem to offer a sharply anachronistic background to the typists of 1904 (Fig. 98).

The Larkin Building originally served as the administrative offices of a large mail order house. It was never, as some have supposed, a soap factory. Wright built, however, one factory in 1905 for Darwin D. Martin, of the Larkin Company, and his brother, W. E. Martin, of Oak Park.

The E-Z Polish Factory in Chicago was long forgotten and only rediscovered two years ago by Grant Manson, who followed up a clue that Wright's only factory lay somewhere along the Galena division of the Chicago and Northwestern Railway by riding back and forth on the line until he spotted it. It is of concrete construction with spandrels surfaced with brick and horizontal windows very similar to those on the sides of the Larkin Building. The plain façade is terminated by open stair bays, their vertical flanking piers framing the composition. The more elaborate scheme for an open court between side wings at the rear, found in drawings at Taliesin, was never executed (Fig. 99).

There is another industrial project for a single-storey varnish factory presumably in the country, interesting in a day when most factories were many storeys tall and set in congested areas for its suggestion of the practice of a much later period.

More appealing to most observers than the E-Z Factory, and actually very well known, though not as a work of Wright, was the remodelling for Edward C. Waller, an even more constant client of Wright's than Darwin D. Martin, of the entrances and the court staircase and balcony in Burnham and Root's Rookery Building in 1906 (Fig. 122). This sumptuous design, simple in general character, but rich in the almost oriental patterns incised and gilded in the polished white marble, is curiously appropriate to the fine glass-covered court of the Rookery.

Most of Wright's other commercial work is of less importance, chiefly interesting for the perfect adaptation of his domestic interior detail to store fittings, as in Browne's Bookstore of 1908. But the Larkin Pavilion at the Jamestown exposition of 1907 (Fig. 133), and the contemporary Pebbles and Balch shop front, both now gone, have a very special character (Fig. 134). They do not remind us of the houses; the design is crisper, more impersonal and more finished. And they have neither the monumental scale of the industrial work nor the luxury of the Rookery marble and gold. The Jamestown pavilion has properly a temporary and festive air, a little like the Wolf Lake project of the mid-nineties. A whole exposition might well have been designed in some such way. Unfortunately when the great Chicago and New York exhibitions came in the thirties, their boards of design not only rejected

Wright as architect, they also rejected as models such work as this which would have set an admirable American standard for exposition design.

The little bank in Dwight, Illinois, of 1906, is a suave exercise in masonry, almost more to be expected in the nineties than at this date (Fig. 115, 116). The Mason City National Bank is more interesting, looking forward and not back, but the hotel which is part of the same project is even more important. Both the bank and the hotel, still building when Wright left for Europe in 1910, have a richness and complexity of form which, even more than the composition of the Gale house of 1909 and the ornament of the Coonley house of 1908, lead the way to the Midway Gardens of 1914.

The bank is of solid brick below, but it opens out under the slab roof into a clerestorey between piers very elaborately ornamented in the spirit of the "capitals" of the Larkin Building interior. Thus the whole bank seems to be a sort of treasure chest (Fig. 168).

The hotel on the other hand forms a U around a court above the open lobby and store fronts below (Fig. 169). The articulation of the wing blocks and of the features of architectural scale, such as the projecting eaves, shades over into the similarly abstract small-scale ornament. The whole effect is somewhat similar to the Larkin Exposition Pavilion, but more solid,—or rather, with more play of solid against void (Fig. 170). In an urban environment, as in the contemporary Stohrs Building in Chicago underneath the Elevated, Wright aimed at a more complex and superficially striking stylistic statement than in industrial or rural settings. Today this reminds us superficially of the cheap ornamental novelties of the last twenty years. Unfortunately the Mason City buildings have been too far remodelled and begrimed to be properly studied in the original. In general, time and accident have somewhat simplified the actual variety of this decade of Wright's work in retrospect. It is easier today to appreciate in drawings the qualities of such designs as the Horseshoe Inn of 1908, projected for Estes Park, Colorado, in which the vocabulary of the Prairie houses is extended to a very large scale, than the significance of the more individual Mason City hotel and the destroyed Stohrs Building.

After the great Prairie houses and the Larkin Building, Unity Church in Oak Park, designed in 1905 and several years in building, is justly the most famous. Wright had been interested in poured concrete for several years, but this was the first time he—or for that matter anyone else perhaps—had used it for a monumental public edifice. He persuaded his Universalist clients on the score of economy and attempted to take the curse off its dead surfaces by exposing the fine pebble aggregate. The building was to Wright an exercise in the "temple" form, square externally with solid stair-towers at the corners, cross-shaped within with the arms above the corridors filled by sloping galleries, and amply lighted by clerestoreys and skylights (Fig. 119). The exterior is solemn and formal, expressive of its monolithic construction, the large scale of the parts established by the necessary thickness of the projecting roof slab. Except for the vines that have sometimes covered it, the solemnity is lightened chiefly by abstract "capitals" at the top of the clerestorey piers (Fig. 122). Such a heavy mass, such restraint in plastic composition, could hold its own in any environment; it is perhaps almost too strong for suburban Oak Park (Fig. 118).

The interior is more complex, with a remarkable sort of space composition (Fig. 120). The auditorium floor is higher than the surrounding corridors into which the space flows beneath the galleries. Four piers define the central square out of which project the short arms toward the clerestoreys. All minor elements, such as the balcony parapets and the grid of the ceiling skylight, repeat an interlocking frame of lines in space. But the lines are not mere lines, they are structural as well and contrast as thick solid members with the voids of the plaid of space between, while the ceiling extends into outside space and is seen through the clerestorey windows as the underside of the cantilevered roof slab. The electric fixtures were heated frankly as part of the architecture and even their wires became a part of the design. This was in its way as revolutionary as the specially designed office fittings in the Larkin Building. Without a congregation the effect may be somewhat severe. And as in all non-ritualistic churches the pulpit end of the auditorium seems to lack focus. Doubtless also the balance and finish of the original colour scheme has been lost with repainting.

The church is entered through colonnades something like "cloisters" which connect the church with the Parish House. These colonnades lighten the composition, recalling the clerestoreys of the main block and of the similar but smaller Parish House block. Thus toward the side street, where the main entrance is, there is considerable breadth and variety, the asymmetrical balance recalling that of the Hillside Home School.

While Wright's early houses, the Larkin Building and Unity Church, are known wherever architecture is studied, his large-scale projects, which would come under the heading of housing or city planning, have been somewhat forgotten. The massive solidity of Unity Church, unavoidable in a first essay in poured concrete, Wright never repeated in later work in this medium. But foreign admirers, as in the case of the Larkin Building, were only too prone to imitate at small scale effects they had never really apprehended in studying the original solely through photographs and drawings. On the other hand the more "sociological" projects of these years ought to have been perfectly comprehensible on paper. Perhaps they may have been more influential abroad than has yet been recognized. For the McArthur apartments in poured concrete were published in the 1910 German portfolio (Fig. 131) as well as the Lexington Terrace project, which Wright had worked on intermittently since 1901, and the Larkin workmen's rowhouse project, which is such a striking premonition of Dutch and German *reihenhäuser* of the twenties and early thirties. The arrangement of the Lexington Terrace flats about an open court with balconies at the second-storey level is not quite as much like Oud's first workmen's housing as the executed Francisco Terrace of the nineties, but the scheme was much more elaborate and on a much larger scale (Fig. 172). The Larkin housing project has wonderfully compact minimal plans with continuous bands of windows above and below. The line of the street is maintained by the roof slab, while the individual houses are marked by the inset doorways between the wide living room bays (Fig. 108, 109). The design might well be a model for government housing today, and is, indeed, being approached in some of the latest Defense Housing projects.

The Roberts project for a large-scale middle-class housing development in Oak Park was confused in the Wasmuth portfolio with the earlier scheme for the *Ladies' Home Journal* of 1900, to which it is very similar. The scheme for Como Orchards, near Darby, Montana, was also in the Wasmuth portfolio, even though it was only partially executed and then without supervision (Fig. 167). Both of these plans, one for a suburban subdivision, the other for a mountain resort, have great interest. But even more interesting were two projects for a town of Bitter Root on much the same site, prepared earlier for the Bitter Root Irrigation Company, though neither of them were published. Of one of these only the plan is to be found at Taliesin, of the other only a bird's-eye perspective. For a study of Wright as a city-planner, they would be documents of major importance, but for this study of Wright's architecture the drawings are at too small a scale to be very revealing.

To many Europeans the corpus of Wright's great work seems to have closed in 1910. Our later sections will make evident what should always have been clear, that Wright's great work no more closed in 1910 than in 1900.

PART FOUR

1911–1920

VII. From the Middle West to Japan and California

THE ample German publications of Wright's early work, the luxurious portfolios of plans and drawings of 1910 and the smaller book illustrated with photographs of 1911, have made the Prairie houses of the first decade of the century and certain non-domestic work of the same years, such as the Larkin Building of 1904 and the Unity Church of 1906, the best-known examples of his architecture. I have discussed elsewhere[1] how the great international influence of Wright is largely derived from these books and how formative that influence was during the next decade upon the development of modern architecture in Europe.

The work of the Prairie years seems in retrospect, despite its very great variety, to form a homogeneous unit. Within that homogeneity there is, between 1902 and 1908 at least, little apparent chronological development. When Wright left for Europe in the spring of 1910 it was hardly evident that upon his return the day of the Prairie houses would be over and that strikingly new developments would henceforth succeed one another at relatively brief intervals. Wright's brief trip to Japan in 1905 had not broken the homogeneity of the work of the decade before 1910; and if he was little or not at all influenced by travel in a country whose art had long been particularly sympathetic to him, it was not to be expected that even a longer stay in Europe, chiefly in Renaissance Florence, would affect him directly. Nor did it do so.

The reasons for the change of phase in 1911 are personal and interior rather than the result of contact with the European architecture of the past. If the European trip had any effect, it was rather to increase his own assurance, to stimulate his imaginative boldness and to encourage a richness of expression already implicit in his work, but possibly somewhat inhibited by the life of suburban Oak Park and by a series of commissions chiefly for suburban houses. Wright was to a considerable extent a regional Middle Western architect before 1910. After 1910, with the wide acceptance of his early work by the European world as the basis of a new architecture, he was conscious of his fame and responsive to a more universal destiny.

The work of the decade 1911–1920 was not homogeneous. Or at least, since it has never been so thoroughly published and studied, it has never seemed so. It is no part of our purpose to refer in detail to the story of Wright's life, so brilliantly told in his own *Autobiography,* but

---

[1] "Wright's Influence Abroad," in *Parnassus,* December, 1940, pp. 11–15.

it should not only be recalled that this decade began with a sharp break with the familiar surroundings in which Wright had worked for a score of years and with all the social implications in the Chicago world of such a break, but that the decade was broken once more in the middle by a personal loss whose external and internal effects we need consider only as they reacted upon Wright's architectural career. The tremendous tragedy at Taliesin in 1914 brought to an end far more completely than the events of five years before Wright's happy relation to the Middle Western environment. And within a very short time the call to Tokio and Wright's many years of work there completed his detachment from the milieu of suburban Chicago with which his earlier career was so closely involved.

Despite his tremendous activity in 1908 and 1909 it may well have been that the enthusiastic response of Chicagoans to Wright's new architecture had passed its peak by 1910. Mrs. Harold McCormick's employment of Charles A. Platt from the East in 1908 to build a traditional house in Lake Forest instead of the palatial project of Wright was probably the symbol of a more general loss of artistic self-assurance in the Middle West. In any case the snobbish imitation of Eastern models seems thenceforth to have increased. Even the members of the Chicago School, who had once been so closely associated with Wright, gradually went over to the tasteful and eclectic traditionalism of the Eastern leaders. It is hard to balance the importance of the particular events of Wright's personal life and their repercussions on his professional career against what seems to have been an almost inevitable general development. Chicago, so capable of accepting and acclaiming architectural innovations since the eighties, so stimulating to Richardson at the end of his career, so capable at the World's Fair of providing the first and happiest illustration of the grandiose dreams of the classicists when those dreams were bold and new, seemed to be growing old and timid.

But if in the second decade of the century Chicago was becoming too smugly conventional to appreciate Wright, the outside world from Berlin to Tokio, and more significantly from Wichita to Los Angeles, now claimed his services. But for the War and his engrossment with the Imperial Hotel, doubtless the extension of his American clientele to regions far from Chicago—there is, for example, one Palm Beach house—would have been even greater.

The work of 1911–1920 cannot conveniently be divided, like that of the previous decade, into a quantity of houses falling into recognizable categories and a limited group of edifices of non-domestic character. The chief works of the period, both before and after the break, are public monuments and not houses; and the most important house was his own Taliesin, built in 1911 and rebuilt after 1914, wholly different in scale and character from the earlier suburban houses. Before 1915 the two chief works, about which the rest may be grouped, are

Taliesin and the Midway Gardens of 1913. In the second half of the decade the Imperial Hotel and the Barnsdall house in California are the landmarks. To a considerable extent each of these four chief commissions is independent of the others in materials, construction, setting and expression; and each is of rather more individual consequence and extent than most of the individual commissions of the earlier period.

Wright was far from being without Chicago commissions of the suburban domestic type on his return from Europe in 1911. The most interesting can best be discussed in relation to his own Wisconsin house. Others are chiefly adaptations of the established Prairie house types. His first important new commission, however, was for the Coonleys, for whom he was also making slight alterations and additions to the house and its adjuncts which had been completed just before he went abroad.

The Coonley kindergarten project of 1911, although it was to stand on the grounds of the Riverside estate, was a wholly independent structure of marked originality of design. The design was completely symmetrical, complex in the relation of its parts and most remarkable for the abstract elaboration of its three-dimensional composition. The slab roof, like that of the Boat Club project of 1902, is the most striking element in the design, emphasizing the varying heights of different parts of the structure, projecting to form pierced pergolas, controlling and harmonizing the complexity of the composition in an extraordinarily original and creative way. Although the roof slab and most of the walls below the high windows are solid and visibly of a considerable thickness, this solidity is not like that of traditional masonry. For the whole design is articulated in terms of plane elements in a fashion already essayed in the Gale house of 1909 (Fig. 183).

The executed Coonley playhouse of 1912 is somewhat smaller and simpler than the kindergarten project, but it incorporates most of its innovations (Fig. 185, 186). Comparison with the Isabel Roberts house of four years earlier, which has a somewhat similar parti, will make evident the marked change of expression. The plan is a formal cross with emphasis on the horizontal arm which is prolonged by the slab roof. However the projecting central wing has a strong balance of horizontal and vertical elements. The tall windows above the flower-box stylobate are filled with gay and festive abstract balloon designs in coloured glass—non-objective pictures designed before non-objective painting had fairly begun in Europe. The far-projecting pergola slab above lets the light through in long vertical or oblique stripes.

In the interior more than the exterior we notice a certain heaviness of membering, which, in general, differentiates the houses of these years from the more delicately domestic work before 1910 (Fig. 184). This is related to the general tendency toward a sort of abstract sculpture at architectural scale, which, as in the Gale house, is differentiated from the later

[61]

European exercises of the Neo-Plasticists by the real sense of thickness in the parts and the clear expression of different sorts of material.

A related project of completely different scale and purpose is that for a concrete skyscraper for the Spreckels Estate in San Francisco. The slab construction dictate a more solid expression than the metal skeleton of typical skyscraper construction. The articulated vertical piers set close together bear a general resemblance to those of Sullivan's Wainwright or Guaranty Buildings of twenty years before. But the great slotted projecting slab roof is quite like that of the Coonley playhouse, and in that version of the project which linked a tall tower to the existing Tower Building with a lower wing, the cross-ties of horizontal slab elements are a remarkable exercise in wholly Wrightian abstract plasticity (Fig. 188). More striking, however, is the other version of which the model was made. In this isolated structure, the great height was expressed by the continuous verticals on all sides of the shaft, and yet the continuity of the shaft was broken some distance from bottom and top by a plaiding of horizontal elements (Fig. 187).

Less than in the case of the epochmaking Luxfer Prism skyscraper project of the nineties and the cantilevered skyscrapers of the twenties need we regret that this project did not come to execution. For a more logical amplification of the new design vocabulary of the Coonley playhouse, justly considered by Wright one of his most perfect works, was the executed Midway Gardens on the South Side in Chicago. The Midway Gardens unfortunately were only destined for a decade of precarious life. They were too European in conception for a country soon to accept Prohibition. But their glories can be re-created from plans and photographs, and even something of the colour of the remarkable abstract murals can be appreciated in the original studies.

The Midway Gardens were designed in the fall of 1913 for Edward C. Waller, Jr., and Oscar Friedman. This Waller was the son of E. C. Waller, who had been from the nineties a recurrent client of Wright's. The construction was nearly complete the following summer when Wright was called away by the tragedy at Taliesin. The Gardens thus represent the culmination of Wright's achievement between his return from Europe and the break in the middle of the decade. They are also his last great Chicago work.

The site lay along the old Midway of the World's Fair at the corner of Cottage Grove Avenue and 60th Street. This was not perhaps, as Chicago was developing, an altogether happy choice for the sort of luxurious outdoor resort that was intended, but the ground was open and extensive, without overshadowing neighbours. The greater part of the site was left clear for outdoor tables, with a tall enclosed structure at the front, terraces down the sides and an orchestra shell at the rear (Fig. 191). It was the sort of open restaurant, casino, or

Kurhaus to be found in most continental countries. Possibly Chicago required some education in sophistication to appreciate its possibilities. At any rate it did not attract the clientèle for which its cuisine and the musical and other entertainment fare—Pavlowa danced here—was originally intended. So it declined to a suburban beer garden and eventually was closed by Prohibition and demolished in the early twenties.

Here Wright, perhaps stimulated by what he had seen of such resorts in Europe, aimed at public instead of private luxury, but not at the stodgy splendours of contemporary urban hotels and restaurants. Instead he sought a festive gaiety, like that with which the Wolf Lake resort project of the nineties had been filled (Fig. 37), a fresh open fantasia in which sculpture and painting, not as independent entities but closely related to the essential architectural conception, should play an important part (Fig. 195).

The elevation of the enclosed structure toward the street was not unlike an amplification of the composition of the Coonley kindergarten project (Fig. 194). The main mass was rather solid but lightened by the open-work towers above and by the textured concrete blocks above the lower walls of brick. For all its solidity this façade was definitely inviting and richer than anything Wright had designed since the nineties. It was also extraordinarily versatile in the way large architectural elements such as the articulated piers and slabs that broke up and capped the walls below, or the interesting open-work frames of the tower tops were combined into elaborate abstract patterns. Similarly such details of plastic ornamentation as the textured wall surface and the free-standing statues were crystallized into forms of geometrical and architectural character. Perhaps Iannelli, the collaborating sculptor, had not the talent necessary to execute satisfactorily Wright's projects for Cubist figure sculpture. But the remarkable thing is that these Cubist figures, like the finer nonobjective murals inside, are not derivative from European work, but rather almost exactly contemporary parallels to the work of the most advanced French and German painters and sculptors. And this parallel invention was made, not by the New York artists who in 1913 organized the Armory Show in which such European work was first shown in America—none of them were yet so advanced—but by an architect who was merely developing abstract painting and semi-abstract sculpture as an essential component of a new architecture.

Toward the gardens the architecture is less enclosed, even the tall restaurant structure is opened up by terraces and projections on this side (Fig. 196). The side wings provide covered terraces and covered galleries to protect diners from the elements and the whole establishment from its none too appropriate surroundings (Fig. 193). The varying levels of the garden build up toward the side wings and the enclosed edifice at the rear, the terrace edges are marked by parapets and flower-filled boxes and urns. Thus Wright made the most of a site without natural advantages to form a sort of amphitheatre facing the orchestra platform and shell (Fig. 192).

It has been said of French architecture that it is either in the *style funèbre* or the *style casino*. The temple form of the Unity Church and the grey pebbled surface of its poured concrete, the solid brick masses of the Larkin Building gave to Wright's earlier non-domestic work a somewhat severe solemnity. The Midway Gardens represents Wright's *style casino* at its apotheosis. It provided an American model which should have been borne in mind in designing the expositions of the thirties. For they were dismal examples of the general American incapacity to achieve a festive spirit in anything but folk building.

Wright's other great work of the first half of the decade was his own house on the family land outside Spring Green, Wisconsin. Taliesin, which has made of Spring Green even more a center of architectural pilgrimage than Oak Park in the last thirty years, was begun for his mother upon his return from Europe. But before it was completed he had decided to live there himself and, despite two fires and long absences in Japan and in California and winters spent at Taliesin West in the last few years, it has been Wright's headquarters ever since. But there is not a Taliesin period as there is an Oak Park one. Oak Park is a suburb of Chicago and the environment was at least symbolic of the location and the character of most of his work while he lived and worked there. But Taliesin is to be found rather upon the map of the United States or the map of the world than on the map of Wisconsin.

Taliesin quite literally grows from Wright's native hillsides both in the choice of most of its materials and in its close adaptation to the site. But it reaches out as well to the whole world and it would be as incomplete without the great works of Oriental art incorporated in its walls as without the great music of the European past which continually sounds from its innumerable musical instruments (Fig. 177). The houses before 1910, even his own Oak Park house (which originally had an upstairs studio and later an attached but separately designed studio building), were houses and no more. But this was a house, a studio, a farm and even eventually a school, a complex linkage of the elements which alone could form the true home of Frank Lloyd Wright. This is not the place to describe the philosophy and the atmosphere of Taliesin. It will be difficult enough to describe its architecture, since the story is complicated by major reconstructions after the fires of 1914 and 1925, and by continual alterations and additions. But it was built once for the first time (Fig. 175): that first form, or at least that first form as rebuilt and somewhat extended immediately after the

[64]

1914 fire, can be re-created from plans and photographs and somewhat distinguished from the ultimate complexity of the Taliesin of today (Fig. 269–275).

Taliesin is not on a hilltop, it is rather wrapped around a hilltop, which rises behind and above the house. It makes no attempt to dominate the natural setting nor is it merged with it. The materials, particularly the local stone laid in loosely projecting layers like natural cliffs, are from the soil, but the house, except for the various solidly anchored chimneys and piers of the stonework, soars and hovers (Fig. 178). There are long bands of plaster, more roughly surfaced than on earlier houses, framed above and below by sturdy moulded wooded strings. Above this are the bands of windows whose wooden mullions as always indicate the stud-structure of the wall (Fig. 174). Over all are the roofs, the most conspicuous feature of Taliesin. But the roofs no longer form a simple geometrical cross shape, indeed their very forms are varied, with gable elements and penthouses introduced among the predominant hips. The roof complex seems like some piece of landscape, slightly abstracted to flat slanting planes, but flowing together as freely as the space of the rooms below.

Hardly distinguishable from the architecture is the treatment of the area which the house and studio and farm wing surround (Fig. 176). The long court is formalized by walls and steps and pools of right angle elements which are tied in under the loggias of the house. The great oak tree higher up the slope is literally nourished by the little fountain in the center of a circular paved area. This forms an outdoor tea room with a curving stone bench. The lawn on the crest of the hill is naturally of almost exactly the same slope as the shingled roofs around and below. Yet it is sharply defined toward the lower court by retaining walls and steps and on the open side by the long stone wall which forms a sort of frame for the view toward Hillside. The out-cropping of rock in the slope of the lawn is cut into shallow polygonal steps. Thus if the house participates in the informality of the landscape setting, the setting as it enters between the wings of the house is formalized by architectural elements. Flowers and small-scale plants in such a lay-out are but a minor embellishment, hardly more important, considering the scale of the out-of-doors, than the flowers and green branches which generally fill the vases in the rooms.

Much of this description of the setting is of today rather than of twenty-five or thirty years ago. For Taliesin is not and never has been static and it is no more possible to describe it fully at a particular stage of its growth than any other living organism. With time parts of it have atrophied. For instance, the original farm wing is today used, if at all, for other purposes, now that a new farm group has been built beyond the next hill. Other parts have changed their purpose slightly. The studio, for a time filled with the apprentices and their drafting tables, has now become again Wright's private atelier, with the work of the apprentices removed to the new Hillside drafting room. But always Taliesin has been something more than a house and more like a medieval manor, with provision, partly below the main living rooms, partly beyond the studio, and now in the former farm wing, for the apprentices and various community facilities.

No other of Wright's houses, even of the period when Taliesin was building, is quite like it, since no other was intended to serve such complex functions. But the best houses of the decade belong recognizably to the same architectural family. They are sturdier and less delicate in design than the Prairie houses and if of wood and plaster usually looser in plan and composition. Moreover, most of them, like Taliesin, have sloping or hill-crest sites, and if not actually in the woods, have the protection of much wild planting. Most of those that were built are small, although the fine project for the Cutten house in Downer's Grove, Illinois, was larger than the original Taliesin. But the fine Angster house, at Lake Bluffs, Illinois, of 1911 (Fig. 179, 180), the later Hunt house in Oshkosh, Wisconsin, and the group of houses at Grand Beach (Fig. 209, 210, 211, 212, 213), Michigan, all of the second half of the decade, if they lack the Taliesin stonework, of which the Cutten house was to have made much use, have nevertheless a commonsense simplicity, a graceful rusticity comparable to that of the best horizontal-battened wooden houses of the previous decade in similar locations.

The few houses of this period which were built in Oak Park and other such suburban locations are more formal and usually have ornamentation in the spirit of Midway Gardens. The early Harry Adams project of 1911, with its elaborate symmetry, rich frieze and other elements of plastic abstract decoration, formed, like the Coonley kindergarten project, a halfway step between the Coonley house or the Mason City hotel and the Midway Gardens. The executed Adams house of 1913 in Oak Park, on the other hand, is a somewhat barren and heavy version of such early brick houses as those of the Littles and the Heaths.

The later Little house in Minnesota beside Lake Minnetonka was designed in 1912 and begun in 1913, but not completed until Wright's return from Japan. Although of masonry, it is both simple and delicate. The long plan, chiefly one-room thick, extends along the hill-crest by the lake side, with subordinate masses loosely disposed at either end of the living room, whose range of arched windows seems at first sight almost an anachronism in Wright's work at this date (Fig. 199, 200a).

In sharpest contrast to the Little house, with its long horizontal extension, its simplicity and the unusually severe and almost traditional use of brick masonry, is the other large house project designed before 1915, that for the Booths in Glencoe. The actual house as finally completed without supervision in 1916 is barely related to the earlier project of

[66]

1911–13. But the Booth site at Racine Bluffs was not a typical prairie suburb site and the original project was wonderfully complex, like a whirling cross, with wings and bridges shooting out over the ravines and a tall central mass with a very open two-storey living room and even a tower (Fig. 182). Not only was the composition very varied in mass and in the interlocking of such structural elements as piers and roof slabs, like an elaboration of the Gale house of 1909, it was also, like the early Adams house project, richly ornamented with plastically patterned surfaces boldly contrasted with plainer elements (Fig. 181).

We must regret deeply that this splendid house project was never executed as designed. But it is perhaps less significant than the American System Ready-Cut scheme of the same years, which likewise came to no real fruition because of the break between Wright and the sponsors of the project, Richards Brothers of Milwaukee, after 1916 and our entry into the War.

The American System envisaged both small and medium-sized houses, as well as duplex apartments, which were to be built of wood and plaster out of prepared units. It was, in other words, a system of prefabrication, or at least partial prefabrication, and so various were the possible combinations of units for which Wright prepared drawings that a very elastic repertory of architectural types was to be available (Fig. 205, 206, 207, 208). The examples that were built in Milwaukee and elsewhere, were unsupervised and do not give a full idea of the possibilities. Once more we note that Wright, far from thinking only in terms of mansions for millionaires, was ahead of most of his contemporaries in facing the problem of mass shelter.

Wright was, in 1914 and 1915, far from being without work. But the tragedy at Taliesin and its aftermath must have made the visit of the Japanese committee seeking an architect for the Imperial Hotel in Tokio seem almost like a miracle. After the completion of the Midway Gardens, actual building seems to have dragged except for the reconstruction of Taliesin. The lapsed projects, the unsupervised works, the prolonged building campaigns, and the generally reduced production of the middle years of the decade are perhaps not entirely due either to Wright's departure to Japan or to the coming of the War. Wright's architectural genius flowed fully in country houses, even at the small scale of the Grand Beach cottages. His artistic genius rose to the opportunities of such a commission as the Midway Gardens. His technical genius expended untold pains on the details of such a tremendous low-cost housing scheme as the Ready-Cut houses and apartments. But neither his genius nor his personality fitted any longer into the middle-class frame, perhaps in any case growing more hidebound, of the suburban Middle West. Frank Lloyd Wright, no longer of Oak Park, but of resurgent Taliesin, was ready to serve the world. In the next

[67]

years the only work which could really hold his interest, beside what the Japanese offered him, were the elaborate project for Olive Hill in Los Angeles for Aline Barnsdall and one fine Kansas house for Henry J. Allen in Wichita.

The first project for the Imperial Hotel, prepared at Taliesin before he left for Japan, was much modified before construction really started a year or two later. The long story of the Japanese episode, which had no very important architectural results other than the Hotel, is told by Wright in the *Autobiography* and need not be repeated here. But when the Hotel was finally completed it must have seemed to Wright worth all the trials, extending over six or seven years, which it had cost him.

From the first Wright had envisaged a type of construction which should provide real protection against the earthquakes to which Tokio was subject and also against the fires which were their inevitable aftermath. The great pools in the court of the Hotel were not primarily for ornament, but to provide an adequate water supply in case of fire (Fig. 223). In 1923 when the earthquake came so soon after the completion of the building, as if to try out its vaunted strength, the Hotel survived, an island of safety in a sea of flames, as much because of its water supply as because of its construction.

Wright has likened the special construction used in the Hotel to the balance of a tray on a waiter's fingers. The paired central concrete supports and the cantilevered floors constitute the essential technical device in a building which is from foundation to roof all of new materials and new devices compounded (Fig. 225, 226, 227). Wright brought out to Tokio Paul Mueller, the engineer from the old Adler and Sullivan office force of the early nineties, to assist him. The many ingenious things they worked out together deserve a detailed engineering analysis for which this is not the place.[2]

The vast H-shaped structure, of which the main plan scheme was determined in the first project of 1915, rests on innumerable concrete piers driven into the shallow crust above the soft lower soil (Fig. 219). The weight of the structure is borne by the central piers and the cantilevered floors. The outer walls are self-supporting shells of specially made brick filled with concrete. The walls lean in against the cantilevered floor slabs and interlocked with their edges (Fig. 220, 222).

The side wings provide the private accommodations on either side of the corridors between the paired central supports. Every feature, from the special arrangement of the plumbing to protect it against earthquake strains, to the built-in cupboards and the new heating units, was the result of detailed technical and artistic study (Fig. 229, 230).

[2] Contemporary accounts both before and after the earthquake will be found in the *Architectural Record,* vol. 53, pp. 332–352 and vol. 55, pp. 118–123. The former is by Louis Sullivan.

The central block between the long side wings contains the public rooms. Lobby, dining room, ball room and many other facilities are on the most lavish scale (Fig. 231, 232). Around this block are the large garden courts with their great pools, terraced and architecturally elaborated by parapets and richly sculptured decoration among the carefully selected and placed Japanese plants (Fig. 223). It is in the courts that Wright's luxurious ornamentation, now with the able Japanese craftsmen to execute it profuse and elaborate beyond his dreams in the Midway Gardens, is seen at its best. The curious spotted greenish lava that cuts like cheese was turned into fantastic shapes of almost geological abstraction among the Japanese evergreens (Fig. 228). The reflections in the pools, the contrast of the lava colour with the dark green foliage and the brick walls behind composed a picture sufficiently Japanese in character, yet wholly original and personal.

Similar carved lava elaborates and enriches the masses of the building itself. To some the solidity of the mass, emphasized by the battered walls and by the rather heavily plastic ornament, has seemed inexpressive of the cantilevered skeleton within. And yet the massiveness of the building is real enough and has a sound reason. Indeed, it was the outside windows which were the chief point of danger during the fire after the earthquake. The lighter, gayer quality of expression of the early project, quite similar to that of the Midway Gardens, had proved inappropriate as an expression of the final structure (Fig. 222).

The necessary solidity of the structure, heavier still around the large voids of the public rooms in the central block, and the desire to lighten, or at least enrich, the structural elements with carved and painted decoration explains the turgidity which seems apparent in photographs of the monumental interior. Doubtless in actuality—I have never seen it—the particular scale, which is often hard to read in Wright's work from photographs alone, the elegance of the execution and above all the colour, would give a quite different impression, more like the quiet grace of the bedrooms and the rich warmth of Wright's own apartment in the annex he built for temporary use while the Imperial Hotel was in construction.

A quite different spirit is evident in the project for a country hotel at Nagoya. Here a really Japanese lightness informs every line of the structure. As always with Wright, despite his genius for using natural elements within an architectural frame as in the courts of the Imperial, he is even happier where he can associate his architecture appropriately with a setting of natural beauty (Fig. 233).

The Fukuhara house at Hakone also had a superb site—indeed, part of it slipped off with the edge of the cliff in the earthquake—and both this and the Hayashi house in a suburb of Tokio belong in construction and expression to the Taliesin group of wood and plaster houses. The projects for the houses for Count Immu and Viscount Inouye, like the Fukuhara

[69]

house, followed Japanese planning in having their chief rooms grouped around a garden court. They were, however, to be of brick with something of the monumentality and the rich carved stone decoration of the Imperial. The Bogk house in Milwaukee of 1916, though a square block in plan, is somewhat similar in expression.

Other American buildings of the Japanese years beside the Bogk house, the German Warehouse in Richland Center, designed before Wright's departure and never entirely completed, and the Allen house in Wichita, begun in 1917, have much in common with the Japanese work. The concrete structure of the Warehouse is masked with sturdy walls of brick and capped with a very heavy and rich ornamental band of concrete blocks superbly contrasted with the blank walls below. This marked the change of function to cold storage on the upper storey. The plastic geometrical patterns of the blocks, so much more severe than the forms the Japanese craftsmen were executing in lava, offer an early hint of the pattern-textured surfaces of the California block houses of the twenties (Fig. 203, 204).

The Allen house is somewhat Japanese in disposition, with a low living room wing and a longer two-storeyed wing enclosing a garden court with terraces and a pool (Fig. 216). But the masonry is handled almost as simply as that of the Little house. The placing of the wings of the house near the lot line and the enclosure of the garden court from the neighbors is quite different from the lay-out of the Prairie houses and possibly superior now that suburban streets were full of automobiles (Fig. 217, 218).

So much too much has been made of Japanese influence upon Wright's work that it is interesting to note that his actual work in the Orient has actually less of a Japanese air than much of his early work. While the specific influence of Japanese architecture in American work in these years, except of course in the continued use of wood stripping on plaster walls now restricted to interiors, is in the Allen plan.

In the Japanese years Wright's chief American commissions were for Aline Barnsdall in Los Angeles and included her own house, two other houses, all three of which were built, and projects for a theater and a terrace of shops and small houses. Preparatory work on these went on intermittently during the years the Imperial Hotel was in construction. Although no actual construction began until 1920, the three Barnsdall houses were in the end completed before the Hotel.

The Barnsdall Theater was an important project related to the Tokio moving picture theater project and exists in several different versions (Fig. 214, 215). It was to have been a tremendous structure of poured concrete, quite unconventional in plan and adapted to the special productions Aline Barnsdall was planning with Ordynsky and Norman Bel Geddes. Most of the versions provide for a great solid cubic block decorated with bands

[70]

of cast ornament, like the main façade of the Barnsdall Residence A (Fig. 242), and with a smaller octagonal mass above covered with abstract patterns somewhat like those on the German Warehouse. Unfortunately the designs for the terrace of shops with houses above beside the theater, running along Sunset Boulevard, were never so far developed. They might well have been one of Wright's most effective large-scale suburban housing schemes.

"Hollyhock House," Miss Barnsdall's own residence at the top of Olive Hill, was finally built in 1920-21, but never entirely completed in accordance with Wright's hopes. On account of vicissitudes of ownership, it has not been very well maintained. It is one of the rare instances of Wright's domestic use of exposed poured concrete, immediately given up for the textile block system of construction in the later California houses. But perhaps it should not be considered domestic in the ordinary sense. Because of the site and the tremendous size—it is one of Wright's most expensive houses, perhaps his most expensive—the composition is rather monumental. Near the top of the hill the main block of the house extends around a central courtyard (Fig. 236). Despite the large windows in the projecting living room bay, the effect except in the court (Fig. 237) is chiefly of solid wall, excluding the excessive heat and light of the region. Perhaps this is because of the curious canted line of the upper part of the wall above the windows, like a sort of mansard. Against this heavy roof-like slope stand little, lacy finials, abstract hollyhocks, catching and breaking up the brilliant light and now partially covered by the over-luxuriant local growth (Fig. 235).

To the left the line of the house is broadly extended by subordinate wings, more open than the main block, and by pergolas, garden walls and terraces which tie the tremendous spread and bulk of the house firmly to the ground (Fig. 240). From a distance beyond the rising slope of the lawn and against the distant mountains, the monumentality of the house is reduced to domestic scale (Fig. 238).

Thinking for a moment of modern architecture abroad in these years, on account of the War still chiefly projects on paper, we can see in Hollyhock House a special significance. The Imperial Hotel, in its luxuriant ornamentation, was akin to the rather similar luxuriance of one branch of European architecture in these years, particularly that of the Dutch school of Amsterdam, whose members on account of Berlage's enthusiasm studied Wright's new work closely. But in the Barnsdall house the use of poured concrete, the bold contrast of plain surfaces and large glass areas, the experimentation with long spans and open frames, was more parallel to the line younger men like Oud and Le Corbusier and Gropius were taking. In the first case there was almost certainly a direct influence. In the second it seems rather doubtful. Since in the next decade the work of Wright, to which as Oud recognized in *Wendingen* the new men owed so much, and the work of the younger Europeans, who were around 1920 beginning to crystallize their "international style," was to seem to both sides sharply opposed, it is worth while to point out the parallelism. This parallelism will be even more apparent in Wright's later California work and attention has already been called to the Yahara Boat Club project of 1902 and the Gale house of 1909, among other prototypes.

But critics inspired by "international" principles in the twenties literally could not see the architecture for the hollyhocks. In retrospect, whether or not we like the particular ornament on Hollyhock House for itself, it is not difficult to see that it was only a minor, if certainly not negligible, element in this important early concrete house. The small house project of 1919 for "Monolith Homes" of concrete, another of Wright's "sociological" projects which never came to execution, we may well feel provides still another astonishing parallel, in this case with Le Corbusier's Citrohan project of the same year. But the more developed version of this, prepared for Dr. Chandler in 1927, is better worth studying today. Happily, after twenty years, the unity of modern architecture and the pre-eminence of Wright are once again generally recognized. But it helps to explain Wright's isolation in the ensuing years that from the end of this decade until the opening of the thirties Wright's work was castigated almost as freely (and he feels, more jealously) from the left as from the right, if the meaningless political terms may be thus used.

At a time when he had to suffer every sort of indignity in his private life, Wright, the long-term leader of modern architecture, the forerunner whose vital contributions every-one admitted, was cast critically and professionally into a minority. Yet if he was attacked now as well as lauded from abroad, it was still the Europeans who continued to study his every current work and make it widely known by frequent publication. He might at fifty, with ludicrous prematurity as it proved, be dismissed as "old," but it could never be for-gotten that he had been a "master" to all the younger generation. Actually he was never more so than at the opening of the twenties.

PART FIVE

1921–1930

VIII. Textile Block Houses and Projects and Cantilevered Skyscraper Projects

THE Imperial Hotel was finally completed in 1922 and Wright then returned from Japan for good. By this time "Hollyhock House" and the two studio houses for Aline Barnsdall in Los Angeles were also finished and it was evident that the other Barnsdall projects would come to nothing. But in the early twenties while Wright was still travelling back and forth between Tokio and Los Angeles new applications of ferro-concrete construction were taking form in his mind. The more dramatic of these for skyscrapers built on the cantilever principle that had been worked out for the Imperial Hotel was in a sense not wholly new nor destined to come to actual execution. Discussion of the cantilevered skyscraper projects, whose hung screen surfaces of copper and glass were perhaps as remarkable as their structure, can well follow that of the other new type of construction, the "textile" cement block process, which was used in most of the buildings actually executed between 1921 and 1930.

The first crystallization of the textile block process was in a house project presumably designed in 1921 for execution in Los Angeles just before Wright's last trip to Japan. The idea was to combine metal reinforcement with precast blocks, running a textile-like warp and woof of metal rods in hollowed joints between the blocks and then filling the hollows with protecting cement. The resulting wall was not of the order of masonry wall, like most cement block construction, nor yet like a continuous slab. It was rather a sort of mosaic shell strengthened by the reinforcements in the joints. Moreover the same shells could be used for inside and outside wall surfaces, with insulating space between.

This block construction was intended to be used in the large projects of 1921 and 1922 which never came to execution, the Doheny ranch development (Fig. 243), the Johnson desert compound, and for the substructure of the Tahoe summer colony cabins (Fig. 245, 246, 247, 248). But its quality can be far better appreciated in the series of houses which were designed in 1922 and built in 1923 and 1924 in Pasadena and Hollywood.

The finest of these and the first to be designed, according to Wright, was that for Mrs. George Madison Millard in Pasadena, whose house in Highland Park he had built fifteen years before. "La Miniatura," as the house is called, compares in quality with the finest of Wright's Prairie houses. And if it seems to differ from them entirely, those differences derive from the most fundamental of Wright's principles. It is, indeed, these recurrent differences, the apparently inexhaustible variety of his individual solutions, which make Wright's architecture universal. The Chicago architect of the nineties, the Middle Western architect of 1900–1910, had in the previous decade received world-wide acclaim. The Imperial Hotel is seriously described in guide books as "Old Japanese" in style! Now in "La Miniatura" Wright seemed at first to be establishing a regional Californian style. Actually, however, although the insulated solidity of the house and the textured surfaces are specifically suited to the California climate with its heat and brilliant sunlight, the house is even more the expression of the new textile block construction. Nor is it adapted just to any Southern California site, but to a particular one at the bottom of a ravine (Fig. 249). In other words, Wright's California houses are not so much an illustration of his adaptation to a general region very different from the prairies of the Middle West as of his capacity to renew again and again his architectural imagination by drawing on the implications of particular uses of materials and the opportunities of very carefully chosen sites.

The plan of the Millard house and its composition are both very simple (Fig. 251). The house is tall, so that it may rise up out of the ravine, and because it is entered from the side at the second floor level. The living room on this level is tall also, corresponding to two storeys of bedrooms behind. The dining room and the services are below at the level of the garden in the ravine. The compact scheme of the plan, the solid plasticity of the mass, contrast sharply with the articulation of earlier houses. Yet there is a complex flow of space, outward between the piers of the living room front onto the exterior balcony, and inward, above and below the interior balcony, on either side of the chimney (Fig. 252). Moreover, some of the blocks are pierced, so that points of light within and of dark without sharpen the moulded patterns suggesting, as in the row-windows of the earlier houses, the penetration of interior and exterior space (Fig. 253). The external mass is varied and lightened by subordinate parts, the cantilevered balcony on the front and the bridge at the entrance (Fig. 250), and by other minor projections. The patterns on the blocks further break up the solid surfaces into a continuous play of light and shade (Fig. 254).

The setting of this house is marvellously beautiful. The delicate romantic foliage softens the cubic severity of the silhouette. The water and the reflections in the pool, with the flat terrace in front of the dining room, provide a magic carpet upon which the house seems to float. The sides of the ravine wholly isolate the house from its unsympathetic neighbors.

One of the most remarkable, if quite coincidental, things about this house is its resemblance to the first houses the "international" architects were building in Europe at this time. The use of concrete, the compact plan, the simple mass, are all quite parallel, for example, to the early houses of Le Corbusier and the projects of the Bauhaus. It is also important to stress the differences. After twenty years the chief difference is that this house, because of its special construction, because of the textured surface of its cement blocks, above all perhaps because it has a definite solidity and is not dependent on linear abstractions and paper-like planes, but upon materials of a definite thickness and certain intrinsic visual qualities, is as beautiful a work of architecture as it ever was. Most of the early "international" houses, unfortunately, are today shabby and cracked, and seem poverty-stricken and barren unless one studies them in renderings in which their abstract qualities are clearest or in the best of contemporary photographs. Other differences, such as the sympathetic site and the more human scale, have, of course, always been of primary concern to Wright.

The other early block houses are not so interesting, although the Storer house should be mentioned for its grace (Fig. 255, 256), and the Ennis house for its majesty (Fig. 257-258). Here—and this perhaps as much as the repeated units of formal pattern explains the suggestion of Mayan influence—the great terrace on which the house stands is almost the most prominent feature, while the varying height of the rooms gives an extremely plastic skyline. But beside the Millard house, the Storer house seems to lack privacy, while the Ennis house, crowning one of the Hollywood hills, has somewhat too much the weight and dignity of a public monument. The Freeman house is difficult to photograph because of its hillside site, but the fine interiors are more appropriately furnished than those of the Millard house (Fig. 259–262) which served as an antique shop.

A few years later, at the depth of his personal troubles, Wright advised his former pupil, Albert McArthur, in the use of the textile block system on the Arizona Biltmore Hotel in Phoenix. The commission and the design were McArthur's, though the character of the design is inevitably quite Wrightian. This led to the commission to design San Marcos-in-the-Desert for Dr. Alexander Chandler near Chandler, Arizona. Although this great project for a hotel and several separate houses never came to execution on account of the depression, the drawings were carried out in the fullest detail. The project remains, far more than the Arizona Biltmore, an exciting demonstration of the large-scale possibilities of the textile block system of construction (Fig. 281). Wright's universal architecture found here, perhaps for the first time in history, an adequate expression specifically suited to a desert environment. This is equally apparent in the designs of the individual Young and Cudney houses (Fig. 285, 286, 287, 288).

Here the texture of the blocks was simplified to the zigzag flutes of the Sajuaro cactus (Fig. 284), while the most cunning use was made in plan of 60°–30° angles, which Wright henceforth was to prefer to his earlier octagonal forms. The vast size of this project, with central lounge, dining room, and services (Fig. 282), and two large wings of private suites

(Fig. 283) opening on to receding stepped terraces makes it somewhat difficult to comprehend from drawings. But the superb relationship to the desert setting, as well as the remarkable consistency in the use of the same angles from the largest plan elements to the section of the flutes, should make plain why Wright himself admires this particularly among the many unexecuted projects of these inactive years. He points out that the dotted line given by the fluted blocks is the characteristic line of the desert.

While work was going forward on the drawings for San Marcos-in-the-Desert Wright built his own temporary Ocotillo Camp near Chandler (Fig. 276, 277). Here canvas is the chief material (Fig. 278, 279, 280). As this camp lasted but a year or two and proved to be, in a sense, only a preliminary study for Taliesin West (Fig. 352–359) of similar construction and much greater size, built ten years later near Phoenix, it is not necessary to discuss it here. The San Marcos Water Gardens, a sort of super-tourist-camp project for Dr. Chandler, which was never executed, also made much use of canvas, which was thus for the first time raised by Wright to the dignity of a serious architectural material (Fig. 291, 292).

Block construction of a modified sort is again being used by Wright on the buildings now in construction for Florida Southern College (Fig. 405–408). But the last block house in the cycle of the twenties was that built for his cousin Richard Lloyd Jones in Tulsa, Oklahoma, in 1929. Oklahoma is neither like Southern California nor like the Arizona desert. Hence we find the treatment of the textile blocks once more modified. Light is introduced not through windows of any ordinary sort, but by alternating vertical rows of blocks with window strips of the same width (Fig. 297). Thus, in a sense, there are neither solid walls nor isolated apertures, but only a screen of closely spaced piers between which space flows as freely, although entirely differently, as between the mullions of the horizontal window bands in the early wooden houses (Fig. 298). Rich and elaborate as is this composition, the house unfortunately had neither the planting nor the furnishing which Wright would have desired (Fig. 299, 300, 301,302). For this reason, and perhaps also because most of the blocks are unpatterned, the scale is somewhat difficult to grasp in photographs, though not in reality. But even those who persist in seeing it as a penitentiary many storeys high can appreciate how perfectly coordinated are all the various heights and plan projections of the complex composition.

In apparent contrast to the somewhat Mediterranean quality of design in his textile block buildings in Southern California and Arizona and Oklahoma—Mediterranean because of the character of the climate and the light, not because of any respect for Spanish traditions—Wright also developed a rather Northern virtuosity of design in wood in the twenties. In some cases such as the Tahoe cabins (Fig. 248) and the Nakoma Country Club projects (Fig. 267), there were in the high pointed roofs intentional references to Indian wigwams.

But in the one executed example of this sort of design, the rebuilding of the upper part of the Nathan G. Moore house in Oak Park after a fire in 1922, Wright was so hampered by the special conditions of the problem, that we can form no real idea whether this phase would have been as successful as the cement block houses.

Among Wright's Job-like trials in the twenties was the second burning of Taliesin. The reconstruction followed in general the character of the earlier house, but the interiors were much superior (Fig. 274). Indeed, the Taliesin living room is perhaps Wright's finest domestic interior, the slanting planes of the roof individualized by different sorts of wood stripping, the stone piers and the magnificent stone fireplace forming sturdy, almost naturalistic accents, and the screen-like bookcases and the various window groupings breaking the space up and recombining it in a fashion defying precise analysis (Fig. 273). But the beauty of the room is so much enhanced by its contents, the built-in Oriental objects of art, the judicious mixture of boughten and specially made furniture, the colours of rugs and upholstery, the flower and plant arrangements in the vases, that the total effect passes beyond what an architect can ever give to a client. If the architect controls equally completely everything that goes into a client's house, the result will be somewhat impersonal and abstract, like, say, the Robie dining room. If he has no control, the result will be like the Lloyd Jones interiors. However, in many of the houses of the last few years—although they are too new, too much on their best behavior to be quite typical—the cooperation between the architect and the client has been happier, now that the taste of clients has been more educated toward Wright's standards.

The house for Darwin D. Martin at Derby, N. Y., begun in 1927 but designed a year or two earlier, has somewhat the same vocabulary as Taliesin. But as it was unsupervised it is not one of Wright's really satisfactory houses (Fig. 290). Since its construction, the growth of the planting, doubtless laid out by Mrs. Martin, who had known Wright's work for more than twenty years, has enormously improved it (Fig. 289).

Before we deal with the skyscraper work of the twenties one or two further projects of a more sociological interest should be mentioned. For Dr. Chandler, in addition to the great resort hotel, the related large private houses, and the tourist camp, a type of small block house was designed which was intended to be erected in considerable numbers. Though slightly larger, this was in many ways an improved version of the 1919 Monolith Homes (Fig. 295). Since some of Wright's work of the twenties laid him open to the silly charge of designing chiefly for millionaires, it is a pity this small house project is not better known. Had some of these houses been built in that era of architectural expansiveness, they might have been as remarkable examples of Wright's ability to design relatively inexpensive houses as the Usonian houses of the thirties. The plans are compact and rather enclosed, which perhaps explains why Wright called them "conventional" houses in a variant version worked out in 1932.

Motoring back and forth between Wisconsin and Arizona, Wright came to realize the importance of the filling station in the American scheme of things. Two projects, one for a village service station, of the sort that in thinly settled areas has many uses besides purveying gasoline, and one for a less elaborate urban station, were prepared (Fig. 293). It is a great pity that in these years, when many of the oil companies were beginning to establish standard models of stations after the stylistic orgies of the earlier twenties, no one made use of these designs.

In comparison with the first decade of the century Wright seems to have built little in the twenties, when unfortunately his compatriots in the last throes of "tasteful" revivalism were building far too much. Never was what Wright stood for so incomprehensible in his own country. Moreover, he was continuously harried in his private life, driven from Taliesin, and to some extent out of contact with his environment after seven years off and on in the Orient. The wonder must be not that he built so little, but that he built as much as he did, and that so many elaborate projects of the greatest consequence came in these years from his fertile brain. Indeed, it would almost seem as if his brain was more fertile than it had ever been, as if after the years in which he had concentrated almost entirely on two clients, the Japanese Imperial Family and Aline Barnsdall, his creative potentialities were wider and yet more expertly canalized than ever before. In retrospect it is ironic to realize how little his range and his depth were realized in those years, how generally he was treated by his compatriots and by foreigners alike—if for rather opposed reasons—as an "old master" whose work in the world had been completed by 1910.

In the last great age of skyscraper building it is even more ironic that Wright, who had actually worked with Sullivan on the first great skyscrapers thirty years before, built none. But there are two skyscraper projects of considerable importance, whose cantilevered construction and copper and glass exterior screens have already been mentioned. In the midtwenties Wright worked for several years developing an idea of 1920 for Albert M. Johnson, for whom he had prepared the Death Valley desert compound project in 1922.

The National Life Insurance Building was to have been erected on Water Tower Square in Chicago. Unlike most of the skyscrapers of the period it was not a solid tower stepped at the top in conformity with the New York zoning law. The main block of the building was very thin and from this block wings projected out on one side with light courts between. Thus in a single building of very large size some of the advantages of widely spaced skyscrapers were achieved. The location, moreover, was well north of the skyscraper areas of Chicago and the building might have been expected to stand alone, at least for some time (Fig. 263–266).

The paired supports were in the center of the main block and of the wings and from them the floors were cantilevered out. Thus, there was no external skeleton at all and the sheathing of copper grilles, almost entirely filled with glass, was to be hung from the edges of the cantilevered floors. No comparable openness of surface was achieved in executed skyscrapers until the very end of the skyscraper building period. But Howe and Lescaze's Philadelphia Savings Fund Society Building in Philadelphia and Hood's McGraw-Hill Building in New York were both more conventional in construction and even in general composition. This project stands with San Marcos-in-the-Desert as one of the really great buildings of the twenties that never came to execution on account of the depression. Indeed, as the real estate boom collapsed very early in Chicago, the project was given up just as the Chandler project was started.

As if pursued by depression, Wright prepared his other skyscraper project, St. Mark's Tower, an apartment house to be built in New York in 1929! But of this a later development for Washington, Crystal Heights, may now at long last be built (Fig. 411–413).

St. Mark's Tower, like the National Life project, has its concrete supports in the center, cantilevered floors and hung wall-screens of copper and glass. It is, however, entirely different in planning. Within a polygon, four apartments are grouped on each floor about the central core of stairs and elevators between the central supports. The apartments are duplex, with high studio living room and balconies, and their various elements are most ingeniously and compactly organized of polygonal and oblique forms within the main polygon of the tower (Fig. 307).

A related project of the next year for a group of apartment towers in Chicago links the polygons of St. Mark's Tower in couples and represents a scheme of greater urbanistic significance, since the towers were intended to rise in a much less congested area than on 2nd Avenue in New York (Fig. 308). Although better known because of ample publication and frequent exhibition of the model, St. Mark's Tower is the inferior as well as the earlier version. It is some consolation to believe that the present Crystal Heights project is superior to both.

The Elizabeth Noble apartment house project is hardly a skyscraper, but it is a model of excellence in small apartment design. The ferro-concrete cantilevers are possibly less audacious, but the ample planning, with rectangular rooms and large terraces before most of the living rooms, provides what is almost like a series of superposed penthouses. The clean contrast of plain concrete walls with very large open areas of copper and glass is curiously parallel to the "international" work of the time, and devoid of the particular decorative virtuosity of the copper grilles of the National Life or the interlocking polygons of St. Mark's Tower (Fig. 303, 304).

Another interesting project of the twenties for a "Steel Cathedral embracing minor cathedrals" is certainly a skyscraper in size. Half again as tall as the Eiffel Tower, still in 1926 the tallest edifice in the world, and intended to contain a million people, it would have been a sort of religious Empire State Building. The designs were never carried very far, although the project appears again later in Broadacre City. And the scale is so tremendous that it is difficult to grasp either the principles of the tenuous steel construction, or the complex intersecting polygons of the plan and triangles of the exterior. It is in spirit curiously like some of the wooden projects of the immediately preceding years, a kind of heavenly wigwam as fantastic as some of Buckminster Fuller's house designs of these years. But if this project is really fantastic, and economically unrealizable even in a boom period like the mid-twenties, it is important to recognize that the other skyscraper projects by Wright in the twenties were not. Indeed, in retrospect we can see that they were far less fantastic than most of the skyscrapers that were erected.

The particular decorative exuberance of Wright's major work of the previous decade, which continued to a considerable extent in the early twenties, definitely diminished after the rebuilding of Taliesin in 1925. The Lloyd Jones house executed and the Elizabeth Noble apartment project compare in directness of structural expression and restraint in ornament with the finest wooden houses before 1910. Yet they are completely free from traditional methods of construction, wholly determined in design by the nature of their reinforced block and slab construction. To the eyes of the time Wright did not, in the twenties, seem always at the forefront of architectural progress. But the eyes of the twenties were in many respects rather blind. In the next decade his reputation, particularly in America—Europeans continued through the twenties to publish new books on his work—rose again. At long last the prophet of modern architecture, so strangely misunderstood in the twenties, began to receive honor in his own country.

PART SIX

1931–1941

IX. Projects of the Depression Years and the Current Revival of Activity

WRIGHT suffered more than most architects from the depression. As we have seen, most of the major projects of the mid and late twenties failed to come to execution. And in the early thirties, he was no busier with actual building than his colleagues. But these years were not inactive. He published several books and lectured widely, while the exhibition prepared for the Chicago Art Institute in 1930 circulated both abroad and at home. If many were still inclined to think of Wright as an "old master," a sort of ancestor of the new European architecture which was beginning to be widely known and even imitated in America, his lectures, publications, and exhibitions now made his work increasingly well known at home and abroad. Most critics were profoundly shocked that the Chicago World's Fair of 1933 made no use of his talents. When Wright's work was included, perhaps without his enthusiastic approval, in the International Exhibition of Modern Architecture held at the Museum of Modern Art in 1932, it was obvious that his work alone balanced the European work that was shown. Most of the other work by Americans appeared derivative.

The "House on the Mesa," prepared for this exhibition and shown in a fine model, was a luxurious mansion, a "five-car house," as Wright effectively described its scale. No project of Wright's, except possibly the Elizabeth Noble apartment house, could have displayed so well the similarities and the differences between Wright's work and that of the European leaders (Fig. 310). No house of theirs was more open or dramatic in the exploitation of cantilevered concrete construction. No plan so clearly segregated general living space from master's and service wings (Fig. 311)—in the tradition of the Coonley house; no composition handled dominating horizontals with more breath-taking ease, or achieved the ultimate in soaring lightness by suspending the metal frames of the windows from the cantilevered roof slab. Above all, no European house was so superbly compounded of interflowing exterior and interior space. Landscape setting there was none, except in so far as the name implied the openness of a western mesa, but the lay-out of pool and terraces, the tremendous volume of the great living room, with its open screen walls, the long anchor of the more solid wings on the entrance side, produced an abstract organism of planes and lines in space beside which the European houses, both executed and projected, appeared earth-bound and two-dimensional. In Wright's own words, "the whole was integral in character, completely in the nature of materials." While a critic has said it "achieved a significant unity and purity of style never excelled by the Greeks, with an integrity of means to ends never dreamed of by them."

Another important project of 1931 was that for the Capital Journal Building in Portland, Oregon. This made use of a quite different sort of ferro-concrete construction with isolated piers. But as this construction was actually used in the S. C. Johnson and Son Administration Building in Racine, Wisconsin, begun in 1936, it can better be discussed later. The chief difference in the Oregon project, in which the principle of the construction was first worked out five years before, is that the walls are but light screens of glass in metal frames suspended from the roof slab (Fig. 328, 329).

The two other major events of Wright's career in these years were the founding of the Taliesin Fellowship and the development of the regional planning model known as Broadacre City.

Earlier in his life Wright had developed schemes by which those who were his draftsmen could share, as in no other architectural office, in a broad educational experience. This had already been true to some extent in the Oak Park days before 1910, and a sort of minor version of the Fellowship had been run at Taliesin in the years 1919–24. Unfortunately in these years Wright was in Japan or in California most of the time. Although the ideal never fell into abeyance and Wright's associates were always to some extent apprentices, it was not until 1929 that Wright first prepared a scheme for adapting the old Hillside Home School buildings of 1887 and 1902 as a School of the Allied Arts, and not for several years more that the present Taliesin Fellowship was actually initiated. A new project for remodelling the Hillside buildings was made in 1932 and in 1933 began the actual work on the Fellowship complex, which is still far from finished. The new drafting room with its tremendously long and light wooden trusses, which Wright delights to describe as an abstract forest, and the moving picture theater, arranged in one end of the old school building, are the elements of greatest architectural interest thus far executed. But as more and more commissions came to Wright after 1935, work on the Fellowship buildings slowed down. It is no part of the present story, which is concerned only with Wright's executed buildings and projects, to deal with his educational programme. But it is an ironic indication of the success of the Fellowship that its own buildings are unfinished. For Wright has kept the members of the Fellowship so busy as real apprentices on major architectural commissions of all sorts that this remodelling on which they set to work in the dull years of the early thirties has properly been neglected.

In all the preceding periods of Wright's work there were important projects which indicated his vital and continuing interest in large-scale problems of planning. But this book is no more concerned with Wright as a city planner or regional planner than as an educator. The subject merits a special volume and fortunately Wright has himself devoted a volume to the subject as well as many minor passages in his other writings. *The Disappearing City* [c1932] offers in its title the essence of Wright's urbanistic, or perhaps one should rather say, anti-urbanistic thesis. The thesis was superbly actualized in the tremendous model of Broadacre City, for which Edgar J. Kaufmann provided the initial fund with which Wright and the members of the Fellowship went to work. They worked for several years on this project before it was first exhibited in New York in the spring of 1935 at Rockefeller Center. It was later circulated rather widely and then withdrawn for safekeeping at Hillside. Additions and improvements to the model were made before it was shown once more in New York at the exhibition at the Museum of Modern Art in 1940.

Broadacre City is, of course, not a city in any ordinary sense. The project covers four square miles at a county seat and contains a vast number of individual edifices of various types. Many of these types had been established by Wright in separate projects in the preceding decade. Of these the members of the Fellowship made tiny models to the scale of the whole vast scheme in order to show them not as microcosms but as parts of a coherent macrocosm. Among the earlier projects which found a new meaning in relation to the rest of Broadacre City were such apparently unique designs as the Gordon Strong Planetarium of 1925 and the Steel Cathedral of 1926. Other items of less special character were many apartment houses on the model of St. Mark's Tower (Fig. 305) and that for Elizabeth Noble of 1929 (Fig. 303), and the gasoline and service stations of 1928 (Fig. 293). The farm units and the market units first prepared for Walter Davidson in 1932 (Fig. 312), were even more important to the total theory of Broadacre City. For according to Wright's basic ideal agriculture of human scale and dignity should balance small industries which were to be housed in units based on the Capital Journal project of 1931 (Fig. 329).

Of houses there were to be many types, from the five-car "House on the Mesa" project at the extreme of luxury, down through some newly designed "two-car" houses, and the smaller Chandler block houses (Fig. 295) of 1927 to the most minimal separate dwellings. In 1940 houses of the Usonian type were substituted for the earlier minimal dwellings. These minimal types of the early thirties undoubtedly prepared the way for the development of the first Usonian project for the Hoult house in Wichita the year after Broadacre City was first completed.

Separate designs were also made for many other types of buildings in Broadacre City. There was a theater based on the project of 1932; a college, the germ of the Florida Southern scheme now in construction (Fig. 405); schools; hospitals; one large factory for building

[87]

aerotors (for Broadacre City was to make use of new and improved methods of air transport); aerotor-ports and hotels. Special bridges were designed for safe route crossings in relation to large scale plans for long and short distance automobile traffic, a premonition of Norman Bel Geddes Futurama of 1939, but, according to Wright, with many traffic-coordinations and detailed solutions not to be found in that project.

One can, indeed, hardly name all the elements of a good life for which architectural provision was made. There were art schools on the model of the Fellowship itself, professional office buildings for architects and others, and, of course, general stores, as well as an administrative center for a minimum of county governmental activities.

So large and complex a scheme can hardly be adequately illustrated or explained here. And indeed in essence Broadacre City is more a frame for architecture than a collection of individual projects. But it does summarize much of Wright's thought throughout a lifetime and brings into coherent relationship the many remarkable individual projects of the ten preceding years when so very little was actually built.

In addition to the remodelling of the Hillside Home School buildings for the Fellowship begun in 1933, there was one house executed before 1935. The Willey house, built in 1934 in Minneapolis, and even more the first project for this house, designed in 1932, seem to open a new cycle of Wright's architecture, the cycle in which production continues so very actively today. But the Willey house is not yet of the Usonian type; nor is it a complex and unique structure like the Kaufmann house or the Johnson Building, begun two years later, which signalized to the world that Wright, the "old master," Wright, the ancestor of modern architecture, was once more in actual building as well as in his ideas leading the world.

The Willey house is not particularly exciting, indeed, it is rather remarkable for a certain reduction of tension. The materials are brick and wood, no more novel than the materials of Wright's great houses of the opening of the century; and they are used with a curiously quiet charm (Fig. 316). The plan has no striking innovations, except for the glazed screen of shelves between the kitchen—in Wright's terminology now the "work-space"—and the living room (Fig. 317). The whole house is on one floor, the hip roof rising higher over the living room, while the terrace is sheltered by an open pergola above). The earlier project was somewhat less conventional in that the bedrooms were below and a cantilevered wooden balcony projected in front of the living room with a parapet of lapped siding canted outward, a favorite motif of the following years (Fig. 314, 315).

In connection with certain work of the previous decade, and even more with the "House on the Mesa" project, exhibited in the same year the first Willey project was designed, the strange parallelism between certain aspects of Wright's work and developments in the work of the European leaders of modern architecture has been noted. Little influence flowed in either direction in these years and yet both Wright and the younger Europeans, for all their lack of sympathy for each other's current work, seemed to respond to some common spirit of the times.

We can feel this once again in the Willey house in the quietness, the discretion and the straightforward use of such traditional materials as had retained their economic advantages in the face of the bold innovations of the twenties. With Wright this was merely to utilize once more a mastery he had never lost, and implied no real break with the immediate past. There was for him no difference between this continued use of brick and wood and the bold exploitation of new materials in new types of construction. The Capital Journal project and the "House on the Mesa" project both, of the year before the first Willey project, in which two quite different sorts of concrete construction were intended, or the Kaufmann house and the Johnson Building begun two years after the Willey house was built, in which these two types of construction were carried to execution, did not exist for him in a different architectural world. For his architectural world was universal. Unfortunately, this was not always the case with the Europeans, when they met the détente of the thirties, or with certain Americans. For they had in principle rejected traditional materials in the twenties, as Wright had never done, and their return to brick and wood was often a little sheepish and hesitant. Wright has pointed out that he was by this time the author of hundreds of executed buildings while the younger architects had built very little either with old or new materials. This may explain a good part of the difference.

It is too much of a paradox to say that the novelty of the Willey house is that it is not very novel, in terms of the innovations of the preceding decade. But it is not too much to say that it opens with particular effectiveness a new period in modern architecture in general, and not in Wright's work alone. The ancestor of modern architecture sensed that the architecture of the middle of the twentieth century need not be as different from that of the opening of the century as everyone, even perhaps he himself for a little, had believed in the twenties.

In 1936 building really began to revive. In Wright's architectural career the upturn is signalized by two of the most remarkable commissions of his fifty years of building activity. "Falling Water," the Kaufmann house in the Pennsylvania woods, which was completed within the year, and the Johnson Administration Building, which was several years in construction, were widely recognized as classic masterpieces even before they were finished, and amply published and exhibited. And doubtless the publicity these two works received and the general recognition that they represented Wright's genius in a new guise explains, quite as much as the general revival of building activity in the following years, the very large number of commissions that have come to him in the last five years. The majority of these commissions were for smaller houses; and Wright believes that after Broadacre City, his most important work has been the development of the Usonian house type for clients of moderate means of which the first project was also of 1936. But architecture lives not alone by the establishment of types and through the solution of generic problems but quite as much by the thrill and the acclaim of unique masterpieces. Moreover, in the preceding years of depression, while the sterling worth of the Willey house was recognized, it represented, as we have said, the general architectural détente of the thirties. Now confidence in the possibilities of a new architecture, so high in the mid-twenties and later so low, rose once more with the recognition that executed buildings, not just pictorial projects, could successfully maintain the high hopes of an architecture of innovation. Moreover innovations as bold as any suggested in previous years had been warmed and humanized by Wright's intuitive respect for the nature of materials, and in the case of the Kaufmann house, by his superb exploitation of an extraordinary site (Fig. 320).

The Kaufmann house combines two sorts of romanticism, the romanticism about nature, which has flourished since the eighteenth century, and the romanticism about scientific feats of construction, often considered of quite opposite character. A house over a waterfall sounds like a poet's dream. A house *cantilevered* over a waterfall is rather the realized dream of an engineer. Through the forest trees, the long horizontals of slabs and parapets seem to float in space (Fig. 322). The metal sash enclosing the rooms are hardly visible and offer no such sense of support as the wooden and masonry mullions of the Prairie houses. The strength of the structure is patently in the rigidity of the slabs alone and in the solidity with which they are anchored at the rear (Fig. 321). They are anchored not only to the rock of the waterfall edge itself, but also to the solid core of masonry at the rear of the house, built up in great rough pylons of native stone. This stone-work offers the sharpest visual contrast of striated naturalistic surfaces and mottled colour to the clean, precise, light-coloured forms of the concrete. Thus, as from the beginning of Wright's mature work, there is a sort of plaiting in space of horizontals and verticals; light tenuous horizontal planes, here more abstract than the sloping eaves of the prairie houses; and sturdy, massive, articulated verticals, rock of nature's rock, core and heart of the whole construction. But the composition is now at once very complex and very free. Although some hint of a cross form above a square remains, the organic order is rather that of a natural product than of geometry, regularly modular like a crystalline structure, but beyond any simple description in geometrical terms.

Although this was a rather large house, it was not expensive for its size. As it was intended for a week-end retreat an openness of plan such as has hitherto been used only in small houses was possible (Fig. 321). The living area was unified, although the many breaks in the basically square shape suggest the functional differentiation of the different parts. Even in the sleeping quarters above, which provide accommodations more in the nature of bed-sitting rooms or private suites than ordinary bedrooms, there is a remarkable openness. In them it is due more to the way in which each suite opens upon its own terrace than to any loss of interior privacy.

As in the block houses of the twenties, inside and outside are essentially one in treatment. In each room both the solid mass of the vertical masonry core and the rigid suspension of the reinforced slabs is evident, while built-in fittings of wood humanize the scale and the surface textures (Fig. 323). Outside steps, actually starting within the living room, lead down into the stream. Pools hold the water for bathing purposes. Projections of the concrete slabs are pierced to form pergola-like grilles over which plants may hang. Yet nothing is done to interfere with the lush natural growth of the woods, or to dam the flow of the torrent. Never, even in Wright's work, has architecture as the product of man been so perfectly balanced and contrasted with the natural setting. For never has the natural setting been wilder or more superb in its original condition, and never has the work of man been bolder or in a sense more arbitrary in its placing. But so perfect, so apparently inevitable, is the juxtaposition that one cannot imagine such a house in a different setting or a different house in this setting. Ordinary questions of functionalism receive new answers, not because this is not a practical house to live in, but because it is so pre-eminently a comfortable house to live in over a waterfall.

There are no projects leading up to the Kaufmann house unless it be the "House on the Mesa." It seems to have sprung as suddenly from the brow of Wright as did the River Forest Golf Club more than a generation earlier, with the difference that the world was now prepared to appreciate it, and to receive with loud acclaim a building that seemed to epitomize the aspirations not of Wright alone, but of all modern architects. After the twenties, in which the direction of the European leaders and the direction of Wright seemed sharply opposed, despite all the coincidences which we now recognize, now in the later thirties as new countries, Finland and England, came to achievement in modern architecture equalling that of France and Holland and Germany in the previous decade, architecture could be seen to be advancing on a deeper and broader, if less "international" front. And the Kaufmann house was one of the first and most striking demonstrations that a new cycle of world architecture had opened, a cycle, alas, destined within two or three years for a premature end in Europe with the coming of war.

Preliminary construction of the S. C. Johnson Administration Building began in the early fall of 1936, when the Kaufmann house was nearly finished (Fig. 327). But so novel were the hollow tapered piers (Fig. 331), reinforced by tissues of expanded metal lath and supporting only their own lily-pad-like tops, that a building permit was not issued until the following spring (Fig. 326). Nor was the building finally completed, with the furniture and fittings designed by Wright and specially made, until the spring of 1939.

In some ways this is a more luxurious structure than the Kaufmann house, but except for the length of the building campaign it was not relatively very expensive for an office building. It has often been pointed out that the area could easily have been roofed with metal trusses and quite unbroken by piers (Fig. 330). Hence the unimaginative—who do not include the general public, which has flocked to visit the building ever since it was finished—have never comprehended the piers. The system of construction is, of course, that intended for the Capital Journal Building in Salem, Oregon, in the project of 1931 (Fig. 326). The piers do not support anything. They stand like so many plants, providing the solid part of the roofs with their own extensive circular tops, in a fashion somewhat like Maillart's Swiss type of mushroom columns, but entirely opposed to the post-and-lintel principle of most American concrete construction (Fig. 336). Amazingly small at their bases, which rest in nine-inch bronze holders, they do not break up the working space in a functional sense. While in an esthetic sense their lithe repeated shafts, as organic as those of some hollow-stemmed plant, really *create* the interior space.

For the interior space is here entirely cut off from the outside (Fig. 333). The light, coming straight down from the open spaces between the lily-pad pier tops, and entering also in bands below the surrounding balcony and at the top of the wall, is extraordinarily even. Perhaps because of its points of origin, perhaps because of the pyrex glass tubes which fill the openings, the light has a very special quality. With the special forms of the piers, there is a certain illusion of sky seen from the bottom of an aquarium.

The walls of the building, which are but screens stopped below continuous bands of glass tubes where the cornice would be on a traditional structure and the more solid core of the building (ventilation system, staircases, etc.) as well as the balcony parapets are of a specially made hard red brick, mechanically perfect, with raked horizontal joints, and a finish as even as that of the waxed linoleum of the floors (Fig. 334). For here nothing is rustic or casual, everything is polished and smooth (Fig. 337). The very plans and sections of the building, with their curved corners and balanced oblique elements, suggest some large-scale piece of machinery more successfully than the work of those architects who have praised more loudly, if not for so long, the machine ideal.

There are many unusual elements outside the main office space of this building—the auditorium, the bridge, the squash courts, the garages, and the tremendous car port—which deserve mention. Moreover, there are several other structural elements, such as the domed slab of the "car-port," almost as remarkable as the hollow piers and the pyrex tube glazing. Nor can the special steel and magnesite furniture, the first executed from Wright's designs since the epoch-making office furniture in the Larkin Building of 1904, be ignored. But by the time this building was completed Wright was in the full flood of a production as extensive as that of the first decade of the century; and already in 1937 and 1938 there are many other outside commissions which must be discussed, as well as the construction of Wright's own winter camp in the Arizona desert.

The Herbert Jacobs house, the first Usonian house, was built in 1937 outside of Madison, Wisconsin, for $5500. It follows closely the project for the H. C. Hoult house in Wichita of the previous year. In 1936 a house was built for Mrs. Abby Beecher Roberts outside Marquette, Michigan, and in 1937 a house for Herbert Johnson north of Racine and a house for Paul Hanna in Palo Alto, California. But in all this revival of activity the very inexpensive Jacobs house is after the Kaufmann house and the Johnson building the most important. Although somewhat larger than the Willey house of 1934, the Roberts house, at least as it has been altered by the client, is not an improved version, and in all this spate of renewed production can be ignored.

The more successful and very much more elaborate Johnson house is a "zoned" house, with four large arms projecting from a central mass in which the living areas are grouped about a chimney. Extending the principle of the Coonley house, one cross arm contains the master's rooms, another the guest's and children's accommodations, a third the services and a fourth the garage space. This tremendous house is in Wright's estimation "the last of the Prairie houses." However, except for the interest in the zoned plan, and the tall spaces of the living areas flowing upward around the chimney shaft to a curiously clerestoreyed roof, it is not perhaps of great importance (Fig. 341). The new vocabulary of form and construction in brick and lapped siding can be more clearly apprehended in other contemporary houses of ordinary scale. The last of the great houses in the Prairie tradition, so magnificently exploited thirty years earlier, is less significant in the thirties than the small Usonian houses and the slightly larger houses of similar type of which the Hanna house is one of the earliest and best.

It may be recalled that optimists in the thirties believed that the tide of depression would be turned and America's housing problems solved by prefabrication. New materials of all sorts were the hope of the prefabricators in the mid-thirties and Wright's Ready-Cut projects of twenty years earlier were ignored because they depended upon traditional materials. But the business world was not able to sell the new prefabricated models of the architects and technicians in any numbers, and real success, as everyone realized, could only come with mass production. Whose was the fault we cannot be sure. But Wright was no more successful than anyone else in finding sponsors for his small block houses of the twenties or his more completely prefabricated "All-Steel" houses of 1937. Wright points out that he offered new houses as well as new methods, while the others generally preferred to offer old types of houses built by inconsistent new methods.

In the Usonian house, as projected for the Hoults in Wichita in 1936 and as executed for the Jacobs in Madison in 1937, Wright, as so often before, analyzed a structural concept, went to the heart of a way of using materials, and evolved a method of production quite different from prefabrication as others envisaged it and more adapted to actual contemporary conditions. The essence of most schemes for prefabrication lies in the ideal of factory production of wall units. The essence of the Usonian house lies rather more, in Wright's words, in the fabrication of the whole as a unit, and in the principle of its heating. Usonian houses rest on a concrete slab under which in broken stone filling are placed the heating pipes. This has proved to be a very simple and efficient sort of heating, "heating by gravity," as Wright calls it, which puts no premium upon an enclosed plan. Thus the Usonian houses can have the large glass areas and the open flow of rooms of Wright's larger houses without any sacrifice of comfort or economy. The floor slab and a masonry core in which are the chimney, the small heater room, and the kitchen, lighted and ventilated by a clerestorey rising above the bedroom wing, are alone of wet construction. The rest of the house is of dry construction, which is, of course, one of the great theoretical advantages of prefabricated construction.

The walls may be but usually are not factory-made nor do they utilize new materials, except in their plywood centers. But they are, in a sense, prefabricated on the job, like a sandwich, the plywood center lined on both sides with building paper and faced on the exterior and the interior with various sorts of wooden siding screwed tightly together. Thus, there is no skeleton of studs, and the wall sections, prepared in advance, are joined together at the corners like a sort of box. In Wright's words, instead of the house going to the factory the factory comes to the house. Banks of wall-high doors between wooden mullions provide large areas of glass in living rooms and bedrooms, while above the other walls similarly framed windows are arranged in clerestoreys (Fig. 343). Since the heights of the different parts of the houses are ordinarily varied, light comes in from above on all sides if desired, while the solid lower walls provide protection from the street or from the North. Such a principle of construction is very elastic and permits infinite variation of plan. Furthermore, the elements in the wall sandwich may be varied. Sunk battens of redwood and wider boards of a cheaper wood were used both externally and internally on the Jacobs house. Several of the later houses are of cypress with lapped siding inside and out, while the Winkler-Goetsch house (Fig. 376) is of redwood throughout.

The roofs of these houses are built up of crossed two-by-fours on four-foot or five-foot centers, the module that underlies the entire plan and the elevations. The roof slabs are lightened by the way in which the upper layer projects beyond the lower and are frequently pierced to form a trellis for vines over and in front of openings like the pergola of the Willey house. In the Jacobs house the underside of the roof was sheathed with wall board, since replaced with a better material. In later examples plywood or the same lapped siding of the walls, arranged with mitered corners to define by the linear pattern the enclosed space of the interior, provide a more elegant finish. In several of the later houses also the walls are set up not as verticals but with a slight batter, one board lapping the next like the battered wooden balcony parapets which are so striking a feature of the cantilevered terraces of the Johnson house, and doors are often but a hinged section of the ordinary walls indistinguishable but for the hardware.

The Usonian type has been much perfected and elaborated since the Jacobs house was completed and there has been an interchange of influence between the very small houses of the scale of the Jacobs house built for from seven to ten thousand dollars and the larger houses in which greater expansion of plan and composition was possible but with no essential difference in construction and expression.

The Hoult project and the Jacobs house were L-shaped with the living room at one end, the bedrooms at the other and the entrance and services in the angle (Fig. 344). Both the living room and the bedrooms open on the partially enclosed garden terrace, while the other walls toward the street and the lot line are blank except for the high clerestorey windows. The long horizontals of the wall sheathing and of the roof slab give extension and serenity to the composition which the differing heights vary and elaborate. The Rosenbaum house in Florence, Alabama, of 1939 is very similar (Fig. 346, 381, 382, 383).

The much larger Hanna house of 1937 in Palo Alto has a plan based on the 60°–30° angles of which Wright had made much use in the projects of the later twenties (Fig. 351). With the hexagonal module the space effects are somewhat richer or, as Wright puts it, "more reflex" than with the four- or five-foot module which has been more generally used.

This house is also superbly placed on a hill-crest (Fig. 347, 348) whose line the broken plan follows, with the living room opening toward the more distant view and the inner side of the house partially surrounding a sort of court. (Fig. 349, 350).

Several later houses, such as the Manson house (Fig. 399) in Wausau, Wisconsin, and the Sidney Bazett house (Fig. 384) in Hillsborough, California, make similar use of the hexagonal module. Oblique wings are also used on the Armstrong house near Gary, Indiana, of 1939, and the Nesbitt house at Cypress Point, on Carmel Bay, California, now in construction.

But rather more of the small houses of the last few years are based on the square module with more compact planning than that of the L-shaped Jacobs house. Of these one of the best is the Winkler-Goetsch house, the only one executed of a group of seven intended to have been built in 1939 near Okemos, Michigan (Fig. 374). Here the large living room has ranges of glass doors on the entrance side and long windows toward the view (Fig. 377). Out of this very open area, further lighted by clerestoreys above, are two partly enclosed areas. One is a sort of very large inglenook with a great fireplace and bookshelves below the low clerestorey (Fig. 378). The other is the "work-space" (kitchen) behind the chimney, with its narrow end open toward the living room, and surrounded by cupboards and other storage facilities. The bedroom wing extends in the other direction, the rooms opening on a grassed terrace protected by a high wooden parapet of the same construction as the house walls. Here, as in most of these houses, the main roof slab is cantilevered very far out at the entrance to provide shelter for the automobile, the "car-port" which in Wright's current practice takes the place of a garage.

So many of these houses have been built, particularly in 1939 and 1940, and so subtly varied are the plans and the external expression, that it becomes as difficult to cover them adequately as the great series of Prairie houses in the years before 1910 (Fig. 401, 402). Moreover, they are all so new that they do not seem to fall into groups as readily as do the early houses seen in retrospect after thirty years. But before closing the subject of Usonian and related houses—a subject which is actually still very open, as several are still in construction and others are being projected—certain houses and projects which if not unique are rather different from the norm of the Jacobs house and of the Hanna house with which the cycle opened in 1937 should be specifically mentioned.

In 1938 *Life* commissioned a "House for a family of $5000–$6000 income" which, of course, received tremendous publicity. In this house there was conspicuous use of masonry in the piers between the garden doors and elsewhere than in the houses that have been discussed above. As the house was of two storeys, at least in part, the composition was also somewhat more compact and complex (Fig. 360). The Bernard Schwartz house at Two Rivers, Wisconsin, built in 1939, follows very closely the *Life* house project (Fig. 362), and the large Nesbitt house in California now in construction will be somewhat of this type, though considerably larger and more in the spirit of Taliesin itself.

The Sturges house in Brentwood Heights, California, is remarkable for its bold cantilevering. The whole house seems to float from the crest of a knoll (Fig. 379). A somewhat similar effect at a larger scale and on a much finer site will be achieved with the Oboler house now in construction in Los Angeles (Fig. 414). Several other late houses, while they do not make so dramatic and extensive a use of the cantilever, are raised off the ground on piers where the ground is low and likely to be damp.

Of these the Pew house, floating among the trees above Lake Mendota, near Madison, Wisconsin, is a particularly striking example, with its fine rough limestone piers and the superb carpentry—practically cabinetwork—of its battered walls and flat ceilings of lapped cypress siding (Fig. 396, 397). The Lewis house at Libertyville, Illinois, is less open below and has a base and core of brick instead of stone (Fig. 388, 391). It is most remarkable for the rich colours and the harmonious forms of its furnishing in what are perhaps the most successful of all the newer interiors. The Affleck house (Fig. 404), now in construction in Bloomfield Hills, Michigan, will also be raised above a slope on brick piers and wall sections in the manner of the Pew and Lewis houses.

Somewhat related to these Middle Western houses in which masonry plays an important part is the Rose Pauson house of 1940 outside Phoenix. This has a solid canted base of the local purple field stone set in concrete and a lighter wooden superstructure quite like that of the other houses of these years (Fig. 392, 394, 395). It is in site and in the rich and solid simplicity of composition perhaps the most striking of the latest houses.

The real prototype of the masonry of the Pauson house is the permanent base of Wright's own camp in the desert on Maricopa Mesa further out of Phoenix (Fig. 352, 353). The whole platform of Taliesin West, begun in 1938 and still being enlarged and completed, the lower portion of the walls defining the plan, and in places the superstructure as well are of a sort of mosaic of great blocks of the purple volcanic stone of the hills behind set in concrete in forms that are now canted in, now canted out in an extraordinarily subtle way (Fig. 356, 357, 358). Above this solid base the camp is of wood and canvas, an amplification of the earlier Ocotillo Camp, with various sorts of ingenious louvers and canvas-filled screens, so that the sun can be kept out and the cool air let in. The almost prehistoric grandeur of this camp, its superb appropriateness to the scale and the colours and textures of the desert, is most successfully echoed in the somewhat more conventional Pauson house.

[97]

Once more we see that Wright is not the sort of regional architect who is responsive only to the landscape, the climate and light conditions of his native region. Most of the newer houses were designed for and built in the Middle Western and North Eastern states. They have, therefore, a certain similarity of character suited to their surroundings and sharply differentiated winter and summer weather conditions. But the newer California houses, and *a fortiori* those designed for the South Western desert, are quite different in expression, although the wooden elements of the construction are essentially the same. The Schevill house, to be built outside Tucson, Arizona, of the local adobe, but with the concrete slab below and the projecting wooden roof above of the Usonian type, will represent still another creative adaptation to special building materials and conditions.

Not yet built for any client, another type of house projected in these years deserves special mention. Intended first for Ralph Jester, in Palos Verdes, California, and then for Martin Pence in Hilo, Hawaii, the plywood house is apparently a sharp break with the Usonian model, though it merely applies the principles to a different material (Fig. 364). Since plywood can be bent and is stronger in curved forms, all the rooms are circles, set under a continuous slab supported on round stone piers and opening toward a covered central area (Fig. 365). Thus a new material leads once more to a new type of planning, beautifully adapted to a warm, equable climate, and to an expression as new and as pure as even Wright has ever devised.

Despite the tremendous production of these last years it is hard to omit the projects, which perpetually suggest potentialities of achievement even yet unrealized. But the Suntop Homes in Ardmore, Pennsylvania, of 1939, of which one quadruple unit was executed, are doubtless more important than the Jester-Pence plywood projects or certain Usonian designs, such as the Jurgenson house and the Carlson house of 1938, in which pitched roofs, used with extraordinary drama and unconventionality, were substituted for the more usual flat slab roofs. In the Carlson house particularly this provides an expression of shelter from the northern winter as specific as the expression of protection from the southern sun in the Jester-Pence project.

In the executed unit of Suntop Homes the Usonian ideas were adapted to group housing. The four dwelling units are linked about a cross-shaped brick wall somewhat like grouped units of the St. Mark's Tower project of 1929 (Fig. 367). Moreover, if more quadruple units had been built, they were to have been placed on the site so as to give each the same privacy which is given in the executed unit to its four separate dwellings (Fig. 368).

The architectural vocabulary of masonry wall sections, great french doors framed in natural wood and canted parapets of lapped siding is that of the Usonian homes, as is the floor-slab heating system only partially in effect in this scheme. However, the visual result is very different, because the dwellings run vertically upward instead of spreading horizontally. Thus the composition, though asymmetrical on all sides, is crystalline and centralized.

In the Usonian and related houses the design effects are extraordinarily integral. The juxtaposition of materials; the expressive variations of height and width; the contrast of open and closed surfaces; the drama of pitched or flat roof slabs, here sweeping out to cover car-ports, there cut through to let more light into the windows; all these elements produce compositions at once geometrically abstract and materially objective. The superb craftsmanship in brick and stone is sturdy and straightforward, expressing the compact structure of units of burnt clay or the natural stratifications of stone. The cabinetmaker-like precision of the fine redwood and cypress is both simple and rich. The only decorative elements, recalling the leaded glass of the period before 1910 rather than the exuberance of the twenties, are the slotted boards used in some places instead of real windows to light a passage and to suggest the thinness and penetrability of the sandwich wall. The patterns of these slotted boards vary considerably. But in the finest, as in the best "gingerbread" of the mid-nineteenth century, the quality of something sawn in wood is skilfully suggested in the long leaf patterns and the thickened stems of the geometrical plant designs. In his apparent harmony with the general character of the architectural détente of the twenties Wright has neither given up his interest in the more dramatic levitated structure of the twenties—indeed, he seems more interested to free his buildings from the ground than ever before—or his belief that the most complete architecture will always have some sort of detailed development beyond that inherent in the structural use of the materials. In the larger projects and executed works of the last few years this is even more evident as fresh ways of achievement are perpetually found and tried.

The largest commission Wright has undertaken since the Imperial Hotel twenty years before, in the number of separate buildings and the organization of the group plan the most elaborate and complex that has ever come to execution, is Florida Southern College in Lakeland, Florida. The project dates from 1938 and the first of the sixteen buildings planned were begun in 1940 (Fig. 405). The Ann Pfeiffer Memorial Chapel (Fig. 407) and three seminar buildings have been completed; the library is now in construction; so that the general character of the whole can now be appreciated, although it will doubtless be many years more before the whole group is completed.

The flat lakeside, hardly above the water level and without any interesting natural growth, is perhaps the most uninspiring with which Wright has ever had to deal, despite its superficial resemblance to the prairies around Chicago. Here there was little cooperation

[99]

from nature and the architect's responsibility was the greater since he had so little assistance from that partner with whom he has always so closely collaborated.

The general plan is rather formal like all of Wright's group plans (Fig. 406). But there is no academic symmetry. The interest and variety which are lacking in the contours of the site are created by the boldly oblique patterns of the communicating covered ways between the buildings, and the variation in height between the major and minor units. Thus the executed chapel rises high, itself a carillon and flower tower, and its oblique planes establish in the air over the site the chief directions of the flat pattern of the general plan. The low seminar buildings, on the other hand, hug the ground, their flat roofs forming with the covered ways a system of linked planes parallel with the plane of the soil and the water. Another major unit, the library, echoes in its stack tower the oblique planes of the chapel, while the great circular reading room, by its size and its shape, forms a nucleus among the lower surrounding units.

The separate buildings, woven together as one by the covered esplanades, are chiefly constructed of cement blocks, their delicately patterned surfaces contrasted with smooth vertical concrete slabs. The scale of the blocks is smaller than in the California work and the Arizona projects of the twenties. The more frequent use of pierced blocks, with the interstices sometimes filled with cast coloured glass, gives a rather textile effect, light, cool and serene, almost feminine in the manner of crisply starched white hamburg lace. Since the natural environment is all a matter of the flat planes of land and water in which the quality of the light and of the air are the most important elements, the architecture, unlike the houses in the wooded North or on the rock-ribbed desert, makes no use of wood or of natural stone. It is, indeed, a very unmaterial architecture and yet not papery, since the blocks give a certain visible thickness to the thin-spun, tenuously interwoven planes, and the whole is penetrated by the air and animated by the delicate pattern of the shadows cast by the brilliant sun.

There is an element of fantasy here, of a fantasy which Northerners may feel is as implicit in the climate of Florida as in that of Southern California. This contrasts with the solider and more workaday quality of the Usonian houses or of the Johnson building. Actually as college architecture goes, this is not a particularly expensive scheme of construction. But the economy which seems to control not only the practical aspects of the Usonian houses, but also the straightforward simplicity of their design, does not hamper here an expression of festive gaiety, of youthful grace, which is perhaps particularly appropriate for a Florida college. Here there is almost nothing of the détente of the thirties, except perhaps in the refinement of an earlier exuberance, but rather an optimism and a happy expansion toward a more glorious future, as in the boldest projects of the twenties.

One of the boldest projects of the twenties was St. Mark's Tower (Fig. 305). The later version of 1930 for Chicago with its double towers linked in a line, was an even more brilliant expression of the possibilities of the clustered skyscraper group such as was about to come to larger scale execution under the hampering conditions of mid-town New York in Rockefeller Center. In 1940 Wright prepared for a Washington client his own version of Rockefeller Center to be erected at the intersection of Florida and Connecticut Avenues in the outer residential area of the city beyond the confines of L'Enfant's original plan. The site was well away from the downtown area, and yet like the isolated skyscrapers on Wilshire Boulevard in Los Angeles, easily approached from all sides. Moreover, the land here rose above the contiguous areas, while the rapid spread of commercial building out Connecticut Avenue would seem to doom it ultimately as a residential area. But all these reasons, which in the light of the most advanced city-planning practice made this an ideal location for such a project, have not thus far seemed to the Washington zoning authorities to justify granting permission for its execution. Of course the essential objection is the height, but so distant and slender a group of towers could hardly destroy the balance of the official architecture around the Mall more completely than do the solid urban blocks that already exist north of Pennsylvania Avenue.

Along the avenues Wright's project provides shops with a theater at the intersection and a series of cantilevered slabs like shelves above to provide the parking facilities which have elsewhere been almost totally ignored in the new buildings of Washington. The hotel towers are grouped around the rear of the raised lozenge-shaped area, whose predetermined form harmonizes with the crystalline patterns of the plans in detail. At the apex one tower rises well above the others to dominate the group (Fig. 411).

Within the towers the suites interlock like the studio apartments of St. Mark's Tower and the Suntop Homes. However the interest of the project does not reside in such details, carried out in terms of polygons with Wright's tremendous and almost perverse ingenuity, but rather in the brilliant urbanism of the total conception. The man who sees the city as disappearing offers here not only a model of how the urban ideal might be maintained in the mid-twentieth century, and a model much more realizable than the projects of the twenties for rebuilding European metropolitan cities, but a masterpiece of urban architecture, beside which Rockefeller Center itself and the accidentally isolated skyscrapers of Wilshire Boulevard appear as timid, half-hearted compromises.

The other great project of the immediate present, the Kansas City Community Church, now nearing completion, also occupies an urban site, but in a Middle Western city which has quite broken its nineteenth century bounds and spread out over the hills to the south leaving its earlier shell behind to die of blight. For all the variety of Wright's architectural production, the many apparently separate threads of development are closely linked through the years and no project is ever quite forgotten. Just as Crystal Heights has its prototypes in the Chicago apartments and St. Mark's Tower of ten years earlier, which in turn were based structurally on the concrete cantilevers of the Imperial Hotel, the Kansas City Church owes much to the Theater project and the Steel Cathedral project of the twenties, which were incorporated in Broadacre City, and ultimately to the Barnsdall theater project of the late 'teens, to Unity Church of 1906 and even to the All Souls Building project of the late nineties. The provision for parking about the edge on shelf-like cantilevered slabs is taken over from the Crystal Heights project and the character of the composition in terms of planes set on edge at oblique angles is a more solemn and solid version of the Florida Southern Chapel (Fig. 409). But this church is too large to constitute in itself a tower. Instead, a tower of light, formed by searchlights, will at night form a rival to the ambiguous red-glowing steam of Magonigle's War Memorial.

Wright is in 1941 in the full flow of production and happily as busy as in the days of his greatest activity before 1910. Many projects already referred to are now building, many more new projects, already commissioned, have hardly yet passed from Wright's brain onto paper. There can, therefore, be no conclusion to this record of more than a half century of building. As we look back over the landmarks of this unprecedentedly long-continued career, to the Charnley (9) and Harlan (21) houses of 1891, the Lake Forest Golf Club (49) of 1898, the great Willitts (73), Heurtley (71) and Ross (77) houses and the Hillside Home School (81) of 1902, the Larkin Building (92) of 1904, the Unity Temple (118) of 1906, the Coonley (148), Robie (166) and Gale (160) houses of the end of the decade, Taliesin, in its three incarnations of 1911, 1914 and 1925 (174, 269), the Midway Gardens (191) of 1914, the Imperial Hotel (220) of the end of that decade, the California block houses (249, 255, 256, 259) and the Lloyd Jones house (297) of the twenties, the Kaufmann house (320) of 1936 and the Johnson Building (330), the Usonian and other houses of the last five years, the Florida Southern College and the Kansas City Church now in construction, it seems almost impossible that one man can have designed and built so many edifices which have entered the canon of the world's great architecture. But the best thing of all is that we need not look backward only. Like Wright, we can look forward to a continuing production of equal vitality. For his creative vigor is in no way reduced, but rather increased by the long years of its continuous exercise. Indeed, after the ten dull years from 1925 to 1935, it is as if Wright's energy, long pent-up as regards executed work, though not, as we have seen, as regards major architectural inventions on paper, now flowed with renewed force. We need not regret that so many major projects remain unexecuted. For we can feel assured that their best qualities will eventually come to execution in the continuing work of succeeding years.

Of Wright, as of Titian, we may believe that in the eighth decade of his life and the sixth of his architectural career more work lies ahead which will equal in every way what is past. Wright has physically outlived the generation of the traditionalists, in the moment of whose triumph Kimball could write of Sullivan's and Wright's architecture as "a lost cause"; professionally he seems to be outliving the generation of the great European innovators of the twenties. In 1941, as forty years ago in 1901, or even a half century ago in 1891, Wright seems to stand poised for new triumphs at the opening of a great phase of his career.

Chronological List of Executed Work and Projects: 1887–1941

ALTHOUGH many lists of Wright's work have been prepared and several of them published, none of them are very complete and most of them are quite inaccurate. The most complete listing, that in Grant Manson's unpublished Harvard doctoral dissertation of 1940, covers only the period through 1910. Manson has very generously permitted me to collate this list with his. To him I owe all the dates established from public records in the early part of the list, but my interpretation of other sorts of evidence often differs somewhat from his. I specifically owe to Manson my knowledge of the Roloson houses of 1894 and the E-Z Polish Factory of 1905. We have also on the basis of our joint familiarity with the Taliesin collection of drawings discussed many points of detail.[1]

Beyond 1910 my list is based on that prepared for the exhibition at the Museum of Modern Art, chiefly the work of Henrietta Calloway. However, the Museum list has been enlarged and altered almost beyond recognition from additional material at Taliesin and by the correction of most of the individual dates through correspondence with clients and others.

I have not included the many new commissions of 1941 which had not taken form on paper when I was at Taliesin in May. The completeness of this list is relative. For both Manson and I have heard of early work about which we cannot obtain adequate information. In the later period, which has been less studied, there are even more likely to be items that I have missed. Among the Taliesin drawings there are hints of projects and possibly even of executed work about which but little can be learned even from Wright. I have included such things only when the existing drawings were relatively complete or the designs themselves of exceptional interest.

The text and the arrangement of plates follows in general a chronological order. In this list an attempt has been made at the impossible; a detailed consecutive itemizing of the architectural production of Wright's brain. It will be realized that much of the diagrammatic appearance of consecutiveness is false. But the only hope of arriving at a generally true sequence was to pretend in detail to a precision which is actually somewhat absurd. Since earlier lists have been so excessively casual in their dating, with certain important

---

[1] I should specifically state that I do not owe to Manson my knowledge of the Orrin S. Goan project, but to information on early drawings.

buildings dated more than five years too early or too late, it seemed worth while to aim, at least, at a high degree of accuracy.

The following notes explain the principles that have been used in preparing the list:

Within each year the items are arranged alphabetically, the executed work preceding the projects, which are always indicated as such.

Boldfaced dates are established by building permits or from similar public records. They are, in a sense, absolute; but they are hardly more accurate than those determined from published announcements of commissions, directory lists, private records or contemporary inscriptions on drawings. Building permits granted late in the year presumably imply construction the following spring. Where construction is known to have begun before the permit was issued or considerably later such facts are given. Sometimes the permit date and sometimes the actual date at which construction started has determined the place in the list, usually the earlier of the two.

Some building campaigns extended over several years. This is indicated, when known, by a dash following the date and a note if the building was not effectively completed within the year following that of the entry. In the absence of any other records, I have used the latest contemporary date on drawings, as this usually agrees with the date of construction where both are known. But there is always a possibility of error in mistaking for contemporary ones approximate dates added later to the drawings.

Projects differing markedly from executed work are separately entered with cross reference to the executed work.

The absence of a date to the left in the list (which is indicated in cross references and illustration captions by putting the date in brackets) may in some cases imply an uncertainty of as much as several years, in others merely the lack of firm evidence. Notes of early publication or exhibition—otherwise usually not included—or of the clients' appearance in directories at the given address often fix a *terminus ante quem*. Such a *terminus,* with other indications, has often been considered sufficient to justify a precise date. Exhibition and publication of early work, unless otherwise noted, was in the Chicago Architectural Club exhibitions held at the Art Institute and in their catalogues in 1894, 1898, 1900 and 1902. There were also later exhibitions at the Art Institute of Wright's work alone in 1907; about 1916 (indicated by [1916]); and in 1930. This last exhibition travelled widely here and abroad in following years, possibly with some changes in the material. Finally in 1940 there was the exhibition at the Museum of Modern Art in New York which this book memorializes.

Bracketted items are not to be considered entirely Wright's work. The various reasons are given in separate notes.

Estimated costs, generally given on building permits and sometimes mentioned in the press, are entered in the list when known. Of course they represent at best only rough approximations of actual cost. Allowance must also be made for changing construction prices in the past fifty years and in different parts of the country. It is unfortunate that this information cannot be more complete, but in most cases it might have offended the clients to give costs for work of the last decade or so.

1887   Project: Misses Lloyd Jones (?) house, Helena Valley, Spring Green, Wis. (effectively a more elaborate preliminary project for the house below; published in the *Inland Architect*, August, 1887)

1887   Project: Unitarian Chapel, Sioux City, Iowa (published in the *Inland Architect*, June, 1887)
Misses Lloyd Jones house,[2] Hillside, Spring Green, Wis. (published in the *Inland Architect*, February, 1888; extensively altered as part of the Taliesin Fellowship complex, 1933–   )

1889   Frank Lloyd Wright house, 428 Forest Avenue, Oak Park, Ill. $4,000 (new dining room and then a playroom added in mid-nineties; studio, v. **1895**; other additions and alterations up to 1909; subdivided into three apartments after Wright's return from Europe in 1911)

1890[3]   [James Charnley house, Ocean Springs, Miss.] (unsupervised; probably modified)
W. S. MacHarg house, 4632 Beacon Avenue, Chicago, Ill. (MacHarg first listed at this address in Chicago Directory, 1891; demolished)

1890[3]   [Louis H. Sullivan house, servants' cottage and stables, Ocean Springs, Miss.] (unsupervised; enlarged)
Project: Henry N. Cooper house and stable, La Grange, Ill. (based, according to Wright, on a design prepared previous to joining Sullivan)

1891[3]   [James Charnley house, 1365 Astor Street, Chicago, Ill.] (later addition to south)

[2] At this time Wright was working in J. L. Silsbee's office. The style of this house is essentially Silsbee's, as is true of the two projects of 1887 listed above.

[3] Works of the firm of Adler and Sullivan. The dates are in general those given by Hugh Morrison in his *Louis Sullivan*, New York, W. W. Norton [c1935]. As Sullivan's chief lieutenant in design from about 1890 until he left Adler and Sullivan in 1893, Wright certainly designed the Charnley house in Chicago and was chiefly responsible for the other works of Adler and Sullivan here listed, particularly the houses. For that matter, Wrightian elements, equally due to his hand, can be readily distinguished in other Adler and Sullivan work of these years. See discussion, above, pp. 6–14.

1892   George Blossom house, 4858 Kenwood Avenue, Chicago, Ill. (garage later, v. 1907)

1892   Robert G. Emmond house, 109 South Eighth Avenue, La Grange, Ill. (porch enclosed, resurfaced)

1892   Thomas H. Gale house, 1019 Chicago Ave., Oak Park, Ill. $3,000

Dr. Allison W. Harlan house, 4414 Greenwood Avenue, Chicago, Ill. (commissioned and possibly begun in 1891; balcony altered)

1892   Warren McArthur house and stable, 4852 Kenwood Avenue, Chicago, Ill.

1892   R. P. Parker house, 1027 Chicago Avenue, Oak Park, Ill. $3,000 (built by Thomas H. Gale for Parker's occupancy)

1892[3]   [Albert W. Sullivan house, 4575 Lake Avenue, Chicago, Ill.] (occupied by Louis H. Sullivan, 1892–96)

1892[3]   [Victoria Hotel, Chicago Heights, Ill.] (remodelled)

1893[4]   Walter Gale house, 1031 Chicago Avenue, Oak Park, Ill. (front terrace destroyed)

1893[3]   [Meyer Building, 307 West Van Buren St., Chicago, Ill.] (cornice removed)

Municipal Boathouse, Carroll Street at Lake Mendota, Madison, Wis. (demolished)

1893   William H. Winslow house and stable, Auvergne Pl., River Forest, Ill. $20,000.

1893   Project: Library and Museum competition, Milwaukee, Wis. (exhibited, 1894)

[1894]   Frederick Bagley house, 101 County Line Rd., Hinsdale, Ill.

Dr. H. W. Bassett remodelled house, 125 South Oak Park Ave., Oak Park, Ill. (Dr. Bassett first listed at this address in Oak Park Directory, 1895; demolished)

Peter Goan house, 108 South Eighth Ave., La Grange, Ill. (upper story resurfaced)

1894   Robert W. Roloson houses (4), 3213–3219 Calumet Avenue, Chicago, Ill. $27,000 (remodelled as apartments)

1894   Francis Woolley house, 1030 Superior Street, Oak Park, Ill. (resurfaced)

1894   Project: Orrin S. Goan house, La Grange, Ill.

[3]Works of the firm of Adler and Sullivan. The dates are in general those given by Hugh Morrison in his *Louis Sullivan*, New York, W. W. Norton [c1935]. As Sullivan's chief lieutenant in design from about 1890 until he left Adler and Sullivan in 1893, Wright certainly designed the Charnley house in Chicago and was chiefly responsible for the other works of Adler and Sullivan here listed, particularly the houses. For that matter, Wrightian elements, equally due to his hand, can be readily distinguished in other Adler and Sullivan work of these years. See discussion, above, pp. 6–14.

[4]The W. I. Clark house, 211 South La Grange Road, La Grange, Ill., was published as Wright's in the *Inland Architect* in 1894, vol. 24, no. 1, but it was actually designed by E. Hill Turnock, an Adler and Sullivan draftsman. It is not clear how Wright's name came to be attached to it; but probably Turnock used Wright's name in announcing the commission.

1894   Project: A. C. McAfee house, on Lake Michigan, Chicago, Ill. (exhibited and published, 1900; a slightly variant plan for James L. McAfee also exists)

1895   Francis Apartments for Terre Haute Trust Company, 4304 Forestville Ave., Chicago, Ill.

1895   Francisco Terrace for Edward C. Waller, 253–257 Francisco Ave., Chicago, Ill.

Nathan G. Moore house and stable, 329 Forest Ave., Oak Park, Ill. (published in the *Inland Architect,* 1898; terra cotta bay windows by Fellows, c. 1914; rebuilt after fire, v. [1923])

1895   Edward C. Waller apartments, 2840–2858 West Walnut St., Chicago, Ill. (designed to be built at the corner of Jackson Blvd. and Kedzie Ave., but actually erected without supervision contiguous to Francisco Terrace)

1895   Chauncey L. Williams house, 520 Edgewood Pl., River Forest, Ill. (dormers on front and left and remodelled after 1900)

1895   Frank Lloyd Wright studio, 951 Chicago Ave., Oak Park, Ill. (remodelled as two apartments after Wright's return from Europe in 1911)

1895   H. P. Young alterations, 334 North Kenilworth Ave., Oak Park, Ill.

1895   Project: Jesse Baldwin house (based on McAfee project of 1894)

Project: Luxfer Prism Company skyscraper (two versions exhibited and published, 1898)

1895   Project: Wolf Lake Amusement Park for Warren McArthur, on Wolf Lake, Ill.

Project: house, name unknown (published in the *Architectural Review,* June, 1900; similar to Walter Gale plan)

1896   H. C. Goodrich house, 534 North East Ave., Oak Park, Ill. $2700 (altered internally)

Misses Lloyd Jones windmill "Romeo and Juliet," Hillside, Spring Green, Wis. (resheathed with siding instead of shingles, 1939)

Charles E. Roberts remodelled interiors, 321 North Euclid Ave., Oak Park, Ill. (executed gradually over several years)

Charles E. Roberts stable, 317 North Euclid Ave., Oak Park, Ill. (altered to serve as a dwelling about 1929)

Project: Mrs. David Devin house, on Lake Michigan, Chicago, Ill. (exhibited and published, 1900)

1896   Project: Robert Perkins apartment house, West Monroe St., Chicago, Ill.

1897   George Furbeck house, 223 North Euclid Ave., Oak Park, Ill. $15,000 (porch enlarged)

1897   Isidore Heller house and stable, 5132 Woodlawn Ave., Chicago, Ill.

Henry Wallis boathouse, South Shore Rd., Delavan Lake, Wis. (demolished)

Project: All Souls Building, Oakwood Blvd. at Langley Ave., Chicago, Ill. $100,000 (published and exhibited in 1900; designed in association with Dwight Heald Perkins; v. [1901], Abraham Lincoln Center)

1898   Rollin Furbeck house, 515 Fair Oaks Ave., Oak Park, Ill. (later additions and internal changes)

River Forest Golf Club, Bonnie Brae Ave., River Forest, Ill. (front wing built first; completed, exhibited and published, 1900; enlarged and altered, v. [1901]; demolished 1905)

1898   George W. Smith house, 404 Home Ave., Oak Park, Ill.

1898   Project: Mozart Garden remodelling for David Meyer, State St. at 55th St., Chicago, Ill.

1899   Joseph W. Husser house, 180 Buena Ave., Chicago, Ill. (demolished)

1899   Edward C. Waller remodelled hall and dining room, Auvergne Pl., River Forest, Ill. (demolished)

Project: Cheltenham Beach for Norman B. Ream and Edward C. Waller, 75th to 79th Streets on the Lake, Chicago, Ill. (published in the *Architectural Review,* June, 1900)

Project: Robert Eckart house, River Forest, Ill. (published and exhibited in 1900)

Project: Edward C. Waller house, River Forest, Ill. (exhibited and published in 1900; a separate and more advanced design than the above; but as Mrs. Eckart was Waller's daughter both probably relate to a single potential commission)

Project: house, name unknown (published in the *Architectural Review,* June, 1900)

1900   William Adams house, 9326 South Pleasant Ave., Chicago, Ill. $6,000 (plan probably provided by the client, Wright's builder since the Winslow house)

1900   B. Harley Bradley house and stables, "Glenlloyd," 701 South Harrison Ave., Kankakee, Ill.

1900   S. A. Foster house and stables, 12147 Harvard Ave., Chicago, Ill.

| 1900 | Warren Hickox house, 687 South Harrison Ave., Kankakee, Ill. |

1900   Warren Hickox house, 687 South Harrison Ave., Kankakee, Ill.

1900   E. H. Pitkin house, Sapper Island, nr. Kensington Point, Desbarats, Ont., Canada.

1900   Henry Wallis (H. Goodsmith) house, South Shore Rd., Delavan Lake, Wis. (unsupervised; sold by Wallis to Dr. Goodsmith upon completion)

1900   Project: "A Home in a Prairie Town" and first version of Quadruple Block Plan, for Curtis Publishing Co. (published in the *Ladies' Home Journal*, February, 1901; there is an alternative unpublished and less advanced version of this house)

1900   Project: "A small house with 'lots of room in it'," for Curtis Publishing Company, (published in the *Ladies' Home Journal*, June, 1901)

1901[5]   E. Arthur Davenport house, 550 Ashland Ave., River Forest, Ill. (front terrace removed)

     E. R. Hills remodelled house, 313 Forest Ave., Oak Park, Ill. (drawings dated 1900; work carried out by Nathan G. Moore for his daughter, Mrs. Hills, a year or two later)

     Fred B. Jones house, boathouse, gate-lodge and barn, "Penwern," South Shore Rd., Delavan Lake, Wis. (unsupervised; the drawings indicate continued construction of the separate edifices through 1903 in the sequence given)

1901[5]   F. B. Henderson house, 301 South Kenilworth Ave., Elmhurst, Ill. $10,000 (second-storey covered porch added over original terrace in front of living room)

     Robert M. Lamp cottage, Governor's Island, Lake Mendota, Wis.

     River Forest Golf Club additions, Bonnie Brae Ave., River Forest, Ill. (altered and enlarged at rear and sides; exhibited and published, 1902; demolished, 1905)

1901[5]   Frank Thomas house, 210 Forest Ave., Oak Park, Ill. $10,000 (built by James C. Rogers, Mrs. Thomas' father; resurfaced)

1901   Universal Portland Cement Co. Pavilion, Pan-American exposition, Buffalo, N. Y. (demolished)

1901   Edward C. Waller gateway, stables and gardener's cottage, Auvergne Pl., River Forest, Ill.

     Henry Wallis remodelled gate-lodge, South Shore Rd., Delavan Lake, Wis. (gate and fence demolished)

---

[5] Most of the work of 1901 and early 1902 was done in association with H. Webster Tomlinson. There is no reason, however, to believe that Tomlinson had any effect whatever on Wright's rapidly maturing style.

1901   T. E. Wilder stables, Elmhurst, Ill. (demolished)

1901   Project: Lexington Terrace for Edward C. Waller, Lexington St., Spaulding Ave., Polk St., and Homan Ave., Chicago, Ill. (this project was reworked in 1909, q.v.)

Project: Abraham Lincoln Center, Oakwood Blvd. and Langley Ave., Chicago, Ill. (exhibited, 1902; a later development of the All Souls Building project of [1897] in association with Dwight Heald Perkins, v. **1903**)

Project: "A Village Bank in Cast Concrete" (published in the *Brickbuilder*, August, 1901)

Project: Henry Wallis house, Delavan Lake, Wis.

1902[5]   William G. Fricke house, 540 Fair Oaks Ave., Oak Park, Ill. $12,000 (remodelled for Emma Martin, v. 1907; detached pavilion since demolished)

George E. Gerts double house, Birch Brook, Whitehall, Mich.

Walter Gerts house, Birch Brook,[6] Whitehall, Mich.

1902   Arthur Heurtley house, 318 Forest Ave., Oak Park, Ill. (remodelled internally as two apartments)

Arthur Heurtley remodelled house, Les Cheneaux Club, Marquette Island, Mich.

1902   Misses Lloyd Jones Hillside Home School, Hillside, Spring Green, Wis. (incorporated in Taliesin Fellowship complex, v. 1933–)

1902   Charles S. Ross house, South Shore Rd., Delavan Lake, Wis. (modified)

George W. Spencer house, South Shore Rd., Delavan Lake, Wis.

1902   Ward W. Willitts house and gardener's cottage, 715 South Sheridan Rd., Highland Park, Ill. $20,000 (cottage altered to serve as garage)

Project: Delavan Lake Yacht Club, Delavan Lake, Wis.

1902[5]   Project: Victor Metzger house, Desbarats, Ont., Canada

Project: John A. Mosher house

1902   Project: Yahara Boat Club, Lake Mendota, Madison, Wis.

1902   Project: Edward C. Waller house, Charlevoix, Mich. (v. 1903)

Project: house, name unknown, Oak Park, Ill.

---

[5]Most of the work of 1901 and early 1902 was done in association with H. Webster Tomlinson. There is no reason, however, to believe that Tomlinson had any effect whatever on Wright's rapidly maturing style.

[6]There may be several other early houses at Birch Brook of Wright's design, probably unsupervised variants, but so modified as to be unrecognizable today; v., however, [1921].

1903   George Barton house, 118 Summit Ave., Buffalo, N. Y. (built by Darwin D. Martin, Mrs. Barton's father)

1903   Susan Lawrence Dana house, East Laurence Ave. at 4th St., Springfield, Ill. (incorporating an older house)

1903   W. H. Freeman house, Hinsdale, Ill. (unsupervised; altered in execution)

1903   [Abraham Lincoln Center, Oakwood Blvd. at Langley Ave., Chicago, Ill.] (executed by Dwight Heald Perkins alone; much simplified externally, although based on the earlier projects, v. [1897]; [1901])

1903   Francis W. Little house and stable, 603 Moss Ave., Peoria, Ill. (additions made for Robert D. Clarke, v. 1909)

1903   W. E. Martin house, 636 North East Ave., Oak Park, Ill. (subdivided into three apartments)

       Scoville Park fountain, Lake St., Oak Park, Ill.

1903   J. J. Walser, Jr., house, 42 North Central Ave., Chicago, Ill. $4,000

       Project: Robert M. Lamp house, Madison, Wis. (different from executed house, v. 1904)

       Project: Chicago and Northwestern (?) Railway station, Oak Park (?), Ill. (3 versions)

       Project: Charles E. Roberts quadruple block plan (24 houses), Chicago, Fair Oaks, Superior and Ogden Aves., Oak Park, Ill. (based on the Quadruple Block Plan of 1900 published in the *Ladies' Home Journal,* February, 1901, but with somewhat different houses; an alternative scheme with still differently planned houses on conventional narrow lots also exists)

1903   Project: Edward C. Waller house, Charlevoix, Mich. (different from 1902 project)

       Project: Frank Lloyd Wright one storey studio-house, Oak Park, Ill.

       Project: house, name unknown.

1904   Edwin H. Cheney house, 520 North East Ave., Oak Park, Ill. (garage later)

1904   Robert M. Lamp house, 22 North Butler St., Madison, Wis. (bricks now painted; storey added on top)

1904   Larkin Company administration building, 680 Seneca St., Buffalo, N. Y. (now Larkin retail store)

1904   Darwin D. Martin house, conservatory, garage, etc., 125 Jewett Pkwy., Buffalo, N. Y. (slight alterations by Wright, 1914)

Project: Hiram Baldwin house, Kenilworth, Ill. (different from executed house, v. [1905])

Project: Robert D. Clarke house, Moss Ave., Peoria, Ill. (before Clarke's purchase of Little house in 1905)

Project: Larkin Company workmen's rowhouses, Buffalo, N. Y.

1904   Project: J. A. Scudder house, Campement d'Ours Island, Desbarats, Ont., Canada

1904   Project: Frank L. Smith bank, Dwight, Ill. (different from executed bank, v. 1905)

Project: H. J. Ullman house, North Euclid Ave. and Erie St., Oak Park, Ill. (the Ullman house built in 1905 by Robert C. Spencer is quite different from Wright's project)

Project: house, name unknown, Highland Park, Ill.

1905   Mary M. W. Adams house, 103 Lake Ave., Highland Park, Ill.

Hiram Baldwin house and garage, 205 Essex Rd., Kenilworth, Ill. (entrance and interiors altered)

1905   Charles E. Brown house (Evanston Model Home), 2420 Harrison Ave., Evanston, Ill.

1905   E-Z Polish factory for Darwin D. and W. E. Martin, 3005–3017 West Carroll Ave., Chicago, Ill. (top floor rebuilt after fire, 1913)

1905   W. A. Glasner house, 850 Sheridan Rd., Glencoe, Ill.

1905   Thomas P. Hardy house, 1319 South Main St., Racine, Wis.

1905   W. R. Heath house, 76 Soldiers Pl., Buffalo, N. Y.

A. P. Johnson house, South Shore Rd., Lake Delavan, Wis. (unsupervised)

1905   Lawrence Memorial Library interior for Mrs. R. D. Lawrence, Springfield, Ill.

1905   River Forest Tennis Club, Bonnie Brae Ave. and Quick St., River Forest. Ill. (burned, 1906; v. 1906)

1905   Rookery Building remodelled La Salle and Adams St. entrance lobbies and balcony in central court, La Salle and Adams Sts., Chicago, Ill. (entrances considerably modified)

1905   Frank L. Smith bank, Dwight, Ill.
Project: Charles W. Barnes house, McCook, Neb.
Project: T. E. Gilpin house, Kenilworth Ave. and North Blvd., Oak Park, Ill.
Project: Single-storey varnish factory

1905   Project: Harvey P. Sutton house, McCook, Neb. (different from executed house, v. 1907)
Project: house on a lake.

1906   P. A. Beachy house, 238 Forest Ave., Oak Park, Ill. (incorporates an earlier house)
K. C. de Rhodes house, 715 West Washington St., South Bend, Ind. (published in 1906)
Grace Fuller house, Hazel Ave. and Sheridan Rd., Glencoe, Ill. (exhibited in 1907; demolished)

1906   A. W. Gridley house and barn, North Batavia Ave., Batavia, Ill.

1906   P. D. Hoyt house, 318 South Fifth Ave., Geneva, Ill.
George Madison Millard house, 410 Lake Ave., Highland Park, Ill.
Frederick Nicholas house, Brassie Ave., Flossmoor, Ill. (unsupervised)
W. H. Pettit mortuary chapel, Belvidere cemetery, Belvidere, Ill. (unsupervised)

1906   River Forest Tennis Club, Lathrop Ave. and Quick St., River Forest, Ill. $3,500 (Charles E. White, Jr., and Vernon S. Watson, associated; moved, 1920, from original site at Quick St. and Bonnie Brae Ave., and enlarged by Vernon S. Watson)

1906   C. Thaxter Shaw remodelled house, 3466 Peel St., Montreal, P. Q., Canada

1906   Unity (Universalist) Church and Parish House, Kenilworth Ave. at Lake St., Oak Park, Ill. $35,000 (designed and possibly begun in 1905)

1906   Project: Richard Bock studio house, Maywood, Ill.
Project: Mrs. David Devin house, Eliot, Me. (exhibited in 1907)

1906   Project: "A Fireproof House for $5000," for Curtis Publishing Co. (published in the *Ladies' Home Journal,* April, 1907)
Project: Walter Gerts (Alex Davidson) house, Glencoe, Ill. (Buffalo, N. Y.) (exhibited in 1907; differs entirely from executed W. V. Davidson house, v. *1908;* slight alterations were made to Walter Gerts' River Forest house at this time)

Project: R. S. Ludington house, Dwight, Ill. (exhibited in 1907)

Project: Warren McArthur concrete apartment house, Kenwood, Chicago, Ill.

Project: C. Thaxter Shaw house, Westmount, Montreal, P. Q., Canada.

Project: Elizabeth Stone house, Glencoe, Ill. (exhibited in 1907)

1907   George Blossom garage, 49th St. at Kenwood Ave., Chicago, Ill.

E. W. Cummings Real Estate office, Harlem Ave. and Lake St., River Forest, Ill. (first listed in Oak Park Directory, 1908; demolished)

Col. George Fabyan remodelled house, Batavia Rd., south of Geneva, Ill. (six houses for rent may have been designed but not executed for Col. Fabyan; no drawings for them remain at Taliesin)

Fox River Country Club remodelling for Col. George Fabyan, Geneva, Ill. (burned about 1912)

Stephen M. B. Hunt house, 345 South Seventh Ave., La Grange, Ill.

1907   Larkin Company pavilion, Jamestown Tercentenary exposition, Jamestown, Va. (demolished)

1907   Emma Martin alterations to Fricke house, and new garage, 540 Fair Oaks Ave., Oak Park, Ill. (v. 1902)

1907   Pebbles and Balch decorating shop, 1107 Lake St., Oak Park, Ill. (extensively altered)

1907   Andrew T. Porter house, Hillside, Spring Green, Wis. (basement dining room, 1938)

1907   Harvey P. Sutton house, 602 Main St., McCook, Neb. (designed in 1905; rebuilt from original plans with some modifications after fire, 1932)

1907   F. F. Tomek house, 150 Nuttall Rd., Riverside, Ill.

1907   Burton J. Westcott house, 1340 East High St., Springfield, Ohio

Project: Harold McCormick house and adjuncts, Lake Forest, Ill. (worked on for several years; a house at Lake Forest for Harold McCormick was built by Charles A. Platt in 1908)

Project: Andrew T. Porter house, Hillside, Spring Green, Wis. (larger, slightly later than executed house)

1908   E. E. Boynton house, 16 East Blvd., Rochester, N. Y.

1908   Browne's Bookstore, Fine Arts Bldg., 410 South Michigan Ave., Chicago, Ill. (demolished)

1908–   Avery Coonley house and stable, 300 Scottswood Rd., Riverside, Ill. (pergola and french windows of playroom, gardener's cottage, [1911]; stable altered as garage, 1912; playhouse, 1912; slight further alterations in 1921; v. [1911], v. 1912)

1908   Walter V. Davidson house and garage, 57 Tillingham Pl., Buffalo, N. Y. (two rooms added lately over garage)

1908   Robert W. Evans house, 9914 Longwood Dr., Chicago, Ill. (porch enclosed about 1913)

1908   E. A. Gilmore house, 120 Ely Pl., Madison, Wis. (altered later to serve as fraternity house)

1908   L. K. Horner house, 1331 Sherwin Ave., Chicago, Ill.

1908   Isabel Roberts house, 603 Edgewood Pl., River Forest, Ill. (resurfaced with brick)

Dr. G. C. Stockman house, 311 First St. S. E., Mason City, Iowa

Project: Frank J. Baker house, Wilmette, Ill. (different from executed house, v. 1909)

1908   Project: E. D. Brigham stables

1908   Project: Dr. W. H. Copeland remodelled house, 408 Forest Ave., Oak Park, Ill. (different from executed alterations, v. 1909)

Project: William Norman Guthrie house, Sewanee, Tenn. (identical with executed Baker house, v. 1909; published in *Ausgeführte Bauten und Entwürfe*, 1910)

1908   Project: Horseshoe Inn for Willard H. Ashton, Estes Park, Col.

1908   Project: Francis W. Little house, Wayzata, Minn. (different from executed house, v. 1913)

Project: J. G. Melson house, Mason City, Iowa (identical, except for site, with Isabel Roberts house above, published in 1910)

Project: Moving picture theater

1909   Frank J. Baker house, 507 Lake Ave., Wilmette, Ill.

1909   City National Bank Building and Hotel for Blyth and Markley, West State St. and

South Federal Ave., Mason City, Iowa (now Adams Building and Park Inn; much remodelled)

1909   Robert D. Clarke additions to Little house and garage, 603 Moss Ave., Peoria, Ill.

1909   Dr. W. H. Copeland alterations, 408 Forest Ave., Oak Park, Ill. (unsupervised and modified in execution)

1909   Mrs. Thomas H. Gale house, 6 Elizabeth Ct., Oak Park, Ill.

1909   J. Kibben Ingalls house, 562 Keystone Ave., River Forest, Ill.

1909   Meyer May house, 450 Madison Ave. S. E., Grand Rapids, Mich. $16,000 (wing added to rear, 1920)

1909   Frederick C. Robie house, 5757 Woodlawn Ave., Chicago, Ill. (garage altered)

Oscar Steffens house, 7631 Sheridan Rd., Chicago, Ill. (published in *Frank Lloyd Wright Ausgeführte Bauten* 1911; altered)

George C. Stewart house, 166 Hot Springs Rd., Montecito, Cal. (published in *Ausgeführte Bauten und Entwürfe* 1910)

Peter C. Stohr building, shops, tearoom, etc., underneath elevated, Wilson Ave., Chicago, Ill. (demolished)

1909   W. Scott Thurber art gallery, Fine Arts Bldg., 410 South Michigan Ave., Chicago, Ill. (demolished)

Project: Harry E. Brown house, Geneva, Ill.

Project: Larwill house, Muskegon, Mich.

1909   Project: Lexington Terrace for Edward C. Waller, Jr., and Oscar Friedman (1901 project reworked with new façades)

Project: Mrs. Mary Roberts house, River Forest, Ill. (different from executed house for Mrs. Roberts' daughter, Isabel, v. 1908)

1909   Project: Edward C. Waller bathing pavilion, Charlevoix, Mich.

1909   Project: Edward C. Waller small houses for rent (3), River Forest, Ill. $3500 each.

Project: Town of Bitter Root for Bitter Root Irrigation Company, nr. Darby, Mont. (two different versions, possibly five years or more earlier)

1910[7]   [J. H. Amberg house, 505 College Ave. S. E., Grand Rapids, Mich.]

---

[7] Upon Wright's departure for Europe in the spring of 1910 several house commissions were handed over to Herman V. von Holst, with whom was associated Marion Mahony from Wright's office. Some drawings for the Irving

Como Orchards summer colony, Darby, Mont. (designs published in *Ausgeführte Bauten und Entwürfe,* 1910; the final form of the Bitter Root project; central clubhouse and group of cottages executed without supervision; part of clubhouse and many of the cottages now demolished)

1910[7]   [E. P. Irving house, Millikin Pl., Decatur, Ill.]

Universal Portland Cement Co. exhibit, Madison Square Garden, Madison Square, New York, N. Y. (exhibited [1916], in exhibition at Art Institute, Chicago, of "Work done since spring of 1911," *sic;* published in *Frank Lloyd Wright Ausgeführte Bauten,* 1911; demolished)

1910   Rev. J. R. Ziegler house, 509 Shelby St., Frankfort, Ky. (unsupervised)

Project: Frank Lloyd Wright house and studio, Viale Verdi, Fiesole, Italy (exhibited, [1916] in exhibition of "Work done since the Spring of 1911," *sic*)

1911   Herbert C. Angster house, 650 Blodgett Rd., Lake Bluff, Ill.

1911   O. B. Balch house, 611 North Kenilworth Ave., Oak Park, Ill.

Avery Coonley gardener's cottage, Scottswood Rd., Riverside, Ill.

1911–   Taliesin I, Frank Lloyd Wright house, studio and farm buildings, Spring Green, Wis. (begun for Mrs. Anna Lloyd Wright, Wright's mother; burned, 1914, then rebuilt; v. 1914– ; v. 1925–)

1911   Project: Harry S. Adams house, Oak Park, Ill. (different from executed house, v. *1913*)

1911–   Project: Sherman M. Booth house, Glencoe, Ill. (different from executed house, v. [1915])

Project: Sherman M. Booth summer cottage

Project: Avery Coonley greenhouse, Riverside, Ill.

1911   Project: Avery Coonley kindergarten, Riverside, Ill. (different from executed playhouse, v. 1912)

1911   Project: Arthur M. Cutten house, Downer's Grove, Ill.

Project: E. Esbenshade house, Milwaukee, Wis. (exhibited, [1916])

Project: Madison Hotel for Arthur L. Richards, Madison, Wis. (exhibited, [1916])

─────────

house are signed by Wright and he made preliminary sketches for the Amberg house. The Adolf and Robert Mueller houses in Millikin Place, Decatur, Ill., were designed and built by von Holst and Mahony. The whole Millikin Place group was landscaped by Walter Burley Griffin from Wright's office.

1911   Project: Andrew T. Porter house, Spring Green, Wis.

1911   Project: Edward Schroeder house, Milwaukee, Wis.

Project: Frank Lloyd Wright house, Goethe St., Chicago, Ill. (exhibited, [1916])

1912   Avery Coonley playhouse, 350 Fairbanks Rd., Riverside, Ill. (now altered to serve as a residence)

1912   Lake Geneva Inn for Arthur L. Richards, Lake Geneva, Wis. (unsupervised and incomplete; now Geneva Hotel)

1912   William B. Greene house, 1300 Garfield Ave., Aurora, Ill. (wing added, 1926, by Harry Robinson, a former Wright draftsman)

Park Ridge Country Club addition and alterations, Park Ridge, Ill., (demolished)

Project: Kehl dance academy, residence and shops, Madison, Wis.

Project: Schoolhouse, La Grange, Ill.

Project: Press (*San Francisco Call*) Building for Spreckels Estate, Market St. between 3rd and 4th Sts., San Francisco, Cal. (two versions, one isolated, one with lower link to existing Tower Building; exhibited, [1916])

Project: Taliesin cottages (2), Spring Green, Wis. (exhibited, [1916])

1913   Harry S. Adams house, 710 Augusta St., Oak Park, Ill.

1913   Banff National Park recreation building, Banff, Alta., Canada (Francis W. Sullivan of Ottawa, associated; demolished, 1939)

M. B. Hilly house, Brookfield, Ill. (not found; possibly only a project)

1913–   Francis W. Little house, II, garage and boathouse, "Northome," R.F.D. 3, Wayzata, Minn. (not completed until Wright's return from Japan much later; the guest house is not by Wright)

house, name unknown, Palm Beach, Fla. (unsupervised)

Project: Art Museum

Project: Carnegie Library, Pembroke, Ottawa, Ont., Canada (Francis W. Sullivan, associated; of two other projects for a double house and a post office in Ottawa also designed in association with Sullivan no traces remain; all three projects exhibited, [1916])

Project: J. W. Kellogg house, Milwaukee, Wis.

Project: Jerome Mendelson house, Albany, N. Y. (exhibited, [1916])

Project: Block of city row houses

1914   Midway Gardens for Edward C. Waller, Jr., and Oscar Friedman, Cottage Grove Ave. at 60th St., Chicago, Ill. (designed and possibly begun late in 1913; demolished, 1923)

1914   S. H. Mori oriental art studio, 801 Fine Arts Bldg., 410 South Michigan Ave., Chicago, Ill. (modified)

1914–   Taliesin II, Frank Lloyd Wright house, Spring Green, Wis. (rebuilt after 1914 fire; studio and students' quarters much modified; rebuilt again after fire, v. 1925–)

Project: Honoré J. Jaxon houses (3)

Project: State Bank, Spring Green, Wis., (a building by another architect was commissioned in 1914; exhibited, [1916])

1914   Project: U. S. Embassy, Tokio, Japan

Project: John Vogelsang dinner gardens and house, Chicago, Ill. (a variant scheme adds hotel accommodations)

1915   Emil Bach house, 7415 Sheridan Rd., Chicago, Ill.

Sherman M. Booth house, 265 Sylvan Rd., Glencoe, Ill. (unsupervised)

E. D. Brigham house, Sheridan Rd., Glencoe, Ill. (unsupervised)

A. D. German Warehouse, Richland Center, Wis. (incomplete; v. project, [1934])

Ravine Bluffs development for Sherman M. Booth, Glencoe, Ill. (unsupervised; entrance features, bridge, and 3 houses for rent were built; possibly designed at the time of the Booth house project, 1911–)

Project: American System Ready-Cut standardized houses and apartments for Richards Brothers, Milwaukee, Wis. (the earliest work on the many alternative designs for these houses and apartments goes back two or three years; the latest revisions on the drawings are dated 1916; eventually some of these designs were executed without supervision; v. 1916)

Project: Chinese restaurant for Arthur L. Richards, Milwaukee, Wis.

Project: Christian Catholic Church, Zion City, Ill.

Project: Model Quarter Section development, Chicago, Ill. (published in *City Residential Land Development Studies in Planning,* edited by Alfred B. Yeomans,

Chicago, [c.1916]; includes Quadruple Block Plan residence areas based on projects of 1900 and [1903] and various public and commercial edifices as well; cf. Town of Bitter Root projects, [1909], and Broadacre City, [1934])

1915 Project: Imperial Hotel, Tokio, Japan (preliminary designs prepared at Taliesin before Wright left for Tokio; exhibited [1916], v. [1917])
Project: Rockefeller Foundation Chinese Hospital
Project: Wood house, Decatur, Ill.

1916 Joseph J. Bagley house, Lakeview and Cedar Aves., Grand Beach, Mich.

1916 F. C. Bogk house, 2420 North Terrace Ave., Milwaukee, Wis. $15,000
W. S. Carr house, Lakeview and Pine Aves., Grand Beach, Mich.
Imperial Hotel Annex, Tokio, Japan (including Wright's own apartment)

1916 Arthur Munkwitz duplex apartments (4), 1102, 1104, 1110, 112 North 27th St., Milwaukee, Wis. $20,000 (unsupervised; built from American system plans)

1916 Arthur L. Richards houses (2), 1835 South Layton Blvd. and 2714 West Burnham St., Milwaukee, Wis. (unsupervised; built from American System plans; the first is resurfaced)

1916 Arthur L. Richards[8] duplex apartments (4), 2720, 2724, 2728, 2732 West Burnham St., Milwaukee, Wis. (unsupervised; built from American System plans; resurfaced)
Ernest Vosburgh house, Crescent Rd., Grand Beach, Mich.
Project: Miss Behn (Voight) house, Grand Beach, Mich.
Project: Clarence Converse house, Palisades Park, Mich.
Project: William Allen White remodelled house, Emporia, Kan.

1917– Henry J. Allen house, 255 Roosevelt Blvd., Wichita, Kan.

1917 Aizaku Hayashi house, Komazawa, Tokio, Japan[9]

[8] Mr. Richards built other houses and duplexes from American System plans at this time in several other cities and towns, but he cannot remember exactly where.

[9] The seven years Wright spent in Japan off and on from 1916, the general lack of dates on the drawings, except perhaps in Japanese, and the failure of Wright's Japanese associate, Endo, to reply to queries make the information on Japanese work and projects particularly vague. The *termini* of the work are probably the 1917 date on the Hayashi house plans, which are preliminary sketches suggesting that the executed work may have been a year or more later, and the 1921 date on the Jiyu Gakuen School drawings. But Wright did not leave Japan for good until 1922 and there is no assurance that the execution of work under Endo's supervision did not continue after his departure.

Stephen M. B. Hunt house, 685 Algoma Ave., Oshkosh, Wis.

Imperial Hotel, Tokio, Japan. 8½ million yen (completed, 1922, after some four or five years in construction)

Project: Aline Barnsdall "Hollyhock House," Theater, etc., Olive Hill, Los Angeles, Cal. (Wright met Miss Barnsdall before going to Japan and these designs were developed concurrently with the Japanese work; the earliest date on a drawing is a revision of 1918; v. **1920**)

Project: Odawara Hotel, Nagoya, Japan

1917   Project: Powell house, Wichita, Kan.

1918   Fukuhara house, Hakone, Japan (damaged by earthquake, 1923)

Yamamura house, Ashiya, Japan

Project: Count Immu house, Tokio, Japan

Project: Viscount Inouye house, Tokio, Japan

Project: Moving picture theater, Tokio, Japan

1919   Project: Monolith Homes development for Thomas P. Hardy (18), Racine Wis. (this scheme, as well as the C. E. Staley and J. P. Shampay house projects of this year, were developed by R. M. Schindler during Wright's absence in Japan. They are hardly to be considered Wright's work, though they issued from his office and the Monolith Homes drawings carry his signature)

Project: W. S. Spaulding gallery for storage and exhibition of Japanese prints, Boston, Mass.

1920   Aline Barnsdall house and garage, "Hollyhock House," Sunset and Hollywood Blvds., Edgemont St. and Vermont Ave., Los Angeles, Cal. $75,000 (execution of the project already worked on for several years, v. [1917])

1920   Aline Barnsdall Olive Hill studio residence A., Hollywood Blvd. and Edgemont St., Los Angeles, Cal. $18,000 (building permit, Dec. 29, 1920; in construction Feb.-Aug., 1921)

1920   Aline Barnsdall studio residence B, 1645 Vermont Ave., Los Angeles, Cal. $21,000 (building permit Dec. 29, 1920; in construction Feb.-Nov., 1921; later altered by R. M. Schindler)

1920   W. J. Weber house, 9th Ave. at 4th St. (city not given on drawings)

1920 Project: Aline Barnsdall Theater, shops, apartments and houses for rent, Sunset Blvd. between Edgemont St. and Vermont Ave., Los Angeles, Cal. (final projects were made at the same time "Hollyhock House" and Residences A and B were in construction, but sketches for the theater may be much earlier, v. [1917])

Project: Cantilevered concrete skyscraper (v. National Life Insurance project, [1924])

1921 Jiyu Gakuen Girls' School of the Free Spirit, Tokio, Japan

Mrs. Thomas H. Gale house or houses[10], Birch Brook, Whitehall, Mich. (unsupervised, date very uncertain)

Project: Cement block house, Los Angeles, Cal.

1921 Project: Edward H. Doheny ranch development, Sierra Madre mountains, near Los Angeles, Cal.

1922 Project: A. M. Johnson desert compound and shrine, Death Valley, Cal.

1922 Project: G. P. Lowes house, Eagle Rock, Cal. (the house as built later by R. M. Schindler was much modified)

1922 Project: Merchandising building, Los Angeles, Cal.

Project: Sachse house, "Deep Springs," Mojave Desert, Cal.

1922 Project: Tahoe summer colony, Emerald Bay, Lake Tahoe, Cal.

1923 Aline Barnsdall kindergarten, "The Little Dipper," Olive Hill, Los Angeles, Cal. $12,500 (demolished, 1924; foundations then made into garden terrace by R. M. Schindler)

1923 Mrs. George Madison Millard house, 645 Prospect Crescent, Pasadena, Cal. $18,000 (the separate library and connecting passage, added in 1926 by Lloyd Wright, does not follow Frank Lloyd Wright's project, v. [1925]; garage enlarged, 1931)

Nathan G. Moore remodelled house, 329 Forest Ave., Oak Park, Ill. (1895 house rebuilt above ground storey after fire of 1922)

Dr. John Storer house, 8161 Hollywood Blvd., Los Angeles, Cal. (begun before an-

---

[10] Mrs. Gale will give no information and she may not have been the client. One house appears to be definitely of Wright's design, although unsupervised; two others are probably builder's copies of this.

nexation of this area by the city of Los Angeles, May 16, 1923; posterior in design to the Millard house)

Project: Darwin D. Martin house for daughter, Buffalo, N. Y.

1924   Charles Ennis house, 2607 Glendower Rd., Los Angeles, Cal. (being reconditioned by Wright for John Nesbitt, 1941)

1924   Samuel Freeman house, 1962 Glencoe Way, Los Angeles, Cal. (laundry remodelled later by R. M. Schindler as separate apartment)

Project: Nakoma Country Club and Winnebago Camping Ground Indian Memorial, Madison, Wis.

Project: National Life Insurance Company skyscraper for A. M. Johnson, Water Tower Sq., Chicago, Ill. (a development of the cantilevered skyscraper scheme of [1920]; worked over for several years, but essentially complete by 1925, the latest date found on drawings)

1925–   Taliesin III, Frank Lloyd Wright house, Spring Green, Wis. (rebuilding begun immediately after fire; 1925; further additions in the mid-thirties; minor changes still being made, 1941)

1925   Project: Mrs. Samuel William Gladney house, Fort Worth, Tex.

Project: Mrs. George Madison Millard gallery, Pasadena, Cal. (the detached library added to the Millard house in 1926 by Lloyd Wright bears little or no relation to this project)

1925   Project: Phi Gamma Delta Fraternity House, Madison, Wis. (the fraternity house as built somewhat later by Law, Law & Potter has little relation, except perhaps in plan, to the Wright project)

Project: Gordon Strong Planetarium, etc., Sugar Loaf Mountain, Md.

1926   Project: Oak Park Playground Association playhouses (6), Oak Park, Ill.

1926[11]   Project: Steel Cathedral embracing minor cathedrals to contain a million people, New York, N. Y.

1927   Darwin D. Martin house and garage, "Graycliff," Derby, N. Y. (garage begun 1926, before house; unsupervised)

---

[11] The Arizona Biltmore Hotel, in Phoenix, Arizona, with whose design Wright was associated in an advisory capacity at this time, has often been incorrectly attributed to him. The commission was Albert McArthur's. McArthur, a former pupil of Wright's, wished to use Wright's textile block system of construction. This was actually much modified when the hotel was built in 1928, but is rather more authentic in the detached cottages.

1927   Ocotillo Desert Camp, Frank Lloyd Wright Southwestern headquarters, Salt Range, nr. Chandler, Arizona (demolished, 1930)

1927   Project: Dr. Alexander Chandler low-cost concrete block houses, Chandler, Arizona (v. 1932)

Project: Dr. Alexander Chandler San Marcos-in-the-Desert winter resort, Chandler, Arizona (this elaborate project, including a hotel and several houses, was worked on for several years before and after the building of the Ocotillo Camp.)

Project: Dr. Alexander Chandler San Marcos Water Gardens tourist camp, Chandler, Arizona (probably later than San Marcos-in-the-Desert)

Project: Wellington and Ralph Cudney house, San Marcos-in-the-Desert, Chandler, Arizona (one of the houses mentioned above)

Project: Owen D. Young house, San Marcos-in-the-Desert, Chandler, Arizona (another of the houses mentioned above)

1928   Project: Darwin D. Martin Blue Sky mausoleum, Buffalo, N. Y. (in construction, 1941)

1928   Project: Standardized village service stations and city gasoline stations

1929   Richard Lloyd Jones house, "Westhope," 3700 Birmingham Rd., Tulsa, Okla.

Project: Richard Lloyd Jones house, Tulsa, Okla. (different and earlier than executed house)

Project: Elizabeth Noble apartment house, Los Angeles, Cal.

1929   Project: Rosenwald Foundation School for Negroes

Project: St. Mark's Tower for the Vestry of St. Mark's-in-the-Bouwerie, New York, N. Y. (published in 1930)

[1930] Project: Grouped apartment towers, Chicago, Ill. (based on the St. Mark's Tower project, above)

Project: Cabins for desert or woods (based on San Marcos Water Gardens project of [1927])

1931   Project: Capital Journal Building for George Putnam, Salem, Oregon

Project: "House on the Mesa," Denver, Col. (exhibited, 1932, at the Museum of Modern Art, New York)

Project: Schemes for "A Century of Progress," Chicago, Ill. (rejecting proposals that he design individual buildings at the 1933 World's Fair, Wright gave considerable thought to several alternative structural and design concepts of the exposition as a whole)

1932   Project: "Conventional House" (practically identical with Chandler block house, project of 1927)

1932   Project: Walter Davidson prefabricated sheet steel farm units
Project: Walter Davidson prefabricated sheet steel and glass markets

1932   Project: New Theater (there was possibly an earlier version of this, c. 1928)

1932   Project: Dean Malcolm M. Willey house, Minneapolis, Minn. (different from executed house, v. 1934)

1933–   Taliesin Fellowship complex, Hillside, Spring Green, Wis. (Misses Lloyd Jones house, v. [1887], remodelled as dormitory; Hillside Home School, v. 1902, adapted as theater, etc.; new drafting room; construction still continues, 1941)

1934   Dean Malcolm M. Willey house, 255 Bedford St. S. E., Minneapolis, Minn.
Project: Remodelling of A. D. German Warehouse as restaurant and apartments
Project: Broadacre City (exhibited and published, 1935; several years in preparation. Includes many projects of the previous decade: Nakoma Country Club, [1924]; Gordon Strong planetarium, [1925]; Steel Cathedral, 1926; Chandler block houses, 1927; San Marcos Water Gardens tourist camp, gasoline and service stations, 1928; St. Mark's Tower and Elizabeth Noble apartment houses, 1929; Capital Journal Building and "House on the Mesa," 1931; New Theater, Davidson farm units and markets, 1932; as well as many new projects for colleges, schools, hospitals, offices, country buildings, factories, hotels, stores, minimum and "two-car" houses, bridges, aerotor-ports, etc. Based on the programme announced in *The Disappearing City* [c. 1932]. Revised for exhibition, 1940, with the addition of various examples of the Usonian house, v. Hoult project, [1936], below, and Jacobs house, 1937)

[1935] Project: Stanley Marcus house, Dallas, Tex. (published in the *Architectural Forum*, January, 1938)

1936–   S. C. Johnson Administration Building, 1525 Howe St., Racine, Wis. (preliminary construction started Sept. 3, 1936, building permit issued April 30, 1937; completed April 1, 1939.)

1936   Edgar J. Kaufmann house, "Falling Water," Bear Run, Penna.

1936   Mrs. Abby Beecher Roberts house, "Deertrack," R.F.D. 1, Marquette, Mich. (altered)

Project: H. C. Hoult house, Wichita, Kan. (the first Usonian house project)

Project: Robert D. Lusk house, Huron, S. Dak. (published in the *Architectural Forum,* January, 1938)

1937   Paul R. Hanna house, 737 Coronado St., Palo Alto, Cal.

1937   Herbert Jacobs house, 441 Toepfer St., Westmorland, near Madison, Wis.

1937   Herbert F. Johnson, Jr., house, "Wingspread," Wind Point, north of Racine, Wis.

1937   Edgar J. Kaufmann office, Kaufmann Department Store, 400 Fifth Ave., Pittsburgh, Penna.

Project: "All Steel" houses development (100), Los Angeles, Cal.

Project: Leo Bramson dress-shop reconstruction, 1107 Lake St., Oak Park, Ill. (published in the *Architectural Forum,* January, 1938; a remodelling of the Pebbles and Balch shop, v. **1907**)

Project: George Parker garage, Janesville, Wis. (published in the *Architectural Forum,* January, 1938)

1938   Ben Rebhuhn house, Myrtle Ave. and Magnolia Dr., Great Neck Estates, Great Neck, L. I., N. Y.

Taliesin farm group, Hillside, Spring Green, Wis.

1938–   Taliesin West, Frank Lloyd Wright winter headquarters in the desert, Maricopa Mesa, Paradise Valley, near Phoenix, Arizona (still being completed and extended, 1941)

1938   Project: Edith Carlson house, Superior, Wis.

1938   Project: Florida Southern College, Lakeland, Fla. (16 buildings in all; Ann Pfeiffer Memorial Chapel and three seminar buildings, v. 1940; Library, v. 1941)

1938   Project: "House for a family of $5000–$6000 income," for *Life* (published in *Life,* September 26th, 1938)

1938   Project: Ralph Jester house, Palos Verdes, Cal.

1938   Project: Herbert F. Johnson, Jr., gatehouse and farm group, Wind Point, north of Racine, Wis.

Project: Royal H. Jurgenson house, Evanston, Ill. (exhibited, 1940)

Project: George Bliss McCallum house, Northampton, Mass.

Project: E. A. Smith house, Piedmont Pines, Cal. (exhibited, 1940)

[1939]   Andrew F. H. Armstrong house, Ogden Dunes, near Gary, Ind. (exhibited, 1940)

1939   Edgar J. Kaufmann guest house, Bear Run, Penna.

1939   Stanley Rosenbaumn house, Riverview Dr., Florence, Ala.

Bernard Schwartz house, Still Bend, Two Rivers, Wis. (based on the *Life* house of 1938; exhibited, 1940)

George D. Sturges house, 449 Skyway Rd., Brentwood Heights, Cal. (exhibited, 1940)

1939   Tod Company "Suntop Homes," quadruple house, Sutton Rd. near Spring Ave., Ardmore, Penna. (4 more units, i.e., 16 more dwellings, were projected)

Katherine Winkler and Alma Goetsch house, Hulett Rd., Okemos, Mich. (exhibited, 1940)

1939   Project: Lewis N. Bell house, Los Angeles, Cal.

Project: Madison Civic Center, Olin Terrace, Monona Ave. at Lake Monona, Madison, Wis. (reworked, 1941)

1939   Project: Edgar A. Mauer house, Los Angeles, Cal.

Project: Ludd M. Spivey house, Fort Lauderdale, Fla. (exhibited, 1940)

1939   Project: Usonian house development (7), Okemos, Mich. (only the Winkler-Goetsch house above was built, and on a different site; the Erling B. Brauner, J. J. Garrison, C. D. Hause, Sidney H. Newman, Alexis J. Panshin, and Clarence R. Van Dusen houses remain unexecuted)

1940   Theodore Baird house, Shays St., Amherst, Mass.

Sidney Bazett house, 101 Reservoir Rd., Hillsborough, Cal. (exhibited, 1940)

1940   James B. Christie house, Jockey Hollow Rd., Bernardsville, N. J. (unsupervised)

1940   Community Church, 4600 Main St., Kansas City, Mo. (construction continues, 1941)

1940   Joseph Euchtman house, Cross Country Blvd. near Labyrinth Rd., Baltimore, Md.

1940   Florida Southern College Ann Pfeiffer Chapel, Lakeland, Fla.

1940   Florida Southern College seminar buildings (3), Lakeland, Fla.

1940   Lloyd Lewis house, Little St. Mary's Rd., Libertyville, Ill.

Charles L. Manson house, 1224 Highland Blvd., Wausau, Wis. (exhibited, 1940)

1940   Rose Pauson house, Orange Rd., Phoenix, Ariz.

1940   John C. Pew house, 3650 Mendota Dr., Shorewood Hills, near Madison, Wis.

1940   Loren Pope house, Locust St., Falls Church, Va.

Clarence W. Sondern house, 3600 Belleview Ave., Kansas City, Mo. (exhibited, 1940)

1940   Leigh Stevens house and adjuncts, Auldbrass Plantation, near Yemassee, S. C. (construction continues, 1941)

1940   Project: Crystal Heights hotel, theater, shops, etc., Connecticut and Florida Aves., Washington, D. C.

Project: John Nesbitt house, Cypress Point, Carmel Bay, Cal.

Project: Martin J. Pence house, Hilo, Hawaii (two schemes, one based on the Jester project of 1938; exhibited, 1940)

Project: Frank A. Rentz house, Madison, Wis. (based on the McCallum project of [1938]; exhibited, 1940)

Project: Franklin Watkins studio, Barnegat City, N. J.

1941   Gregor Affleck house, Bloomfield Hills, Mich.

1941   Florida Southern College Library, Lakeland, Fla.

1941   Arch Oboler house, Ventura Blvd., Los Angeles, Cal.

1941[12]   Project: Margaret Schevill house, Tucson, Ariz.

---

[12]The following additional houses are now being designed or are already in construction October, 1941:

    1941   John Barton house, Pine Bluff, Wis.
    1941   Alfred H. Ellinwood house, Deerfield, Ill.
    1941   Parker B. Field house, Airport Road, Peru, Ill.
    1941   William Guenther house, East Caldwell, N. J.
    1941   Roy Petersen house, West Racine, Wis.
    1941   Stuart Richardson house, Livingston, N. J.
    1941   Vigo Sundt house, Madison, Wis.
    1941   Carlton David Wall house, Detroit, Mich.
    1941   Mary Waterstreet Studio, nr. Spring Green, Wis.
    1941   Project: Sigma Chi Fraternity House, Hanover, Ind. F. Ll. W.

Illustrations

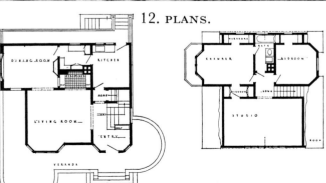

12. PLANS.

11. FRANK LLOYD WRIGHT HOUSE, 428 FOREST AVE., OAK PARK, ILL. 1889.

The Suburban Richardsonian manner is already regularized here. Moreover the stylobate-like terrace and the hovering eaves foreshadow more individual developments, though the planning is still of the eighties.

13. FRANK LLOYD WRIGHT HOUSE, 428 FOREST AVE., OAK PARK, ILL. 1889. LIVING ROOM.

The view of the Wright living room empty shows clearly the open planning in the Queen Anne tradition. The treatment of the openings without architraves beneath a continuous string course is new and personal to Wright. Such refinements of detail enhance the feeling of spatial flow and suggest that the interior walls are no more than movable screens. The small photograph shows the inglenook with the original furniture and decorations.

FIREPLACE INGLENOOK.   14.

15. FRANK LLOYD WRIGHT HOUSE, 428 FOREST AVE., OAK PARK, ILL. LATER DINING ROOM.
[1895.]

16. FRANK LLOYD WRIGHT HOUSE, 428 FOR-
EST AVE., OAK PARK, ILL. LATER PLAY ROOM.
[1895.]
17. R. P. PARKER HOUSE, 1027 CHICAGO AVE.,
OAK PARK, ILL. 1892. FRONT.
18. ROBERT G. EMMOND HOUSE, 109 SOUTH

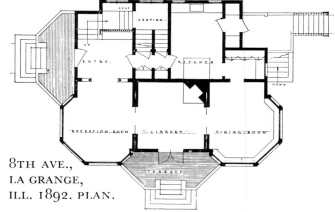

8TH AVE.,
LA GRANGE,
ILL. 1892. PLAN.

19. GEORGE BLOSSOM HOUSE, 4858 KENWOOD AVE., CHICAGO, ILL. 1892.   20. PLANS.

Wright's one executed work of academic design has a very personal elegance. It displays his early ability to rival the Eastern traditionalists at their own game. But it has further significance. The axial discipline orders the looseness of Queen Anne planning, and a new clarity of external design replaces earlier quaintness. The later dormers are not by Wright.

21. DR. ALLISON W. HARLAN HOUSE, 4414 GREENWOOD
AVE., CHICAGO, ILL. 1892.

Wright's best house of the early nineties, remarkable for its premonitions of his ma-
ture Prairie houses a decade later
such as the hovering roof, the balcony, the articulation of the front and
the absence of stylistic reminiscence.

22. PLAN.

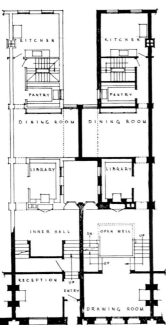

24. PLANS.

23. ROBERT W. ROLOSON HOUSES, 3213–3219 CALUMET AVE., CHICAGO, ILL. 1894.

These are effectively Wright's only executed examples of the city rowhouse. They show unexpected mastery of an unsympathetic problem.

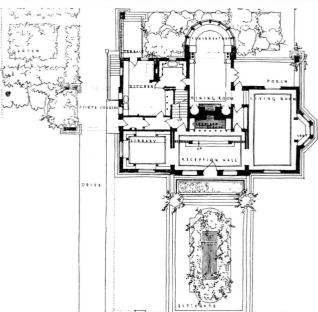

25. W. H. WINSLOW HOUSE, AUVERGNE PL.,
RIVER FOREST, ILL. 1893.   26. PLAN.

The Winslow house was Wright's first independent commission after leaving Sullivan. The fine roman brickwork recalls the Charnley house; while the rich terra cotta frieze is like that on the Victoria Hotel, and the design of the stonework about the entrance is close to that of the Wainwright tomb. Thus the house has generally been considered very Sullivanian. But as these works of the Adler and Sullivan office owed so much to Wright, it is evident that the house rather continues a particular line of design which Wright himself had initiated.

27. W. H. WINSLOW
HOUSE, AUVERGNE PL.,
RIVER FOREST, ILL. 1893.
ENTRANCE HALL.

28. REAR.

The resemblance of the formal plan to that of the Blossom house, over which it is a great improvement, and of the sheltering roof to that of the Harlan house should make plain how little of Sullivan's influence there is here. The composition of the front of this house and the refined and more Sullivanian elegance of the interior detail were enormously influential on the work of George Maher and other members of the later Chicago School in the next ten years.

The fine composition of the rear of the house with its bold conjunctions of horizontal and vertical elements, its contrast of solid and void and of rectangular and polygonal forms was hardly understood by early imitators.

29. CHAUNCEY L. WILLIAMS HOUSE, 520 EDGEWOOD PL., RIVER FOREST, ILL. 1895.
30. FREDERICK BAGLEY HOUSE, 101 COUNTY LINE RD., HINSDALE, ILL. 1894.

The Bagley house is still essentially Suburban Richardsonian, though much chastened in composition and detail. Its virtues are almost conventional for the period. The Williams house is much more original, with a first hint of Japanese rather than Queen Anne quaintness.

31. FRANCIS APARTMENTS, 4304 FORESTVILLE AVE., CHICAGO, ILL. 1895.

The Francis Apartments resemble the earlier Charnley and Winslow houses in their urbane dignity. At the client's insistence Wright used Tudor forms in this house. But the design is rational in character like good old work, while the piazza Americanizes the scheme.

32. NATHAN G. MOORE HOUSE, FOREST AVE., OAK PARK, ILL. [1895].

33. FRANCISCO TERRACE, 253–257 FRANCISCO AVE., CHICAGO, ILL. 1895. COURT.

34. SECOND FLOOR PLAN.

This was an important early low-cost housing development, unfortunately now poorly maintained. The galleries foreshadow twentieth century European practice.

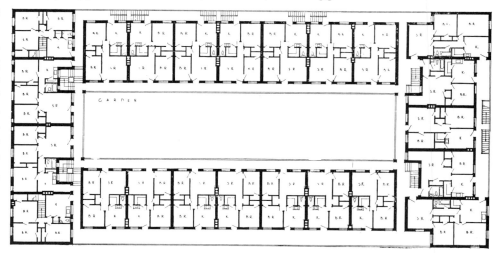

35. FRANCISCO TERRACE, 253–257 FRANCISCO AVE., CHICAGO, ILL. 1895. ENTRANCE FRONT.

36. APARTMENTS, 2840–2858 WEST WALNUT ST., CHICAGO, ILL. 1895.

The monumental dignity and simplicity of these low rental apartment houses is still impressive.

37. PROJECT: WOLF LAKE AMUSEMENT PARK, ON WOLF LAKE, ILL. 1895.

The gaiety, variety and boldness of Wright's greatest later works are foreshadowed here.

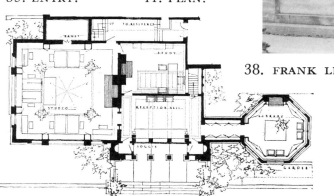

39. ENTRY.   41. PLAN.

38. FRANK LLOYD WRIGHT STUDIO, 951 CHICAGO AVE., OAK PARK, ILL. 1895.   40. ENTRANCE.

Remodelled after 1911 as two apartments.

42. MISSES LLOYD JONES WINDMILL, HILLSIDE, SPRING GREEN, WIS. 1896.

Trained as an engineer, Wright in this windmill and watertower (still one of the conspicuous landmarks of his career) displayed his structural ingenuity in the embrace of lozenge and polygon —hence the name Romeo and Juliet —and in the bracing floors within, like the strengthening membranes within a hollow plant stem. To Wright biological analogy was from the first full of architectural suggestion, since he always emulated a principle rather than imitated a form. The battens represent a step toward the later more structural use of horizontal sheathing.

43. ISIDOR HELLER HOUSE, 5132 WOODLAWN AVE., CHICAGO, ILL. 1897.　PLAN. 44.

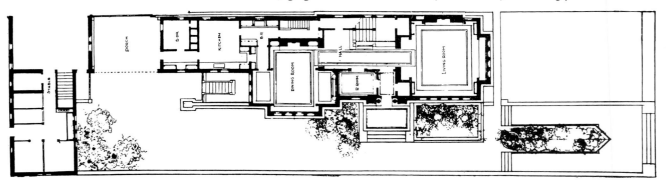

45. JOSEPH W. HUSSER HOUSE, 180 BUENA AVE., CHICAGO, ILL. 1899.

Developed from the MacAfee and Baldwin projects of the mid-nineties, this is the first of Wright's cross-shaped houses. The living floor is raised to make the most of the lake view. The rooms are barely separated by wall spurs and columns, yet the long articulation of the plan gives them considerable independence. The rich frieze about the upper storey recalls that of the Winslow house. The elaborately moulded arches are likewise unexpectedly Sullivanian. But this is the last appearance of such decorative profusion. Already the masses of the stable block illustrate a more severe and abstract tendency.

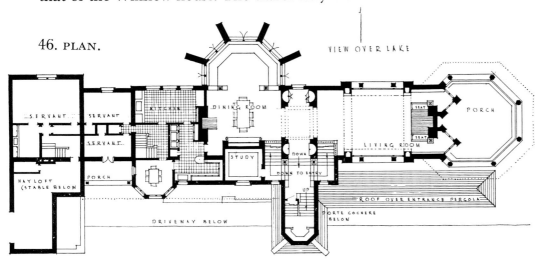

46. PLAN.

47. FRONT WING.
[1898.]
The Golf Club in
its original front
wing already dis-
plays complete
maturity of de-
sign. Note hori-
zontally sheathed
walls and contin-
uous window
bands.

48. RIVER FOREST GOLF CLUB, BONNIE BRAE AVE., RIVER FOREST, ILL. AS ENLARGED. [1901.]

49. RIVER FOREST GOLF CLUB, BONNIE BRAE AVE.,
RIVER FOREST, ILL. [1901.]   PLAN. 50.

As enlarged the Golf
Club maintains the
structural and com-
positional principles
already mature in
the original front
wing of 1898; though
there is some loss of
clarity, perhaps, in
the composition of
the octagonal lounge
with its paired chim-
neys. The perspec-
tive reveals the way
the partially en-
closed volumes inter-
sect better than
photographs.

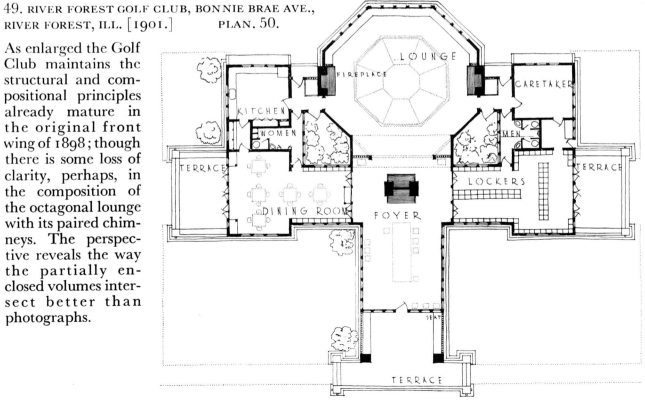

51. EDWARD C. WALLER DINING ROOM, AUVERGNE PL., RIVER FOREST, ILL. 1899.

The interweaving and overlapping of spatial elements in an interior reached mature expression in this remodelled room.

52. PROJECT: EDWARD C. WALLER HOUSE, RIVER FOREST, ILL. 1899.

53. WARREN HICKOX HOUSE, 687 SOUTH HARRISON AVE., KANKAKEE, ILL. 1900.

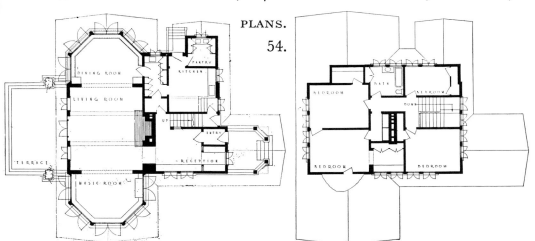

PLANS.

54.

The Hickox house is remarkable for the clarity and consistency of its open planning. The formal but asymmetrical composition owes something to Japanese prints; but the oriental look is more due to coincidence than to actual influence.

55. B. HARLEY BRADLEY HOUSE, 701 SOUTH HARRISON AVE., KANKAKEE, ILL. 1900.

The larger Bradley house is less radical in plan than its neighbor the Hickox house. But the crossing of axes, more conspicuous in the external design than in the plan, prepares the way for such a mature masterpiece as the Willitts house two years later. The plane-like character of the roof slopes, the sheathing of the wooden construction with plaster, the stud-skeleton revealed in the window mullions, express as clearly and boldly as the River Forest Golf Club Wright's wholly personal mastery of the American building tradition.

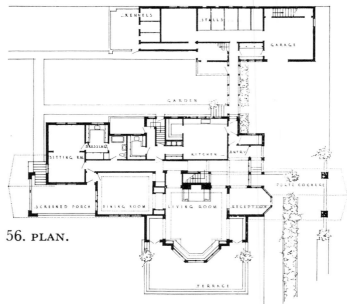

56. PLAN.

57. B. HARLEY BRADLEY HOUSE, 701 SOUTH HARRISON AVE., KANKAKEE, ILL. 1900. LIVING ROOM.

With specially designed furniture and fittings Wright achieved a total unity in his Prairie house interiors from the first. Although this house is less open in plan than its neighbor, the Hickox house, the living room space is extended into subordinate areas and well lighted by the great projecting bay window. The leaded patterns in the glass are characteristic of Wright's mature ornamental style based more on his early Froebel training than on Sullivan.

58. PERSPECTIVE

FROM "LADIES' HOME JOURNAL,"
FEBRUARY, 1901.

59. PLANS.

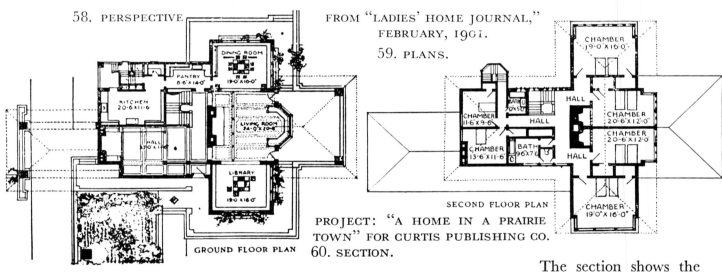

GROUND FLOOR PLAN

DINING ROOM
19·0"X16·0"

PANTRY
8·6"X14·0"

KITCHEN
20·6"X11·6"

LIVING ROOM
24·0"X20·6"

HALL
13·0"X14·0"

LIBRARY
19·0"X16·0"

SECOND FLOOR PLAN

CHAMBER
19·0"X16·0"

CHAMBER
11·6"X9·6"

CHAMBER
13·6"X11·6"

BATH
10·X5·0"

BATH
9·6"X7·6"

HALL

HALL

HALL

CHAMBER
20·6"X12·0"

CHAMBER
20·6"X12·0"

CHAMBER
19·0"X16·0"

PROJECT: "A HOME IN A PRAIRIE
TOWN" FOR CURTIS PUBLISHING CO.
60. SECTION.

The principles of the Prairie house are more completely illustrated here than in the executed houses of this same year.

The section shows the living room extended upward; the plan indicates how two bedrooms may replace this spatial luxury.

61. PROJECT: "A SMALL HOUSE WITH 'LOTS OF ROOM IN IT'" FOR CURTIS PUBLISHING CO., 1900.

62. PLANS.   63. SECTIONS.

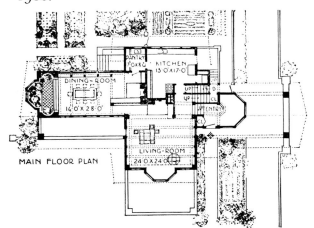

MAIN FLOOR PLAN

SECOND FLOOR PLAN.

The second *Ladies Home Journal* house is less radical than the first with the living room and dining room connected at an interior angle rather than in a continuous suite. The "Japanese" gabled roofs of the Hickox house and its open terrace used here are somewhat less characteristic of the Prairie type than the hip roofs and covered porch of the other.

SECTIONAL VIEW OF DINING ROOM   SECTIONAL VIEW OF LIVING-ROOM   SECTIONAL VIEW OF ENTRY

64. WILLIAM G. FRICKE
HOUSE, 540 FAIR OAKS
AVE., OAK PARK, ILL.
1902.

The bank project,
though significant for
its intended concrete
construction, and the
Fricke house still sug-
gest the nineties.

65. PROJECT: "VIL-
LAGE BANK IN CAST
CONCRETE." For *Brick-
builder*, August, 1901.

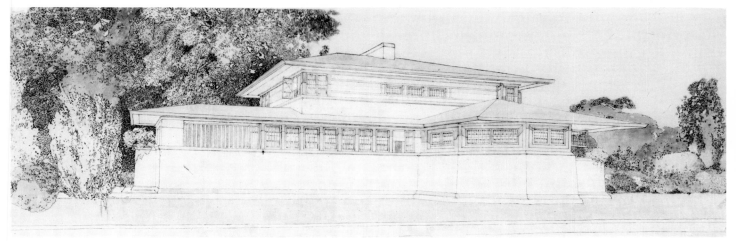

66. F. B. HENDERSON
HOUSE, 301 SOUTH
KENILWORTH AVE., ELM-
HURST, ILL. 1901.

Unfortunately, as the photograph indicates, this house has been damaged by the addition of a covered second storey porch over the open terrace in front of the living room.

68. PLAN.

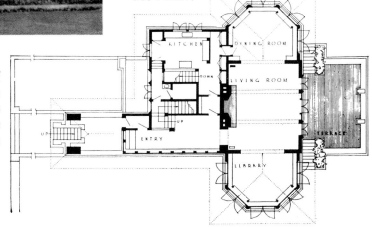

67. THE HOUSE AS ALTERED.

The more mature and slightly larger twin of the Hickox house of the previous year, the Henderson house is also superior. The hip roofs are more serene in feeling and the simple straight line patterns in the leaded glasses are unusually delicate.

69. FRANK THOMAS HOUSE, 210 FOREST AVE., OAK PARK, ILL. 1901. 70. PLANS.

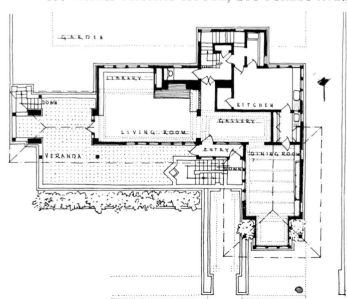

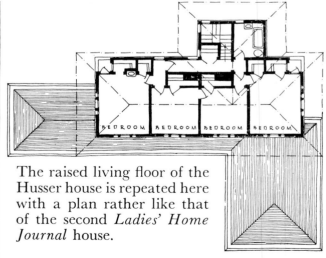

The raised living floor of the Husser house is repeated here with a plan rather like that of the second *Ladies' Home Journal* house.

71. ARTHUR HEURTLEY HOUSE, 318 FOREST AVE., OAK PARK, ILL. 1902.　72. PLANS.

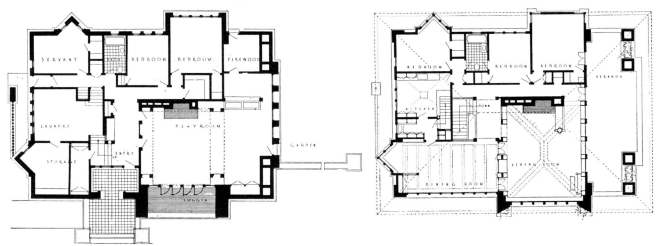

73. WARD W. WILLITTS HOUSE, 715 SOUTH SHERIDAN RD., HIGHLAND PARK, ILL.

This is the first masterpiece among the Prairie houses. The brilliant extension of the cruciform plan, the repeated hovering lines of the upper and lower eaves, the banking of the windows, bring to final maturity the promise of the houses and projects of the preceding transitional years.

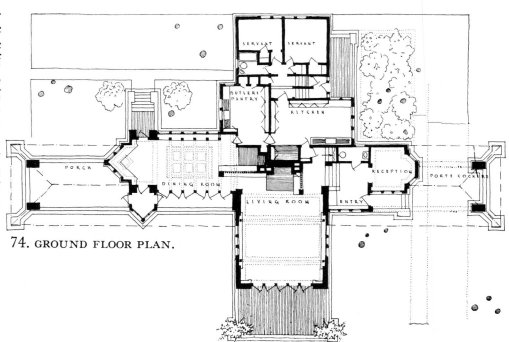

74. GROUND FLOOR PLAN.

75. WARD W. WILLITTS HOUSE, 715 SOUTH SHERIDAN RD., HIGHLAND PARK, ILL. 1902. LIVING ROOM.

The horizontals of the house are effectively crossed by the vertical window mullions and wood-strips suggesting the stud-skeleton beneath.

No photograph can give a just sense of the continuous flow of interior space in the early Prairie houses, but the harmony of the stained plaster walls, natural wood trim and the specially designed furniture, with accents of bright pattern in the leaded glass, is characteristically represented in this living room.

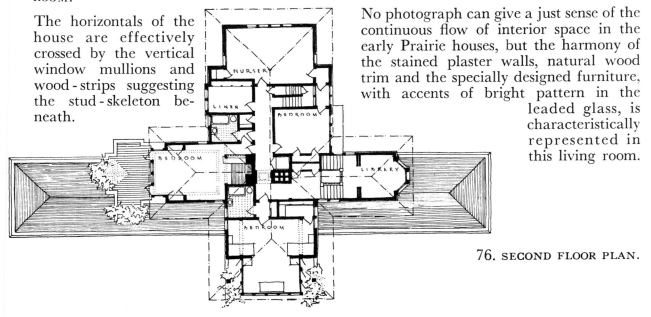

76. SECOND FLOOR PLAN.

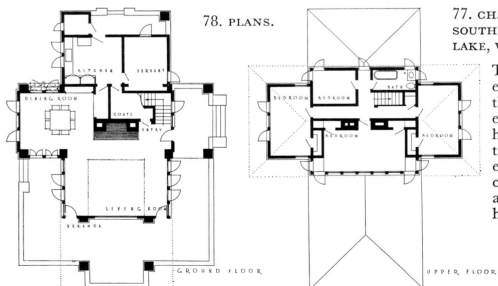

78. PLANS.

GROUND FLOOR

UPPER FLOOR

77. CHARLES S. ROSS HOUSE, SOUTH SHORE RD., DELAVAN LAKE, WIS. 1902.

The finest of the "Forest" houses which are the more rustic brothers of the Prairie houses. The implications of the River Forest Golf Club are here compactly realized in a lake side summer house.

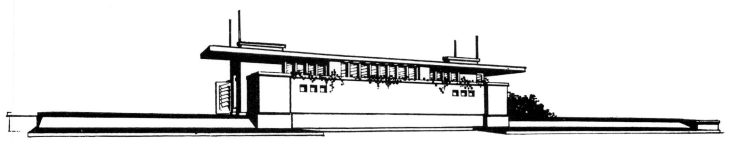

79. PROJECT: YAHARA BOAT CLUB, MADISON, WIS. 1902. PERSPECTIVE AND PLAN.

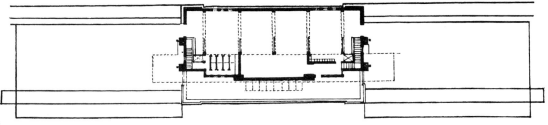

Despite the great production of executed work in the Oak Park years, some of Wright's finest architectural conceptions found expression at first only in projects. The little Yahara Boat Club was the first design in which Wright carried to its logical conclusions his interest in abstract composition, unless perhaps the lost Universal Portland Cement pavilion at the Pan-American Exposition in Buffalo of the previous year was similar, as seems probable. Here in embryo we have the spirit of some of the most famous later work of this decade and the next, the formal symmetry and emphasis on the cantilevered slab of Unity Church, 1906, and the dexterous and subtle elaboration of thickened planes and voids in space of the Coonley kindergarten project, 1911, and the executed Coonley play-house, 1912, which lead up to the Midway Gardens, 1914. The house project, of about the same date, is similarly striking for the tremendous extension of the living room, opening not only into the dining room, but into the studio and a bedroom as well. This is almost a one-room house and foreshadows clearly the planning of the Usonian houses of Wright's present practice. Note the double fireplace.

80. PROJECT: FRANK LLOYD WRIGHT STUDIO HOUSE, OAK PARK, ILL. [1903]. PLAN.

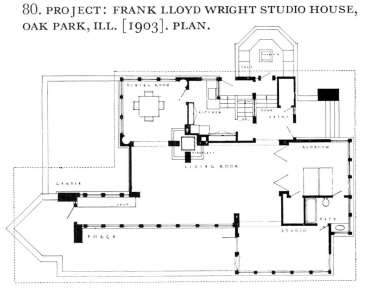

81. HILLSIDE HOME SCHOOL, HILLSIDE, SPRING GREEN, WIS. 1902.   82. PLAN.

The relation to the hill-slope, the sturdy base of rock-faced, flesh-coloured stone, the heavy timber mullions above, produce an effect at once monumental and appropriate to the countryside. The balance of the asymmetrical pavilions, the skilful utilization of different levels within the living room and the gymnasium and by the connecting bridge contrast with the severe character of the industrial Larkin Building, designed immediately afterward, and suggest how his native landscape was ultimately to inspire Wright in the creation of his own house nearby.

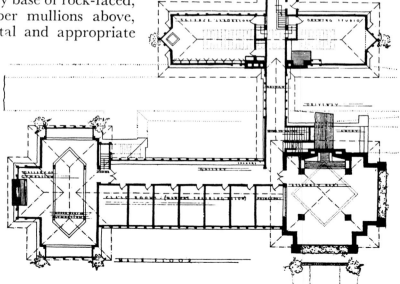

83. HILLSIDE HOME SCHOOL, HILL-SIDE, SPRING GREEN, WIS. 1902. LIVING ROOM PAVILION.

84. LIVING ROOM FIREPLACE.

The batter of the random masonry, the structural window mullions and the red-tiled roofs give monumental character to the exterior, which is echoed in the stone and rough wood of the interior.

85. SUSAN LAURENCE DANA HOUSE, EAST LAURENCE AVE. AT 4TH ST., SPRINGFIELD, ILL. 1903. DINING ROOM. 86.

88. GALLERY.   BRONZE AND GLASS SCREEN. 87.

89. FRANCIS W. LITTLE HOUSE AND STABLE, 603 MOSS AVE., PEORIA, ILL. 1903.

The photographs and plan show the house as enlarged by Robert C. Clarke in 1909. The house is set well back against the lot line to provide an ample lawn about the projecting porch. The stable echoes most effectively the composition of the main house.

PLAN. 90.

91. ENTRANCE.

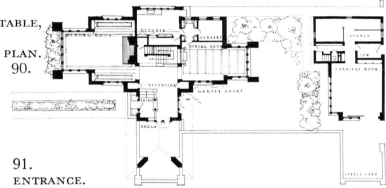

92. LARKIN COMPANY ADMINISTRATION BUILDING, 680 SENECA ST., BUFFALO, N. Y. 1904.

The massive front of the Larkin Building expresses consciously the innate monumentality of industrial architecture. The fine brickwork. the skilfully placed accents of sculpture suggest how severity may be dignified and lightened without loss of scale.

93. LARKIN COMPANY ADMINISTRATION BUILDING, 680 SENECA ST., BUFFALO, N. Y. 1904. OFFICE INTERIOR.

94. SIDE VIEW.

The Larkin Building exists for its interior, the office-floors grouped around the top-lighted court and further lighted from the high horizontal windows between the articulated piers of the side walls.

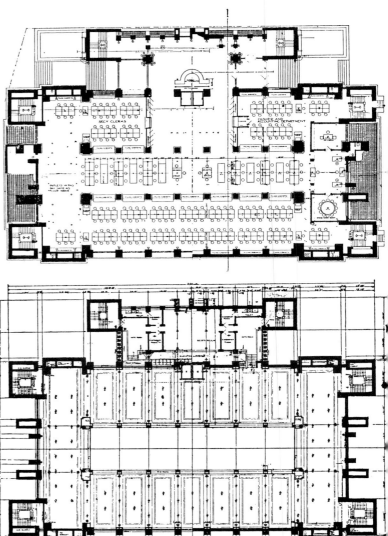

95. LARKIN COMPANY ADMINISTRATION BUILDING, 680 SENECA ST., BUFFALO, N. Y. 1904. INTERIOR OF COURT.   96. FIRST AND THIRD FLOOR PLANS.

97. LARKIN COMPANY ADMINISTRATION
BUILDING, 680 SENECA ST., BUFFALO, N. Y.
1904. ENTRANCE. 98. OFFICE FURNISHINGS.

99. E.-Z. POLISH FACTORY, 3005–3017 WEST
CARROLL AVE., CHICAGO, ILL. 1905.

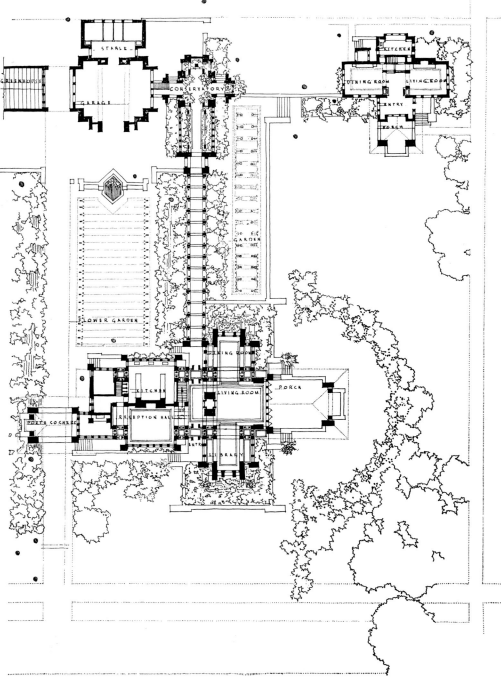

Within the plan, the following labels appear:

- STABLE
- GREENHOUSE
- GARAGE
- CONSERVATORY
- KITCHEN
- DINING ROOM
- LIVING ROOM
- ENTRY
- PORCH
- GARDEN
- FLOWER GARDEN
- KITCHEN
- LIVING ROOM
- PORCH
- RECEPTION HALL
- PORTE COCHERE
- ENTRY
- LIBRARY

100. DARWIN D. MARTIN
HOUSE AND ADJUNCTS,
125 JEWETT PKWAY,
BUFFALO, N. Y. 1904.
ESTATE PLAN.

The small Barton house for Martin's daughter was begun the year before the big house with its conservatory, connected with the house by a gallery, and its garage with living quarters above. There is thus a complex of related structures of similar materials and details rather than a single house. In the many interlocking sub-spaces of the living room in the big house there is a more ample development of the organization of space seen at its most compact in the front suite of rooms of the small Barton house. But the big house has also a separate reception hall of considerable size.

101. DARWIN D. MARTIN HOUSE, 125 JEWETT PKWAY, BUFFALO, N. Y. 1904.

The great size of the Martin house makes possible a subtle extension of the characteristic Prairie house composition. The fine materials inside and out have stood up well despite the long period the house has been empty. But the planting has now overflowed the terraced beds to which it was once confined, giving the exterior an unkempt air. The lower photograph, which is an old one, shows better the intended relationship between the architecture and its original setting. The elaborated latin cross plan provides widely varied silhouettes in perspective from different angles; thus different photographs hardly seem of the same house.

102. VIEW FROM LAWN.

104. DARWIN D. MARTIN HOUSE, 125 JEWETT PKWAY, BUFFALO, N. Y. 1904. LIVING ROOM.

103. GALLERY.

The Martin house once contained some of Wright's most successful early furniture. The round chairs were repeated in 1937 for the Johnson house in Racine. The exterior detail shows the superb masonry, including birdhouses of stone.

105. PERSPECTIVE.

107. PLAN.

106. EDWIN H. CHENEY HOUSE, 520 NORTH EAST AVE.,
OAK PARK, ILL. 1904. SIDE VIEW.

An unusually compact and original plan type.

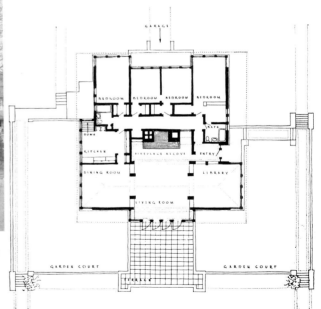

108.

PROJECT: LARKIN
COMPANY WORKMEN'S
ROW HOUSES, BUFFALO,
N. Y. [1904].

109. PLANS.

A remarkable
early scheme for
a worker's hous-
ing development
approximating
the type widely
used in Europe
in the twenties
and the thirties
and now fre-
quent in Defense
Housing in this
country.

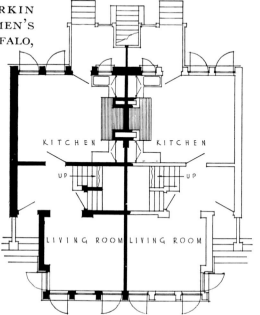

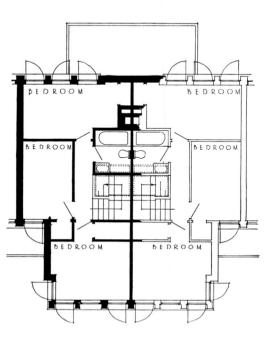

110. W. A. GLASNER HOUSE, 850 SHERIDAN RD., GLENCOE, ILL. 1905.

111. PLAN.

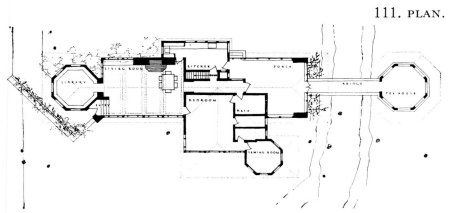

Perhaps the first instance of an all-year house in which there is no separate dining room. The extended plan and attached octagons give scale and interest to a one storey house of no great size.

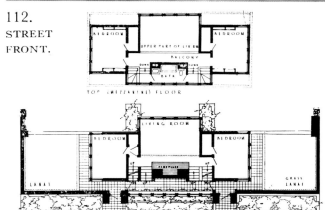

112.
STREET
FRONT.

BEDROOM | UPPER PART OF LIV RM | BEDROOM
BALCONY
DOWN | BATH | DOWN

TOP (MEZZANINE) FLOOR

LIVING ROOM
BEDROOM | BEDROOM
FIREPLACE
LANAI | GRASS LANAI

MAIN FLOOR

113. PLANS.

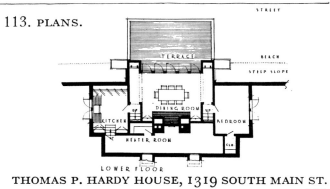

STREET

TERRACE | BEACH
STEEP SLOPE

DINING ROOM
UP | UP
KITCHEN | BEDROOM
HEATER ROOM | CLO

LOWER FLOOR

THOMAS P. HARDY HOUSE, 1319 SOUTH MAIN ST.
RACINE, WIS. PERSPECTIVE FROM LAKE.   114

115. FRANK L. SMITH BANK, DWIGHT, ILL. 1906.

The bank displays a simple, formal dignity rarely seen in small prairie towns.
Wright was rightly so pleased with the Walter Gerts project that he proposed it for another client. The plan, with its free use of solid wall planes and long glass areas set at right angles, is very like the boldest European projects of twenty years later.

117. PROJECT: WALTER GERTS (ALEX DAVIDSON) HOUSE, GLENCOE, ILL. (BUFFALO, N. Y.). 1906.

116. PLAN.

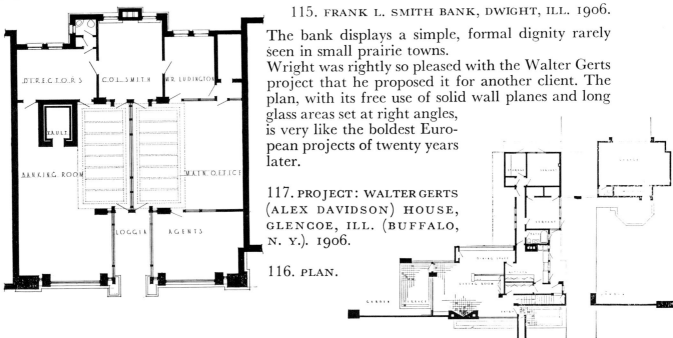

118. UNITY CHURCH, KENILWORTH AVE. AT LAKE ST., OAK PARK, ILL. 1906. SIDE VIEW.

Wright's first executed building of poured concrete. The pebble aggregate provides a textured surface.

119. PLAN.

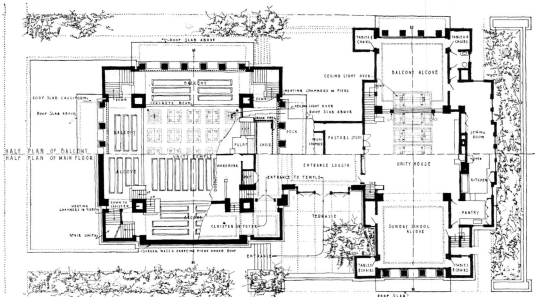

120. UNITY CHURCH, KENILWORTH
AVE. AT LAKE ST., OAK PARK, ILL.
1906. INTERIOR OF AUDITORIUM.

121. INTERIOR OF PARISH HOUSE.

The composition of the interiors is
very rich, with interpenetrating cross
spaces at different levels below and
above the balconies.

Almost exactly contemporary, the rich marble and gold detail of the Rookery entrance contrasts with the geometrical severity of the cast-concrete detail of Unity Church. The patterns at the Rookery are still almost Sullivanian in their curvilinear opulence, suitable to the "Moorish" detail of Root's masterpiece of the mid-eighties.

124. P. A. BEACHY HOUSE, 238 FOREST AVE., OAK PARK, ILL. 1906.

125. W. R. HEATH HOUSE, 76 SOLDIERS PL., BUFFALO, N. Y. 1905. LIVING ROOM.

An unusual Prairie house exterior of masonry and plaster and a typical contemporary living room and dining room.

126. A. W. GRIDLEY HOUSE, NORTH BATAVIA AVE., GENEVA, ILL. 1906.

Although the main block of the house appears square, actually this is an articulated cross plan of considerable extension, yet boldly asymmetrical balance between the low open porch to the left and the high closed wing to the right.

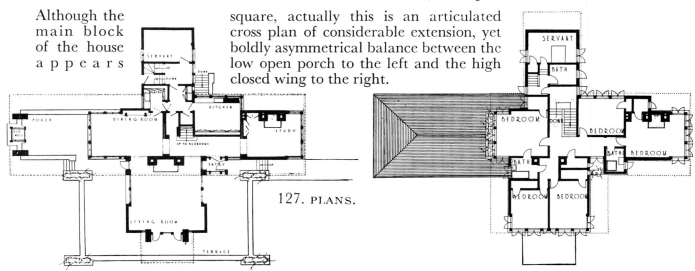

127. PLANS.

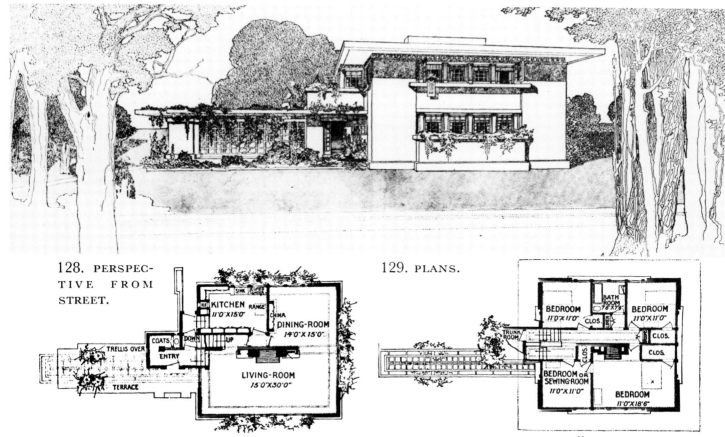

128. PERSPEC-
TIVE FROM
STREET.

KITCHEN
11'0" X 15'0"

SINK
CUPBD UNDER

RANGE

CHINA

DINING-ROOM
14'0" X 15'0"

COATS

DOWN

UP

ENTRY

TRELLIS OVER

TERRACE

LIVING-ROOM
15'0" X 30'0"

129. PLANS.

BEDROOM
11'0" X 11'0"

BATH
ROOM
7'6" X 7'6"

BEDROOM
11'0" X 11'0"

CLOS.

CLOS.

TRUNK
ROOM

CLOS.

BOOKS

CLOS.

CLOS.

BEDROOM OR
SEWING-ROOM
11'0" X 11'0"

BEDROOM
11'0" X 18'6"

PROJECT: "A FIREPROOF
HOUSE FOR $5000" FOR
THE CURTIS PUBLISHING
CO. 1906.

130. STEPHEN M. B.
HUNT HOUSE, 345
SOUTH SEVENTH AVE.,
LA GRANGE, ILL. 1907.

This executed house is
nearly identical in plan
and design with the
project above.

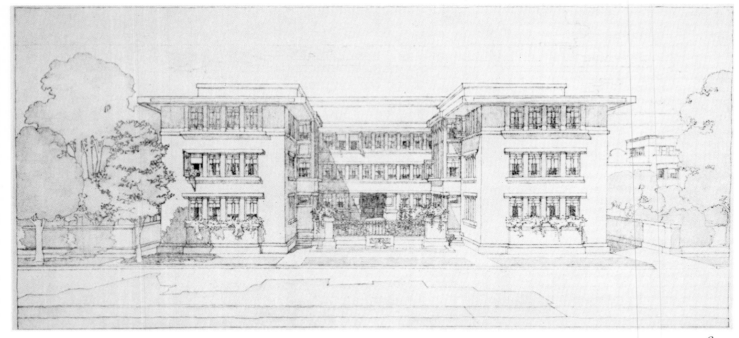

131. PROJECT: WARREN MC ARTHUR CONCRETE APARTMENT HOUSE, KENWOOD, CHICAGO, ILL. 1906.

132. PLAN.

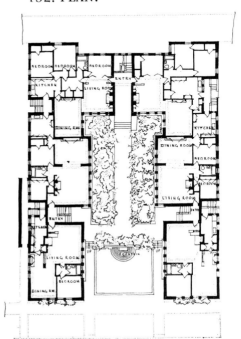

Wright's projects for multiple dwellings in the Oak Park years rarely came to execution. This apartment house scheme is interesting for its intended construction of cast-concrete and for the way in which the breaks in plan about the open court, which let a maximum of light into the apartments, are ordered and harmonized by the fenestration scheme and the projecting slab roof. The importance of material to Wright appears in the contrast between the solid design of this or the Unity Church and the light open feeling of the temporary pavilion and the shop front on the opposite page. This type of low apartment house about a court open at one end to the street was much used in the Chicago area and has many urbanistic advantages over both rowhouses and solid apartment blocks. It is a great pity this design of Wright's was not executed.

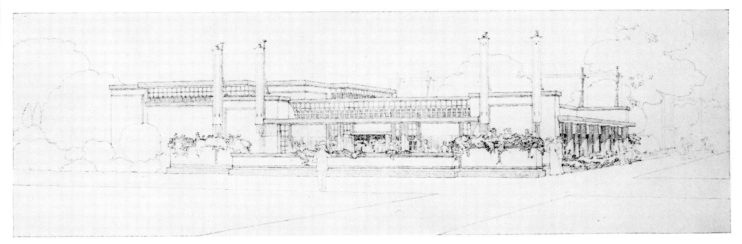

133. LARKIN COMPANY PAVILION, JAMESTOWN EXPOSITION, JAMESTOWN, VA. 1907. PER-SPECTIVE.

134. PEBBLES AND BALCH DECORATING SHOP, 1107 LAKE ST., OAK PARK, ILL. 1907. (Demolished.)

135. BURTON J. WESTCOTT HOUSE, 1340 EAST HIGH ST., SPRINGFIELD, OHIO, 1907.

Two exceptions to the more usual cruciform Prairie house type. The Westcott house is a large example and the Horner a small one of a type in which the main block is nearly square in plan, or at least appears to be so.

136. L. K. HORNER HOUSE, 1331 SHERWIN AVE., CHICAGO, ILL. 1908.

137.

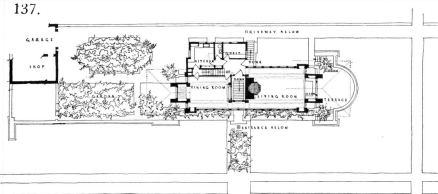

F. F. TOMEK HOUSE, 150 NUTTALL RD., RIVERSIDE, ILL. 1907.

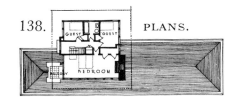

138.　　　　　PLANS.

With raised living floor and entrance below, the long ship-like form of the Tomek house is anchored at the center by the chimney and the small bedroom storey above.

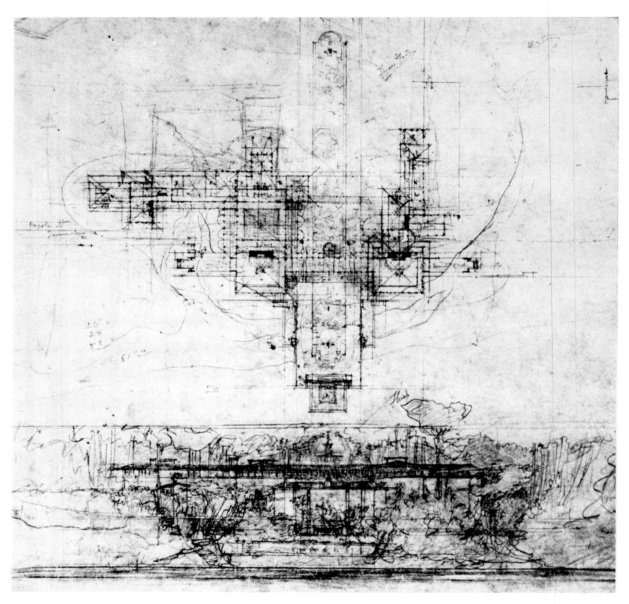

139. PROJECT: HAROLD MC CORMICK HOUSE, LAKE FOREST, ILL. [1907]. HOLOGRAPH PLAN
AND ELEVATION STUDY.

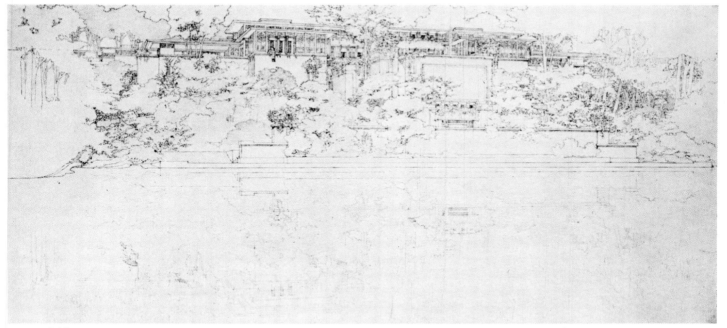

140. PERSPECTIVE OF LAKE FRONT.

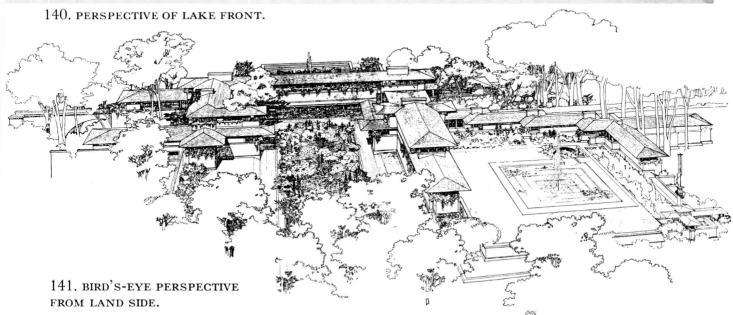

141. BIRD'S-EYE PERSPECTIVE
FROM LAND SIDE.

PROJECT: HAROLD MC CORMICK HOUSE, LAKE FOREST, ILL. [1907].

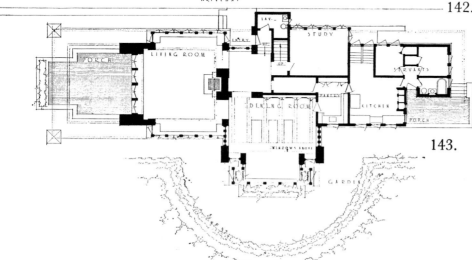

DRIVEWAY

143.

142. E. E. BOYNTON HOUSE, 16 EAST BLVD., ROCHESTER, N. Y.

The Boynton house has a type of plan which is extended chiefly along one axis, at right angles to the street. Later owners have glazed the porches. The Evans house, however, square in plan, is extended in composition to crown the hill slope by the flanking porch and porte cochère on either side.

144. ROBERT W. EVANS HOUSE, 9914 LONGWOOD
DR., CHICAGO, ILL. 1908.

145. DINING ROOM.

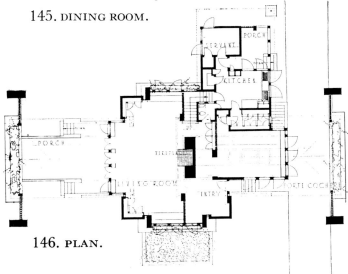

146. PLAN.

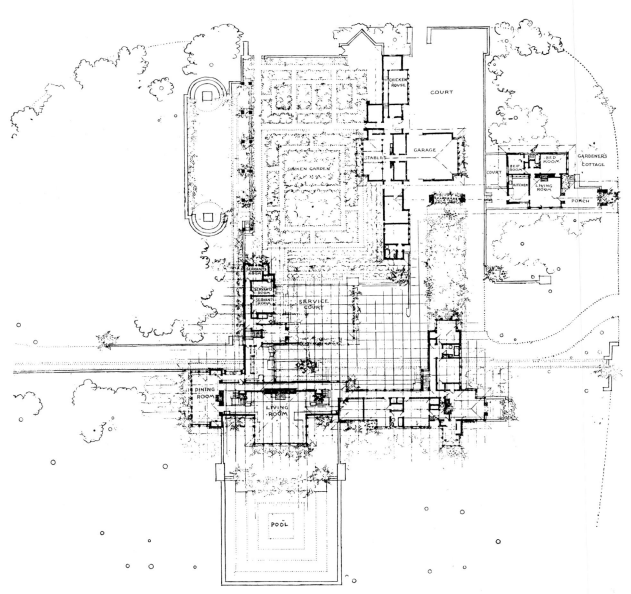

147. AVERY COONLEY HOUSE, 300 SCOTTSWOOD RD., RIVERSIDE, ILL. 1908. ESTATE PLAN.

148. AVERY COONLEY HOUSE, SCOTTSWOOD RD., RIVERSIDE, ILL. 1908. ORIGINAL GARDEN FRONT.

149. AVERY COONLEY HOUSE, 300 SCOTTSWOOD RD., RIVERSIDE, ILL. 1908. GARDEN FRONT WITH ADDED PERGOLA. Wood beams with bronze-metal trimming.

150. AVERY COONLEY
HOUSE, 300 SCOTTS-
WOOD RD., RIVERSIDE,
ILL. 1908. MASTER'S
WING.

The driveway enters
the courtyard at the
rear of the house un-
der the bridge to the
right of the master's
wing.
The ornament of the
upper walls is partly
of incised lines in the
plaster and partly of
inset coloured tiles.

151. DETAIL OF WALL
PATTERN.

152. AVERY COONLEY
HOUSE, 300 SCOTTS-
WOOD RD., RIVERSIDE,
ILL. 1908. LIVING ROOM.

153.   TERRACE.

The sloping ceilings,
stripped with wood and
pierced by grilles for
overhead lighting, are
the most striking ele-
ments in this spacious
Coonley house living
room.

154. ISABEL ROBERTS HOUSE, 603 EDGEWOOD PL., RIVER FOREST, ILL. 1908.   155. PLANS.

One of the most perfect of the early houses is that for Miss Roberts. The "utility room", as it came to be called later, with the heater, is above ground; the kitchen is small and skilfully laid out; the sweep of space is like that in the large Willitts house from the dining room, across below the gallery and in front of the living room fireplace, and out on to the balancing porch. The original plaster has since been replaced with brick veneer by later owners of the house.

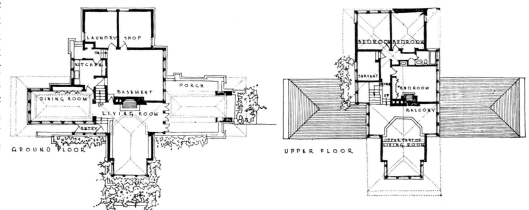

156. ISABEL ROBERTS HOUSE, 603 EDGEWOOD PL., RIVER FOREST, ILL. 1908. LIVING ROOM.

The first *Ladies' Home Journal* project proposed a two-storey living room between a lower library and dining room and in the large Dana house of 1903 several rooms were carried high. This was the first example of such dramatic vertical extension of space in a small house.

157. E. A. GILMORE HOUSE, 120 ELY PL., MADISON, WIS. 1908. Known as the "Airplane House."

158. FRANK J. BAKER HOUSE, 507 LAKE AVE., WILMETTE, ILL. 1909.   159. PLANS.

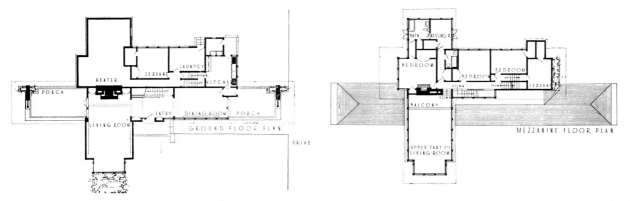

The tall living room of the Isabel Roberts house is here associated with a larger asymmetrical plan. The stopping of the long horizontal eaves and bands of windows against the high living room wing and its great vertical bay produces a most effective composition.

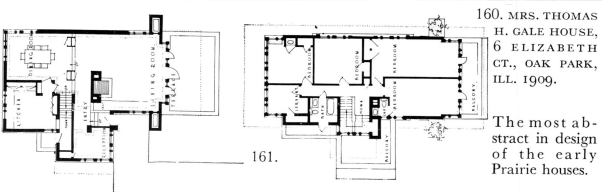

161.

160. MRS. THOMAS
H. GALE HOUSE,
6 ELIZABETH
CT., OAK PARK,
ILL. 1909.

The most ab-
stract in design
of the early
Prairie houses.

162. MEYER MAY
HOUSE, 450 MAD-
ISON AVE., S. E.,
GRAND RAPIDS,
MICH. 1909.

The May house
is of interest for its
copper - sheathed
window detail.
The Ingalls house
was always in-
tended to have
painted trim, as
the detailing in-
dicates.

163. J. KIBBEN
INGALLS HOUSE,
562 KEYSTONE
AVE., RIVER FOR-
EST, ILL. 1909.

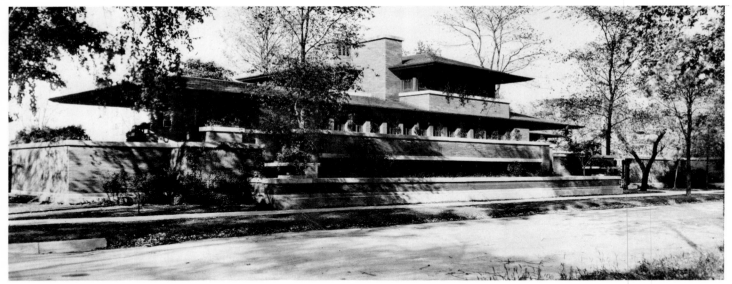

164. FREDERICK C. ROBIE HOUSE, 5757
WOODLAWN AVE., CHICAGO, ILL. 1909.

The raised living
floor, the radical plan,
the long decklike bal-
conies and the superb
masonry of the Robie
house make it one of
Wright's finest works.
The intersection of
planes in space is al-
most as abstract, des-
pite the hip
roof, as at
the Gale house, and
the "lift" of the balco-
nies and eaves is such
as to suggest, as much
as the Gilmore house,
an airplane.

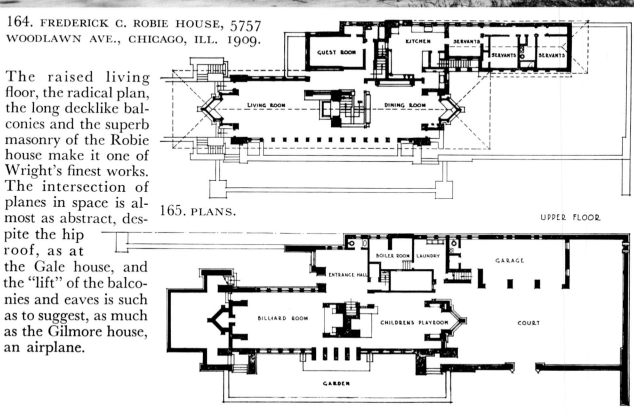

165. PLANS.

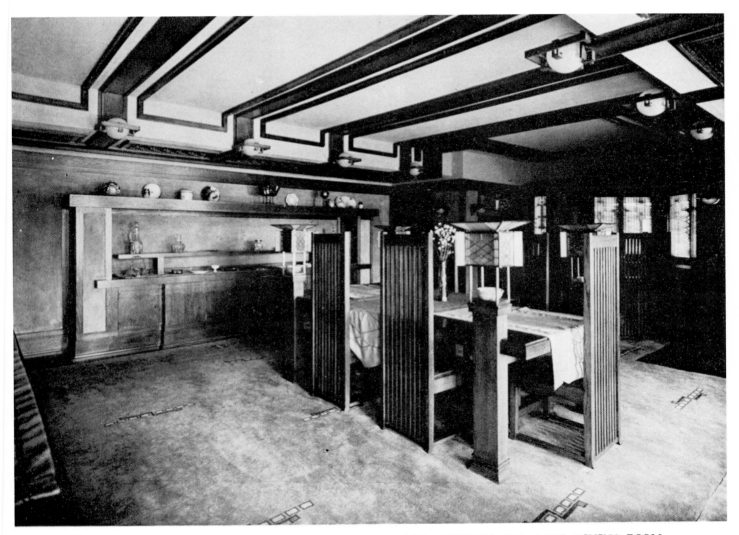

166. FREDERICK C. ROBIE HOUSE, 5757 WOODLAWN AVE., CHICAGO, ILL. 1909. DINING ROOM.

The Robie interiors have been maintained by the Chicago Theological Seminary with all their original furniture and fittings. The very architectural character of much of Wright's early furniture is evident in the dining room table with its corner lighting standards. The specially woven rugs which, together with the upholstery and hangings, completed the somewhat forest-like harmonies of these years can be well seen here. The wood of the furniture is usually identical with that of the trim.

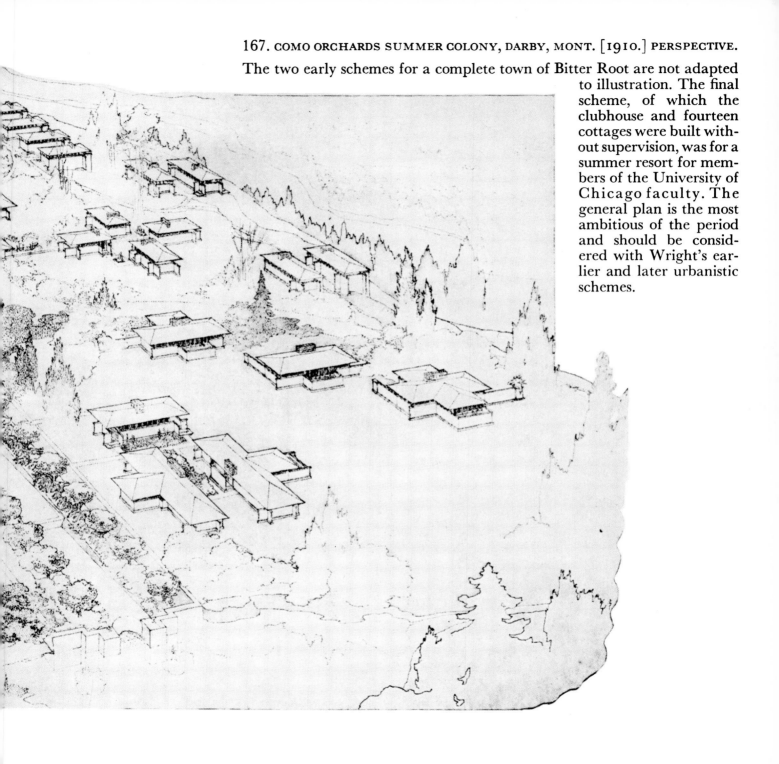

167. COMO ORCHARDS SUMMER COLONY, DARBY, MONT. [1910.] PERSPECTIVE.

The two early schemes for a complete town of Bitter Root are not adapted to illustration. The final scheme, of which the clubhouse and fourteen cottages were built without supervision, was for a summer resort for members of the University of Chicago faculty. The general plan is the most ambitious of the period and should be considered with Wright's earlier and later urbanistic schemes.

168. CITY NATIONAL BANK BUILDING. WEST STATE ST. AND SOUTH FEDERAL AVE., MASON CITY, IOWA. 1909.

The Mason City Bank 169. CITY NATIONAL BANK BUILDING is a remarkable exam-AND HOTEL. WEST STATE ST. AND ple of real monumen-SOUTH FEDERAL AVE., MASON CITY, tality properly scaled IOWA. 1909. GROUND FLOOR PLAN. to a small prairie city. Unfortunately it has now been altered almost beyond recognition by store fronts cut in the lower walls.

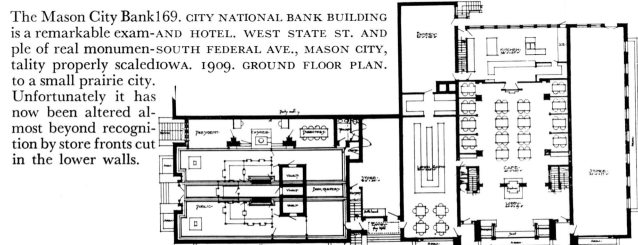

170. HOTEL, WEST STATE ST. AND SOUTH FEDERAL AVE., MASON CITY, IOWA. 1909.

171. CITY NATIONAL BANK BUILDING AND HOTEL, WEST STATE ST. AND SOUTH FEDERAL AVE., MASON CITY, IOWA, 1909. THIRD FLOOR PLAN.

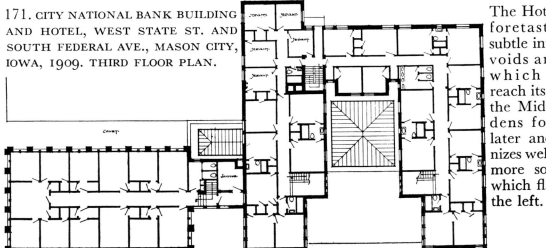

The Hotel gives a foretaste of the subtle interplay of voids and solids which was to reach its climax in the Midway Gardens four years later and harmonizes well with the more solid bank, which flanks it on the left.

This is one of the most important unexecuted projects of the period of the Prairie houses.

First projected in 1901, the Lexington Terrace scheme for large-scale middle class housing was revived in 1909 with somewhat simplified facades. Two ranges of apartments were set back to back with an open passage between. The inner apartments opened on the large interior court. The scheme was an advance over Francisco Terrace.

172. PROJECT: LEXINGTON TERRACE, CHICAGO, ILL. 1909.

173. PLAN.

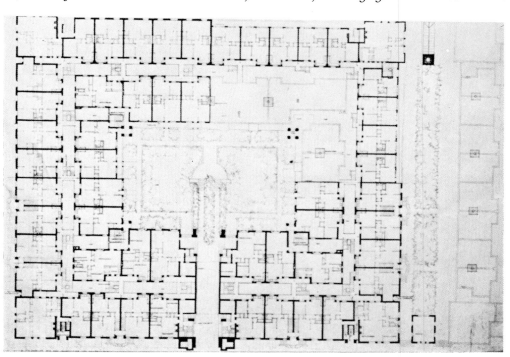

174. TALIESIN I, SPRING GREEN, WIS. 1911.   175. PLAN.

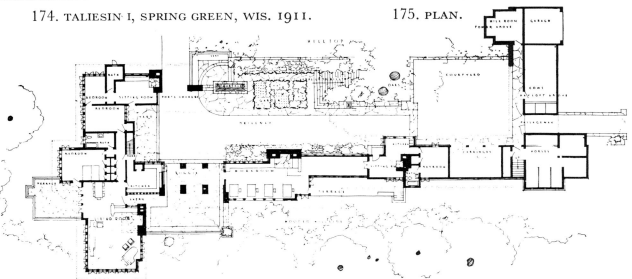

176. TALIESIN II, SPRING GREEN, WIS. 1914. THE GARDEN.

Originally Taliesin was quite small, but it was replaced on a larger scale after the 1914 fire. House and garden alike have grown continuously and are still growing.

The interiors of Taliesin
from the first were rich
with the art of the Orient,
not introduced as some-
thing alien, but built into
and up to in all aspects of
the design.

177. DINING GROUP, LIVING
ROOM.

178. ENTRANCE LOGGIA.
TALIESIN I, SPRING GREEN,
WIS. 1911.

The late Prairie houses as a group are less interesting than those before 1910, nor were there many of them. The best, such as the Angster house, are more like Taliesin itself than like the earlier houses, with very open plans and rather solid massive exteriors. The Angster house, like many of the houses of this decade, is so set among trees it cannot be adequately photographed.

It is unfortunate that the Booth house, erected in 1915, is but a pale shadow of the original project. This remarkable design, illustrated on the opposite page, has an extraordinary plan, whirling out on bridges over the ravines, yet knit together by the great richly surfaced block of the tall living room. Like the earlier McCormick project, this, although effectively unexecuted, belongs in the canon of Wright's major domestic work.

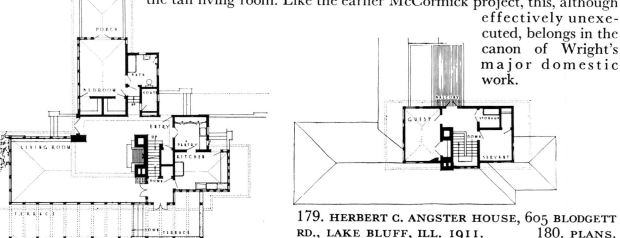

179. HERBERT C. ANGSTER HOUSE, 605 BLODGETT RD., LAKE BLUFF, ILL. 1911.   180. PLANS.

181. PROJECT: SHERMAN M. BOOTH HOUSE, RAVINE BLUFFS,
GLENCOE, ILL. 1911.

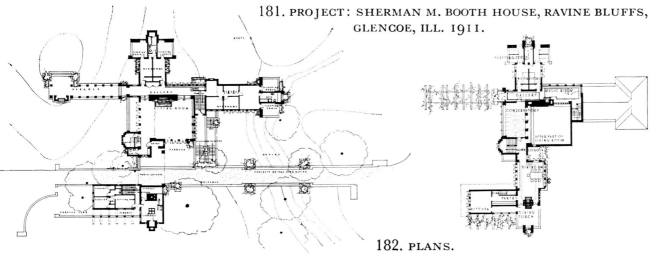

182. PLANS.

183. PROJECT: AVERY COONLEY KINDERGARTEN, RIVERSIDE, ILL. 1911.

184. AVERY COONLEY PLAYHOUSE, 350 FAIRBANKS RD., RIVERSIDE, ILL. 1912. INTERIOR.

185. AVERY COONLEY PLAYHOUSE, 350 FAIRBANKS RD., RIVERSIDE, ILL. 1912.

186. PLAN.

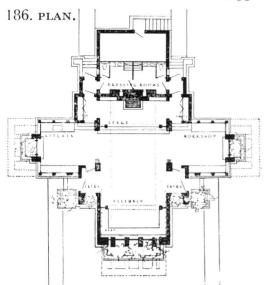

The Coonley kindergarten project was as ambitious and important as the Booth house project. Fortunately the smaller executed playhouse preserves with little loss its virtuosity of poised planes and balanced masses. This sort of design goes back to the Yahara Boat Club project of 1902 and leads immediately into the vastly greater complexity of the Midway Gardens. The interior is somewhat heavier and more architectural in its membering than those before 1910, as if with increasing penetration of interior and exterior space Wright sought to realize an identity of scale outside and inside his buildings of this decade.

187. PROJECT: PRESS BUILDING, SAN FRANCISCO, CAL. [1912]. Model of isolated tower.
188. PERSPECTIVE. With link to Tower Building.

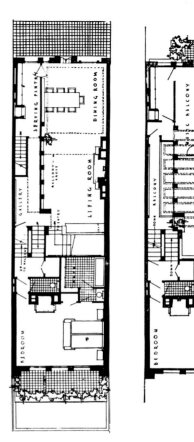

190. SECOND AND THIRD FLOOR PLANS.

PROJECT: FRANK LLOYD WRIGHT HOUSE, GOETHE ST., CHICAGO, ILL. [1911]. PERSPECTIVE. 189.

The ground floor of the house would have contained an entry and Wright's offices. But the chief interest lies in the vertical flow of space at the rear between the second and third storeys.

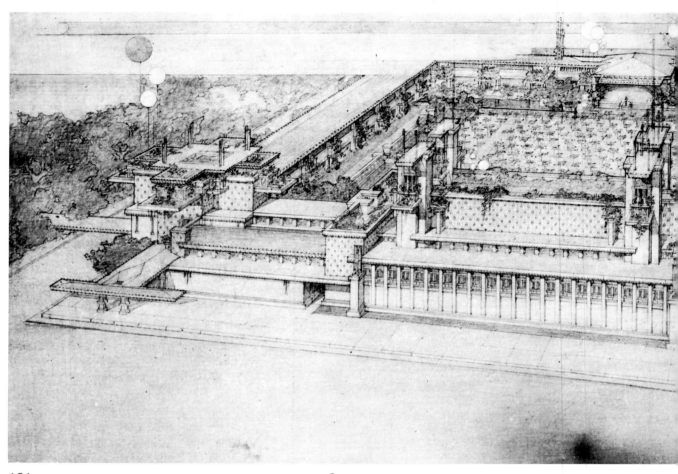

191. MIDWAY GARDENS, COTTAGE GROVE AVE. AT 60TH ST., CHICAGO, ILL. 1914.

After hardly a decade of life the Midway Gardens, ruined by Prohibition, were destroyed in 1923. Fortunately they can be fairly clearly recreated from drawings and photographs. The birdseye perspective shows the tall restaurant building against the street, the open space beyond set with outdoor tables and flanked by raised and covered terraces, and at the rear the orchestra shell. The section should help more than a plan to make the scheme clear, while many photographs display the various aspects of the large and complex whole as it was in its heyday.

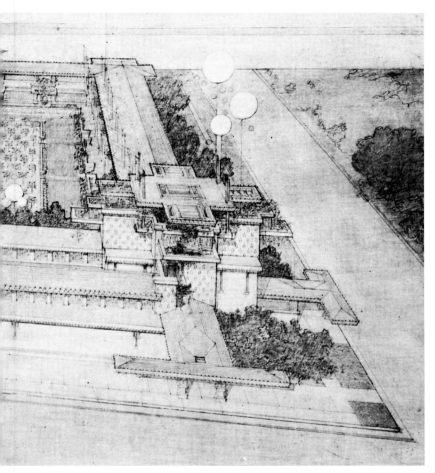

With the Midway Gardens Wright's work arrives at a richness and complexity of architectural form only prepared for in earlier work. Nowhere was interior and exterior space more elaborately interwoven and freely composed, while the ornamental effects are of endless variety and novelty. Concrete blocks provide surfaces of abstract repeating patterns which were to be once more much utilized in the California work of the twenties. Sculpture and wall paintings designed by Wright parallel the most advanced forms of European painters, barely known at this time in America through the Armory Show. And the open frames of the tower tops, a sort of linear sculpture of space, reach forward to aesthetic concepts hardly imagined abroad at this date. But, alas, the luxury, the gaiety, and the utilization of the outdoors had a sophistication for which the urban world of Chicago was not prepared twenty five years ago.

192. MIDWAY GARDENS, COTTAGE GROVE AVE. AT 60TH ST., CHICAGO, ILL. 1914. SECTION.

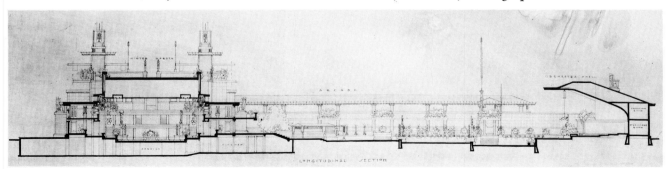

193. MIDWAY GARDENS, COTTAGE GROVE AVE. AT 60TH ST., CHICAGO, ILL. 1914.

194. MIDWAY GARDENS, COT-
TAGE GROVE AVE. AT 60TH ST.,
CHICAGO, ILL. 1914. STREET
FRONT. 195. UPPER TERRACES.

The detail of the brickwork and
the patterned concrete blocks
shows the underlying solidity
and seriousness behind the festive trappings. The roof terraces
show the virtuosity of architectural form and ornament at its
finest and most expansive.

196. MIDWAY GARDENS, COTTAGE GROVE AVE. AT 60TH ST., CHICAGO, ILL. 1914. INTERIOR.

197. DINING ROOM FURNITURE. 198. WIRE FURNITURE.

The wire furniture designs, like the metal furniture of the Larkin Building, indicate Wright's wide interest in materials.

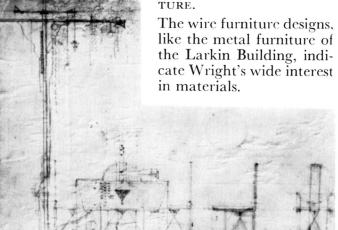

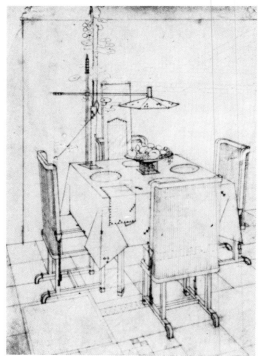

199. FRANCIS W. LITTLE HOUSE, "NORTHOME," R.F.D. 3,
WAYZATA, MINN. 1913- .

200. PLAN.

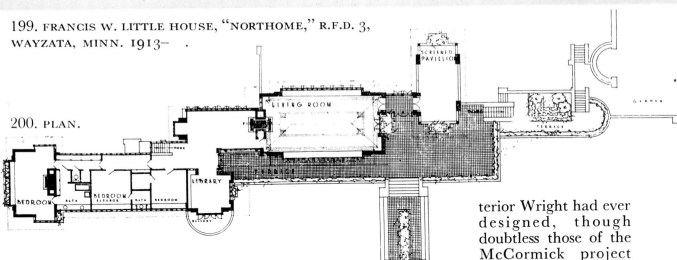

The great extension of the Little house and the surrounding trees make it impossible to photograph as a whole. The exterior view overleaf shows that the arches of the project were omitted in execution. This is effectively a one-storey house, but the dining room and kitchen are below on the left.

The great living room, illustrated on the second page following, is the most spacious domestic interior Wright had ever designed, though doubtless those of the McCormick project might have been similar. Characteristically the height is measured for the observer by the projection at transom level, while the external pitch of the roof is echoed in the slanting planes at the sides of the ceiling.

200A. FRANCIS W. LITTLE HOUSE, "NORTHOME," R.F.D. 3, WAYZATA, MINN. 1913–

200B. FRANCIS W. LITTLE HOUSE, "NORTHOME," R.F.D. 3, WAYZATA, MINN. 1913–   . LIVING ROOM.

201. EMIL BACH HOUSE, 7415 SHERIDAN RD., CHICAGO, ILL. 1915.
202. PLANS.

The Bach house uses the square plan which was a frequent alternative to more articulated types in the Prairie period. But in this later period, when Wright was active on larger edifices, the membering of the small houses is often somewhat heavy. The projecting trellises are most successful elements of detail.

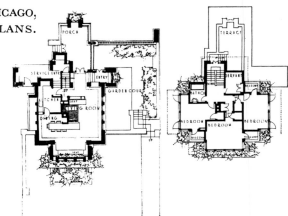

203.   204.

A. D. GERMAN
WAREHOUSE,
RICHLAND CEN-
TER, WIS. [1915]
(NEVER COM-
PLETED).

Finer than the
patterned blocks
of the Midway
Gardens are
those of this
Warehouse. They
face the top
storey which was
for cold storage.

205. PROJECT: AMERICAN SYSTEM READY-CUT DUPLEX FLATS. 1915.   206. PLANS.

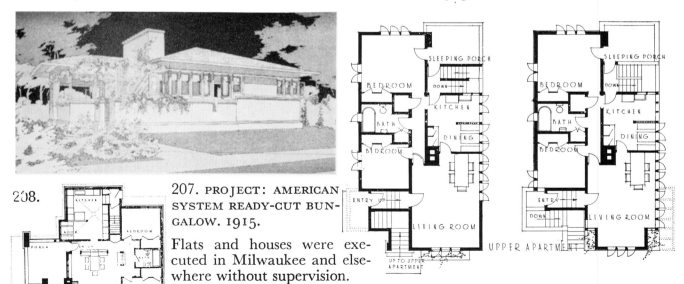

208.

207. PROJECT: AMERICAN
SYSTEM READY-CUT BUN-
GALOW. 1915.

Flats and houses were executed in Milwaukee and elsewhere without supervision.

209. JOSEPH J. BAGLEY HOUSE, LAKEVIEW AND CEDAR AVES., GRAND BEACH, MICH. 1916.

The group of summer cottages at Grand Beach designed in the middle of the decade are quite different from the cottages of the opening of the century at Delavan and White Lakes. The breadth and boldness of composition, curiously formal yet very simple, and the Taliesin-like treatment of the wood and plaster make these among the most agreeable of Wright's smaller houses. The parti of the Vosburgh house (next page) resembles that of the Isabel Roberts house, while that of the Bagley house has, at much smaller scale, something of the pavilion treatment of the McCormick project. Unfortunately the sites make photographs difficult to obtain.

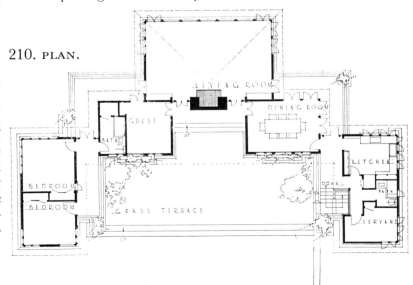

210. PLAN.

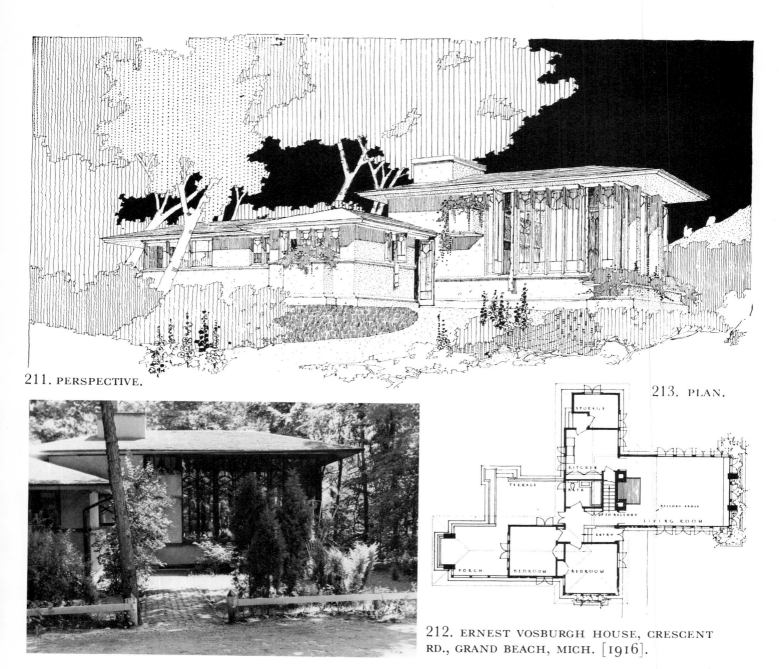

211. PERSPECTIVE.

213. PLAN.

STORAGE

KITCHEN

TERRACE

BATH

UP TO BALCONY

BALCONY ABOVE

LIVING ROOM

ENTRY

PORCH

BEDROOM

BEDROOM

212. ERNEST VOSBURGH HOUSE, CRESCENT RD., GRAND BEACH, MICH. [1916].

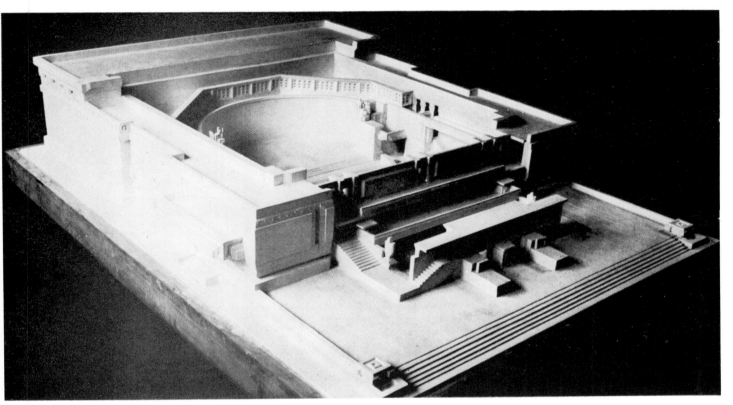

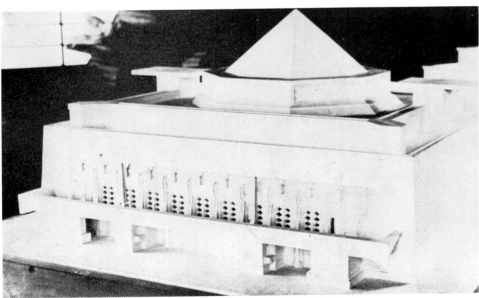

214. PROJECT: ALINE
BARNSDALL THEATER,
OLIVE HILL, SUNSET
BLVD., LOS ANGELES,
CAL. [1920].
MODEL CUT OPEN.

Work on Barnsdall
project began about
1915.

215. PROJECT: MOV-
ING PICTURE THEATER,
GINZA, TOKIO, 1918.
MODEL.

216. HENRY J. ALLEN HOUSE, 255 ROOSEVELT BLVD., WICHITA, KAN. 1917. GARDEN.

The lovely garden of the Allen house, around which the wings of the house, the garage and a wall form an enclosure, is doubtless a Western version of the garden courts of Wright's contemporary houses built in Japan, of which photographs are today unobtainable. Certainly the L-shaped plan, with one low wing for the living room, is rather new, and emphasizes the enclosed garden rather than the crossing of axes at the core of the houses before 1910. Reflecting pools are henceforth an important feature of Wright's larger houses of succeeding decades.

217. HENRY J. ALLEN HOUSE, 255 ROOSEVELT BLVD., WICHITA, KAN. 1917.   218. PLANS.

The heavy rough-surfaced brickwork of these years has less elegance than that of the two preceding decades. But it accords with the larger scale and the firmer articulation of the architectural elements. The rear tower was not executed as designed.

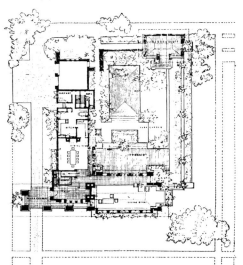

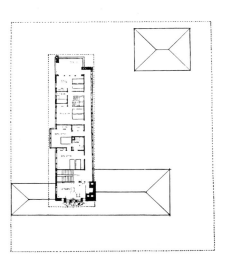

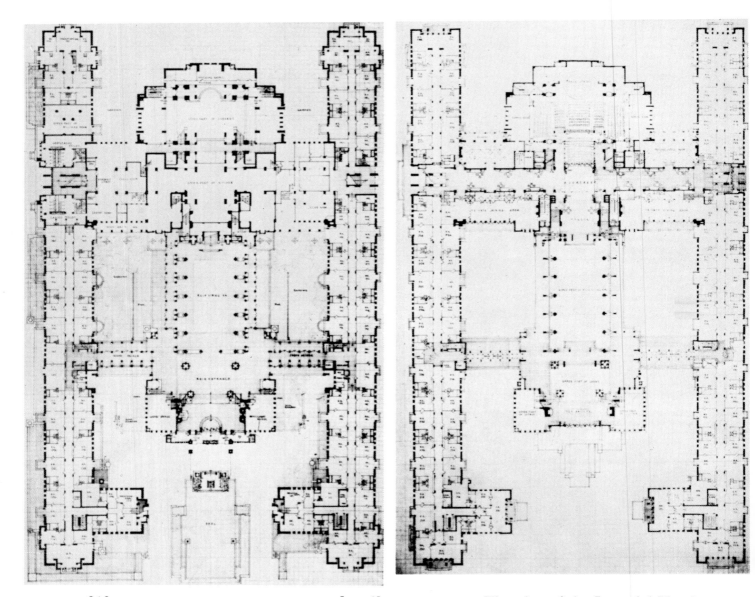

219. IMPERIAL HOTEL, TOKIO, JAPAN, [1916]–1922. PLANS. The plan of the Imperial Hotel forms a great H with the large open public rooms in the thick cross bar and the small bedroom units in the side wings.

220. IMPERIAL HOTEL, TOKIO, JAPAN, [1916]– 1922.

The garden courts with their useful pools of water and their terraces for outdoor service are protected from the streets by the high side wings.

221. TEA TERRACE.

222. IMPERIAL HOTEL, TOKIO, JAPAN, [1916]–1922. GENERAL VIEW.

The monumental scale of the Hotel can be grasped by comparing this and the preceding view with the exterior details which follow.

223. IMPERIAL HOTEL, TOKIO, JAPAN, [1916]–1922. GARDEN COURT.

Water and evergreens are as important as brick and lava in the composition of the exterior.

224. IMPERIAL HOTEL, TOKIO, JAPAN, [1916]–1922. EMPEROR'S
ENTRANCE.

225.
226.
STRUCTURAL
DIAGRAMS.

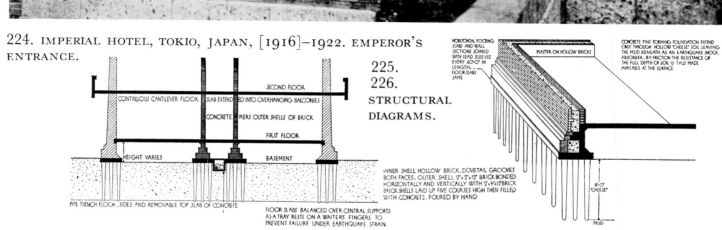

SECOND FLOOR

CONTINUOUS CANTILEVER FLOOR — SLAB EXTENDED INTO OVERHANGING BALCONIES

CONCRETE PIERS. OUTER SHELLS OF BRICK

FIRST FLOOR

HEIGHT VARIES   BASEMENT

PIPE TRENCH FLOOR, SIDES AND REMOVABLE TOP SLAB OF CONCRETE

FLOOR SLABS BALANCED OVER CENTRAL SUPPORTS
AS A TRAY RESTS ON A WAITER'S FINGERS TO
PREVENT FAILURE UNDER EARTHQUAKE STRAIN

HORIZONTAL FOOTING
SLABS AND WALL
SECTIONS JOINED
WITH LEAD SLEEVES
EVERY 60'-0" IN
LENGTH.
FLOOR SLABS
SAME

PLASTER ON HOLLOW BRICKS

CONCRETE PINS FORMING FOUNDATION EXTEND
ONLY THROUGH HOLLOW "CHEESE" SOIL, LEAVING
THE MUD BENEATH AS AN EARTHQUAKE SHOCK
ABSORBER. BY FRICTION THE RESISTANCE OF
THE FULL DEPTH OF SOIL IS THUS MADE
AVAILABLE AT THE SURFACE

INNER SHELL HOLLOW BRICK, DOVETAIL GROOVES
BOTH FACES. OUTER SHELL 2"x7"x12" BRICK BONDED
HORIZONTALLY AND VERTICALLY WITH 2"x9"x12"BRICK
BRICK SHELLS LAID UP FIVE COURSES HIGH THEN FILLED
WITH CONCRETE. POURED BY HAND

8'-0"
"CHEESE"

MUD

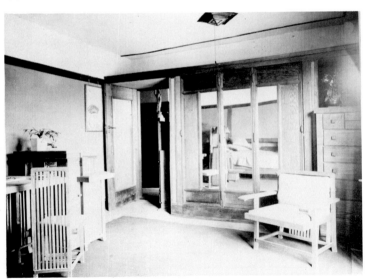

229. BEDROOM.   230. BEDROOM.

228. IMPERIAL HOTEL, TOKIO, JAPAN, [1916]–1922.
Details of the abstract lava sculpture of the exterior.

231. IMPERIAL HOTEL, TOKIO, JAPAN, [1916]. –1922. LOBBY.

Those who have not seen the vast, richly decorated public rooms of the Hotel find them hard to understand in photographs. The lobby in its materials and spatial composition is closely related to the exterior treatment.

232.   BALLROOM.

With its open balconies the lobby is an enlarged version of the Midway Gardens interior. The subordinate spaces leading off in various directions suggest admirably that this is the core of the circulation of the whole structure. The great trusses of the ballroom are elaborately decorated with abstract designs in colour. The carved lava panels represent conventionalized peacocks. Of these there are eight altogether.

233. PROJECT: ODAWARA HOTEL, NAGOYA, JAPAN. [1917].

234. JIYU GAKUEN SCHOOL, TOKIO, JAPAN. 1921.

The Odawara Hotel project is more Japanese than the Imperial in its delicately articulated structure. The setting on the hillcrest would have been particularly effective. The group of buildings at the Jiyu Gakuen School are Wright's most considerable Japanese work after the Imperial. The wood and plaster construction is more conventionally Wrightian and forms a good background for the delicate and varied native flora. The moderate scale is well established in the structural members.

235. "HOLLYHOCK HOUSE," SUNSET AND HOLLYWOOD BLVDS., EDGEMONT ST. AND VERMONT AVE., LOS ANGELES, CAL. 1920. 236. PLAN.

Wright had met Miss Barnsdall before leaving for Japan and work on the designs for her Olive Hill house and other projects went on parallelly with the building of the Imperial Hotel whenever Wright came on brief trips to America in these years. The house design was essentially complete with the revisions dated 1918, but construction fell in the last Japanese years.

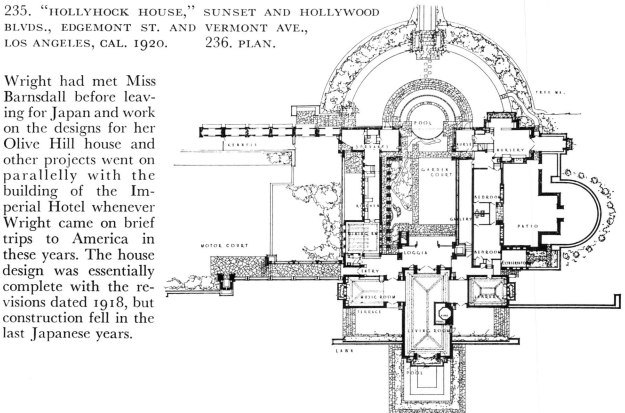

237. "HOLLYHOCK HOUSE," SUNSET AND HOLLYWOOD BLVDS., EDGEMONT ST. AND VERMONT AVE., LOS ANGELES, CAL. 1920. COURT.

238. "HOLLYHOCK HOUSE," SUNSET AND HOLLYWOOD BLVDS., EDGEMONT ST. AND VERMONT AVE., LOS ANGELES, CAL. 1920. SIDE VIEW.

239.   LIVING ROOM.

The superb Olive Hill site permitted the great solid masses of the exterior of the house to stand clean against the Sierra Madre mountains to the north.

240. "HOLLYHOCK HOUSE," LOS ANGELES, CAL. 1920.
VIEW FROM BELOW.   241. DINING ROOM.

ALINE BARNSDALL RESIDENCE A., HOLLYWOOD BLVD.
AND EDGEMONT ST., LOS ANGELES, CAL. 1920.   242.

243. PROJECT: EDWARD H. DOHENY RANCH DEVELOPMENT, SIERRA MADRE MOUNTAINS, NEAR LOS ANGELES, CAL. 1921.

During the Japanese years Wright had spent some t'me each year in Los Angeles working on the Barnsdall commissions and the decade of the twenties opens with a series of important projects and executed works in California. The largest project for a vast development in the Sierra Madre mountains was already to make use of the textile block process.

More significant than the construction and plans of the individual Doheny houses is the general layout by which the mountains north of Los Angeles would have been enhanced by the romantic variety and strategic placing of many separate structures rather than ruined by the chaotic and unplanned developments which were already taking place in Hollywood. But like Wright's important earlier projects for large-scale residential developments this and the contemporary Desert Valley project and the Tahoe Lake Summer colony unfortunately came to nothing. Its possibilities can only be glimpsed in the remaining general perspectives, such as that illustrated here.

244. PROJECT: MERCHANDISING BUILDING, LOS ANGELES, CAL. 1921.

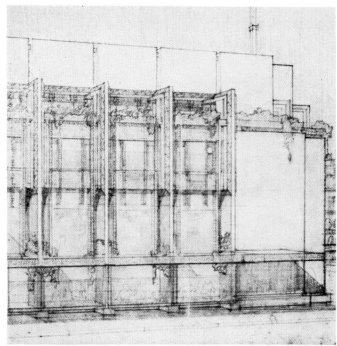

During 1921 Wright also made designs for California in more conventional concrete construction. In the store project the chief interest is the clean surface, twenty years later become commonplace in Los Angeles commercial building, and the way natural light is brought down into the shopwindows behind a sheltering slab.

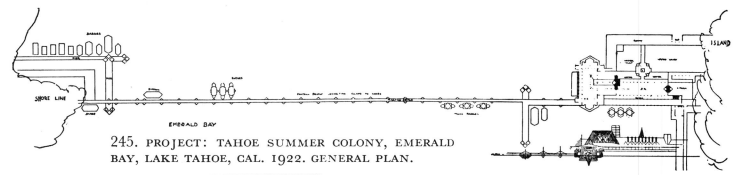

245. PROJECT: TAHOE SUMMER COLONY, EMERALD
BAY, LAKE TAHOE, CAL. 1922. GENERAL PLAN.

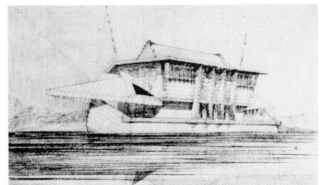

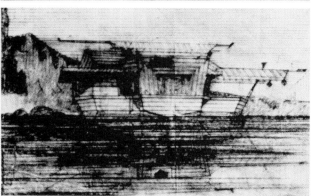

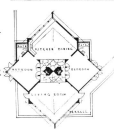

248. FAMILY
BARGE.

247. BARGE FOR
TWO.

246. BIG TREE TYPE CABIN.

Some families were to be housed
in cabins on land, more in
houseboats moored in the lake:
a new sort of summer resort.

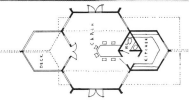

249. MRS. GEORGE MADISON MILLARD HOUSE, 645 PROSPECT CRESCENT, PASADENA, CAL. 1923.

The first to be designed of the California textile block houses was Mrs. Millard's "La Miniatura" in its unusual site at the bottom of a ravine. The entrance is on the middle level at the rear of the three-storey house. The dining room opens on the terrace at the level of the reflecting pool. The two-storey living room opens on the projecting gallery above. Services and bedrooms—reached by a gallery above the living room—are at the rear. The simplicity and compactness of the plan and composition scheme with the bold extension of space inward, outward and upward of the living room are very parallel to the early projects of Le Corbusier, first coming to execution in the same year. But the evident thickness of the textile block walls, their patterned surfaces and sparkling penetrations make the visual result entirely different, as does the intimate relation to the site and the luxurious planting.

250.
ENTRANCE.

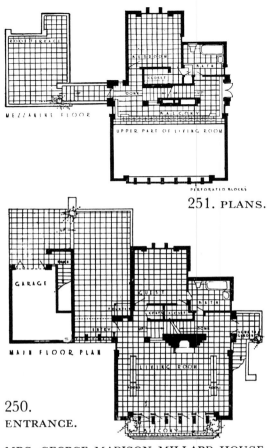

251. PLANS.

MRS. GEORGE MADISON MILLARD HOUSE,
645 PROSPECT CRESCENT, PASADENA, CAL. 1923.

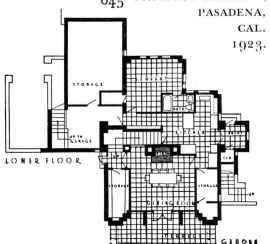

254. MRS. GEORGE MADISON MILLARD
HOUSE, 645 PROSPECT CRESCENT,
PASADENA, CAL. 1923.   DETAIL.

252. LIVING ROOM.   253. LIVING ROOM.

The way the perforated blocks ani-
mate the interior with points of light
repeats at small scale the spatial penetrations between the piers of the front
windows and around the fireplace
above and below the gallery. The antique furniture which Mrs. Millard
had on sale is unfortunately not very
appropriate to the setting the interiors provide.

255. DR. JOHN STORER HOUSE, 8161 HOLLYWOOD BLVD., LOS ANGELES, CAL. [1923].

256. PLANS.

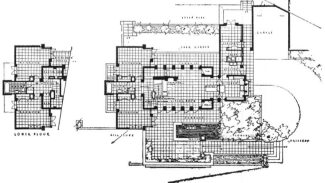

This elegant pavilion has not so happy a site as "La Miniatura"; but the composition is looser and freer with changes of height in the silhouette due to the varying internal heights of the different rooms and terraces.

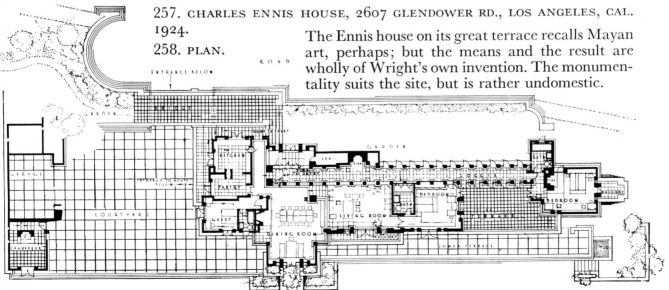

257. CHARLES ENNIS HOUSE, 2607 GLENDOWER RD., LOS ANGELES, CAL.
1924.
258. PLAN.

The Ennis house on its great terrace recalls Mayan art, perhaps; but the means and the result are wholly of Wright's own invention. The monumentality suits the site, but is rather undomestic.

259. SAMUEL FREEMAN HOUSE, 1962 GLENCOE WAY, LOS ANGELES, CAL. 1924. DINING ROOM.

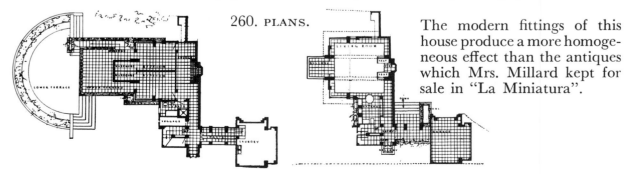

260. PLANS.

The modern fittings of this house produce a more homogeneous effect than the antiques which Mrs. Millard kept for sale in "La Miniatura".

261. SAMUEL FREEMAN HOUSE, 1962 GLENCOE WAY, LOS ANGELES, CAL. 1924.

The hillcrest sites of Hollywood are magnificent to look out from, but they make it hard to photograph the exteriors.

262.
LIVING ROOM.

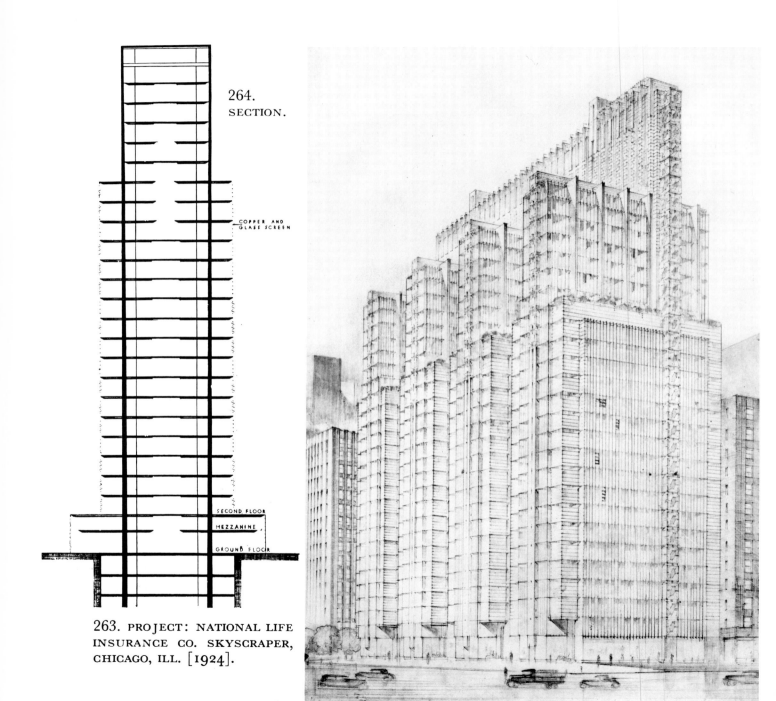

264.
SECTION.

COPPER AND
GLASS SCREEN

SECOND FLOOR
MEZZANINE
GROUND FLOOR

263. PROJECT: NATIONAL LIFE
INSURANCE CO. SKYSCRAPER,
CHICAGO, ILL. [1924].

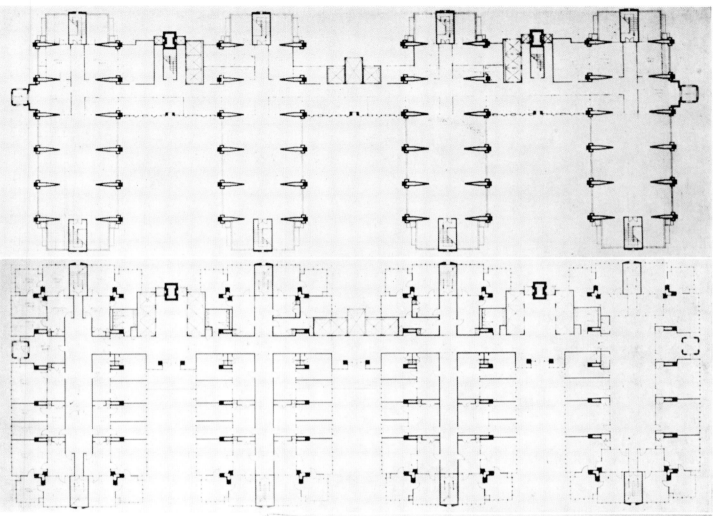

265. PROJECT: NATIONAL LIFE
INSURANCE CO. SKYSCRAPER,
WATER TOWER SQ., CHICAGO,
ILL. [1924].
Plan of 1st to 17th floors. (27th
floor at top.)
266. OFFICE INTERIOR.

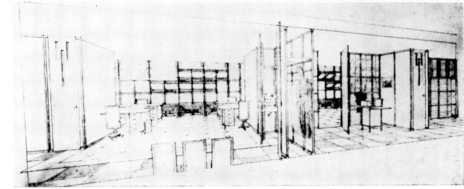

267.   PROJECT: NAKOMA COUNTRY CLUB, MADISON, WIS. [1924].

268.
PLAN.

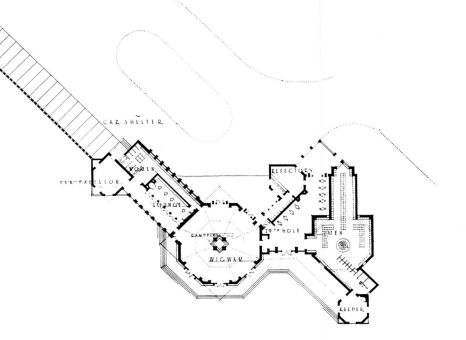

As the Nakoma Country Club was to occupy the historic Winnebago Indian Camping Ground site, Wright echoed in the form of the main roof, as in some of the Tahoe cabins a few years before, the pitch of a wigwam. It is one of the rare instances of Wright's specific inspiration from an artistic form of the past.

269. TALIESIN III, SPRING GREEN, WIS. 1925–

271. PLAN.

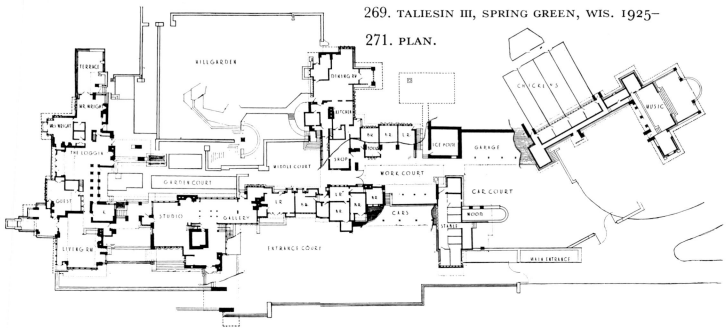

273. TALIESIN III, SPRING GREEN, WIS. 1925–   . LIVING ROOM.
Above the low ceiling bands at either side rise the slanting planes, differentiated by varied wooden stripping, which follow the roof pitch. Japanese screens, Chinese sculpture, and great tree branches complete the furnishing of the room. The furniture is scaled to the architecture.

TALIESIN III,
SPRING GREEN,
WIS. 1925–

The particular character of the living room is carried through into the bedrooms as in all Wright houses. Richly textured fabrics and furs create an effect of luxury as well as comfort.

BEDROOM. 274.

Taliesin is a Northern house and accepts the blanketing snow as gracefully as the hills around. The blue Ming jar is one of the fine oriental objects of art with which Taliesin is surrounded.

ENTRANCE IN WINTER. 275.

276. OCOTILLO DESERT CAMP, FRANK LLOYD WRIGHT WINTER HEADQUARTERS, SALT RANGE, NEAR CHANDLER, ARIZONA. 1927.   277.

The Ocotillo Camp was built for Wright and his assistants to use while designing and building San Marcos-in-the-Desert. The battened lower walls with canvas over wooden frames above provide a sort of supertent admirably suited to the climatic conditions of the desert in winter. Here Wright worked both with a new environment and with materials hardly considered architectural before.

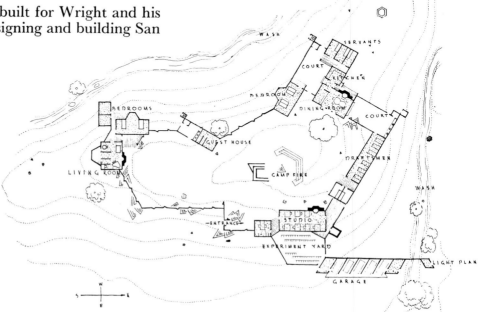

278. OCOTILLO DESERT CAMP, FRANK LLOYD WRIGHT WINTER HEADQUARTERS, SALT RANGE, NEAR CHANDLER, ARIZONA. CABINS.

279. DETAIL.

280. INTERIOR.

Wright's power of simple and elementary abstract composition is boldly illustrated in these tent-cabins.

281. PROJECT: SAN MARCOS-IN-THE-DESERT, NEAR CHANDLER, ARIZONA. [1927.] PERSPECTIVE FROM GATE LODGE.

283. SECTION.

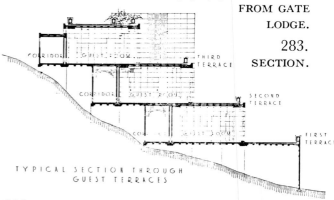

282. TEXTURE MODEL.

The samples of the blocks to be used were set up at the Ocotillo Camp.

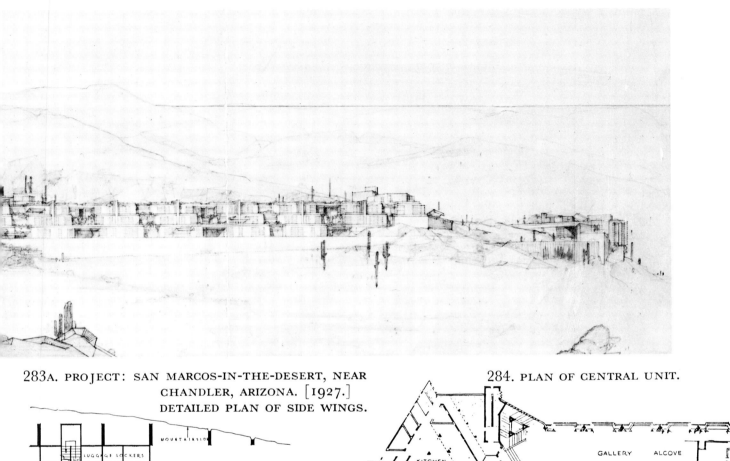

283A. PROJECT: SAN MARCOS-IN-THE-DESERT, NEAR
CHANDLER, ARIZONA. [1927.]
DETAILED PLAN OF SIDE WINGS.

284. PLAN OF CENTRAL UNIT.

The entrance was beneath the main block; above were lobby and lounge, and on top the
dining room and kitchen whose plans are given. Flanking the long facade of the hotel were
the independent houses—two are illustrated on the next page. The second terrace plan indicates how the individual guest balconies were given considerable privacy by interpolated
planting.

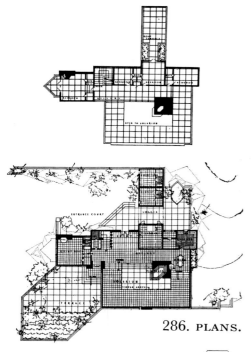

285. PROJECT: OWEN D. YOUNG HOUSE, SAN MARCOS-IN-THE-DESERT, NEAR CHANDLER, ARIZONA. [1927.]

286. PLANS.

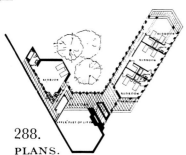

288. PLANS.

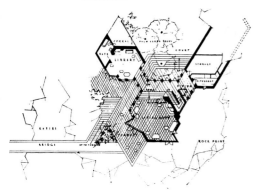

287. PROJECT: WELLINGTON AND RALPH CUDNEY HOUSE, SAN MARCOS-IN-THE-DESERT, NEAR CHANDLER, ARIZONA. [1927.]

The Young project was rather like the Los Angeles houses. But the diagonal placing of the blocks and the use of window lights of the same measure as the blocks were innovations. The Cudney project used the same blocks as the hotel, but its more "reflex" composition makes the inspiration of the Saguaro cactus more evident.

289. DARWIN D. MARTIN HOUSE, DERBY, N. Y. 1927.

290. PLANS.

Built without the architect's supervision, this house is somewhat clumsy in detail compared with the contemporary work at Taliesin. But the rich growth of planting now gives it a grace worthy of Wright, and it is well maintained.

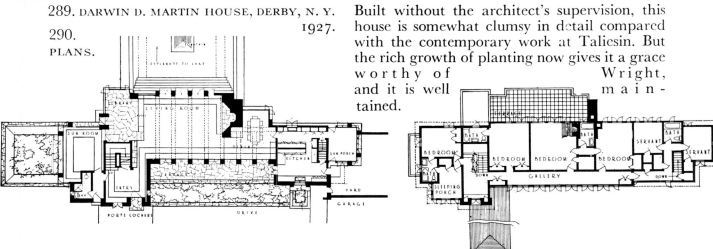

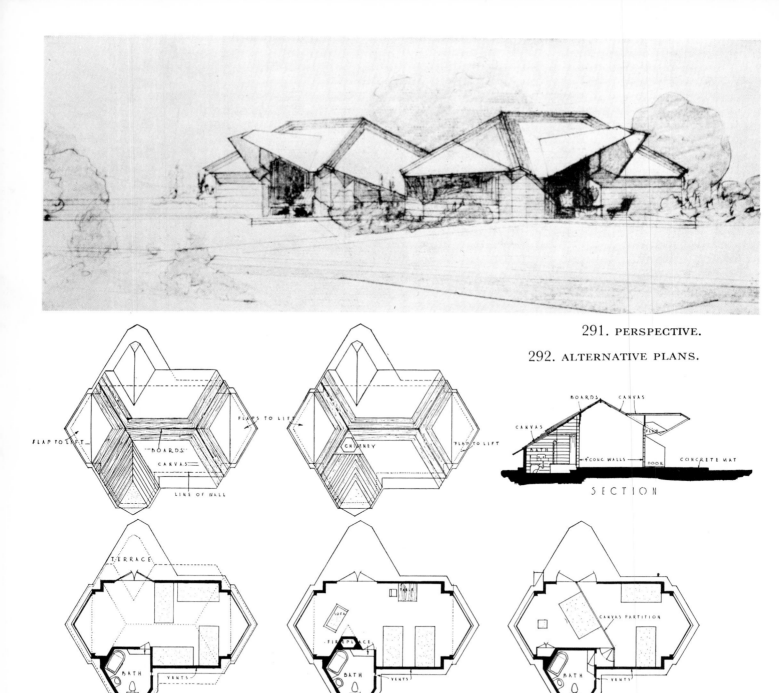

291. PERSPECTIVE.

292. ALTERNATIVE PLANS.

SECTION

PROJECT: SAN MARCOS WATER GARDENS, CHANDLER, ARIZONA. [1927.] TOURIST CABINS.

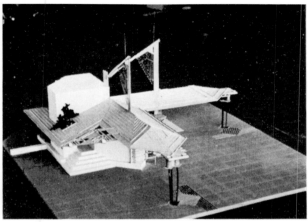

293. PROJECT: VILLAGE SERVICE STATION. 1928. MODEL.

294. PLAN AND SECTION.

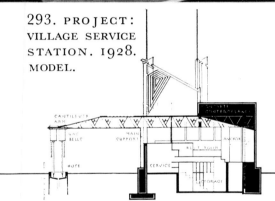

295. PROJECT: ALEXANDER CHANDLER BLOCK HOUSE, CHANDLER, ARIZONA. 1927. 296. PLANS.

The Chandler block houses, based on the Monolith Homes project of 1919, were among the most successful of Wright's small house schemes. Despite their very different construction they lead toward the Usonian houses of today.

297. RICHARD LLOYD JONES HOUSE, 3700 BIRMINGHAM RD., TULSA, OKLA. 1929.   298. PLANS.

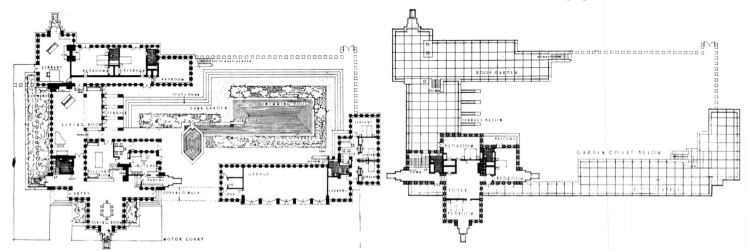

299. RICHARD LLOYD JONES HOUSE, 3700 BIRMINGHAM RD., TULSA, OKLA. 1929. ENTRANCE.

The human figures help to give a true conception of the scale of this house.

300. COURT.

301. RICHARD LLOYD JONES HOUSE, 3700 BIRMINGHAM RD., TULSA, OKLA. 1929.
DINING ROOM.

The remarkable interior effect of the very open construction should be clear.

302.
BILLIARD ROOM.

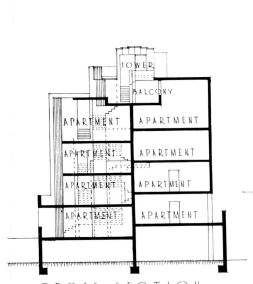

CROSS SECTION

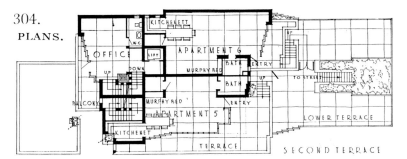

303. PROJECT: ELIZABETH NOBLE APARTMENT HOUSE, LOS ANGELES, CAL. [1929].

This is one of the most remarkable of Wright's many fine unexecuted projects of the twenties. The planning produced what is practically a series of superposed penthouses, each with its own large terrace. The bold contrast of plain concrete surfaces and large open glass areas, through which the cantilevers can be seen, parallels remarkably closely the principles, supposedly so antithetical, of the "international" architects of Europe at this time. But the clarity of the conception and the design is as much the natural product of Wright's genius as the rich elaboration of the projects of the earlier twenties.

304. PLANS.

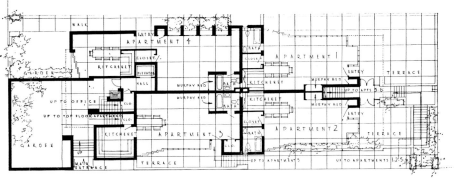

FIRST TERRACE

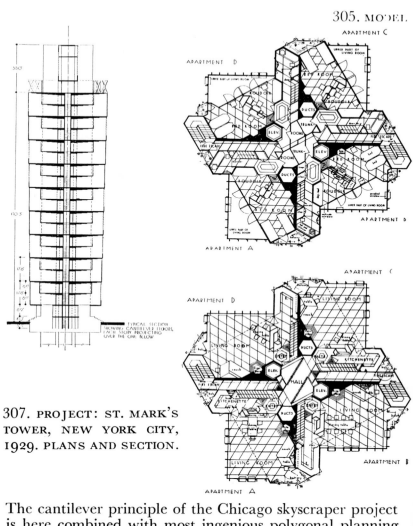

305. MODEL

APARTMENT C

APARTMENT D

APARTMENT A

APARTMENT C

APARTMENT D

APARTMENT B

APARTMENT A

307. PROJECT: ST. MARK'S
TOWER, NEW YORK CITY,
1929. PLANS AND SECTION.

The cantilever principle of the Chicago skyscraper project
is here combined with most ingenious polygonal planning
in a small apartment tower intended for a New York site.
Somewhat similar interlocked duplexes were used a decade
later in the Suntop Homes in Ardmore, while the general
character of the project is repeated in the grouped towers
of the next year for Chicago and the Crystal Heights hotel
project for Washington of 1940.

The grouped apartment towers of the later Chicago project have a wider urbanistic significance than the Noble and St. Mark's Tower apartment projects of the previous year, leading directly to the great Crystal Heights scheme of 1940, which is also unfortunately still only a project.

309. PLANS.

308. PROJECT: GROUPED APARTMENT TOWERS, CHICAGO, ILL. 1930.

It is curious to recall how fantastic these Wright skyscraper projects of the late twenties once seemed. For it should now be evident to almost every one that they were more practical and straightforward in every way than most contemporary skyscraper building.

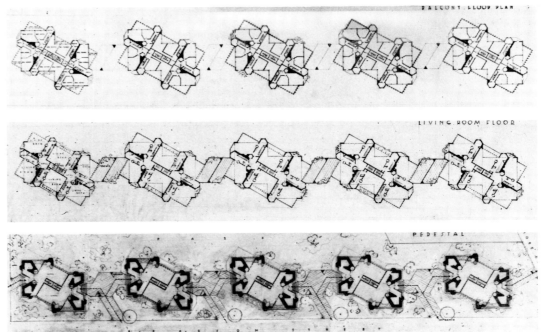

310. PROJECT: "HOUSE ON THE MESA." [1931.] MODEL EXHIBITED AT THE MUSEUM OF MODERN ART, NEW YORK, 1932.

311. PLAN.

When Wright's work was brought into direct conjunction with that of the "international" architects at the Museum of Modern Art exhibition in 1932, how much the "old master" was a master and how youthful his achievement continued to be was made manifest. Four years later the Kaufmann house realized the boldness of this design, but with perfect adaptation to a quite different site. For this project was designed for a Western mesa, while the Kaufmann house was to be cantilevered over an Eastern forest stream.

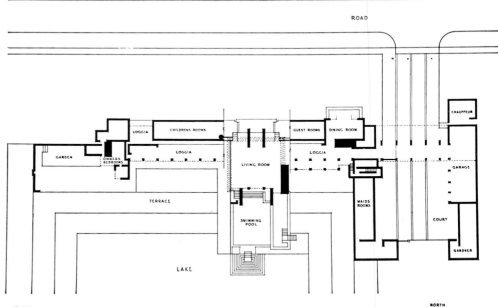

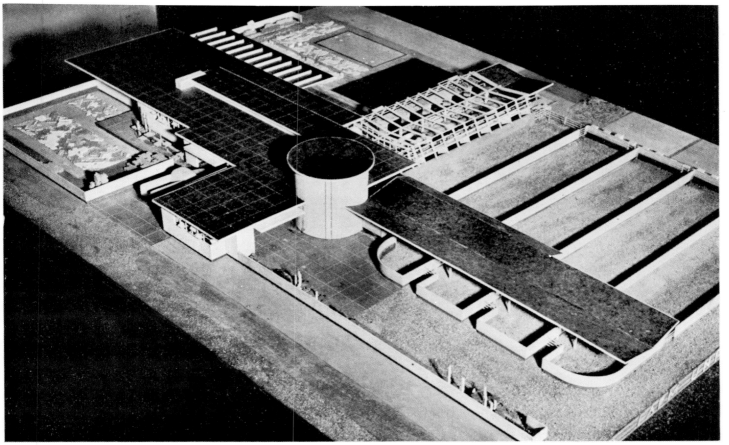

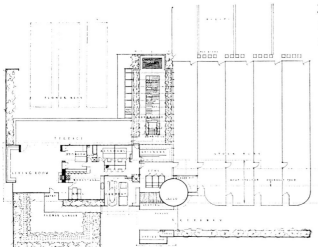

312. PROJECT: WALTER DAVIDSON SHEET STEEL
FARM UNITS. 1932. MODEL EXHIBITED AT
MUSEUM OF MODERN ART. 1940. 313. PLAN.

Wright, always close to the land in thought
sought in these units to bring to the farmer
the advantages of modern architecture in
general and of prefabrication in particular.
The compactness, the rational organization of a complex of dwelling and working
elements, and the relation to road and land
are all worth noting.

314. PROJECT: MALCOLM WILLEY
HOUSE, MINNEAPOLIS, MINN. 1932.
MODEL EXHIBITED AT MUSEUM OF
MODERN ART, 1940.

The Willey project
opens a new cycle of
house designs. The solid
and essentially tradi-
tional construction of
brick and wood is boldly
rethought. The living
quarters are placed on
the upper level. The
particular motif of the
balcony parapet of
lapped siding is one that
was destined to be much
used in later houses.

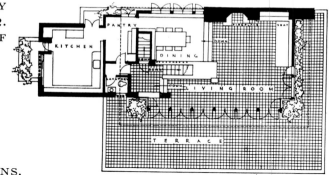

315. PLANS.

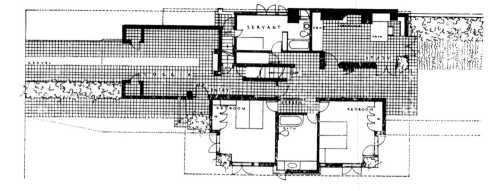

316. MALCOLM WILLEY HOUSE,
255 BEDFORD ST., MINNEAPOLIS,
MINN. 1934.   317. PLAN.

318. LIVING ROOM.
The executed Willey house is at
first sight rather more conventional than the earlier project.

Here for the first time
the space of the
kitchen, now called by
Wright the "work-
space", is joined to that
of the living room.

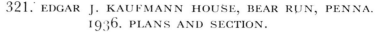

The drama of the "House on the Mesa" is realized in this house over a waterfall. Here the cantilevered floor slabs are anchored to a masonry core and the natural rock.

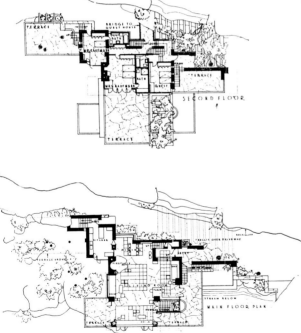

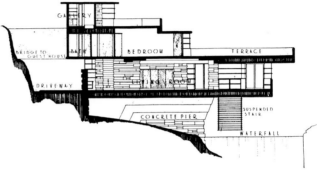

The main storey consists almost entirely of one great room opening out into various subordinate spaces and connected with the stream below by a staircase. The upper floors consist of various individual suites each opening upon its own terrace. The house is very solid to the rear where the masonry walls connect with the natural rock below. But between the parapets and the roof slabs above, the front walls are all of glass set in metal frames. The view on the opposite page from below the waterfall reveals the audacity of the conception; it is unequalled, perhaps, in contemporary architecture and justly one of the most famous modern houses in the world.

322. EDGAR J. KAUFMANN
HOUSE, BEAR RUN, PENNA.
1936. 323. STEPS TO POOL.

The side of the Kaufmann
houses reveals a characteristic plating of horizontals
and verticals, but the composition is richer than
ever, despite the simplicity
of the means. The relation
of the rough ashlar base
to the concrete slabs and
parapets is clearer in the
small view.

324. EDGAR J. KAUF-
MANN OFFICE, KAUF-
MANN DEPARTMENT
STORE, 400 FIFTH
AVE., PITTSBURGH,
PENNA., 1937.

325. CYPRESS PLY-
WOOD MURAL: DETAIL.

The walls above and
to the left of the desk.

328. PROJECT: CAPITAL JOURNAL BUILDING, SALEM, OREGON, 1931. PERSPECTIVE.

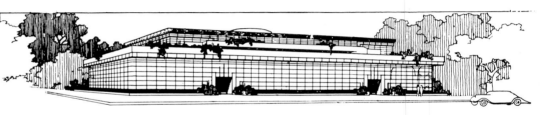

The Capital Journal project was the prototype of the Johnson Building of five years later. There the scheme of hollow concrete piers reinforced with metal tissue and supporting only their own lily-pad-like tops was worked out in theory. The Capital Journal building was not so large and complex and its side walls would have been of metal and glass instead of the brick screens of the Johnson Building.

To test the strength of the new type of piers, one was erected in Racine on the Johnson site in the summer of 1936 and loaded far beyond anything it would ever have to carry.

329.

HALF PLAN
AND
SECTION.

327. S. C. JOHNSON AND SON, INC., ADMINISTRATION BUILDING, 1525 HOWE ST., RACINE, WIS. 1936–1939.

TESTING
SAMPLE PIER,
1936.

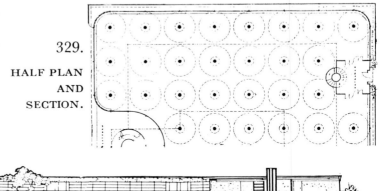

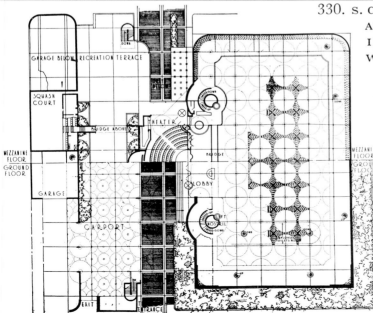

330. S. C. JOHNSON AND SON, INC., ADMINISTRATION BUILDING, 1525 HOWE ST., RACINE, WIS. 331. SECTION OF PIER. 332. PLAN.

The plan and the interior, with the section of a pier, reveal the remarkable construction and the resultant new space composition of this famous building. The special lighting effect is merely suggested.

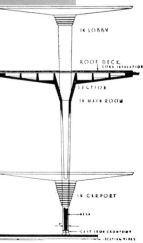

333. S. C. JOHNSON AND SON, INC., ADMINISTRATION BUILDING, 1525 HOWE ST., RACINE, WIS. 1936–1939.

334. ENTRANCE.

The night view reveals more clearly than the day view the bands of glass tubing at the point where a conventional cornice would be expected. This emphasizes that the walls are merely non-supporting screens.

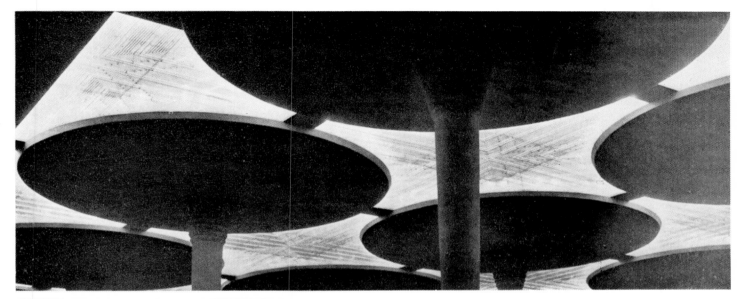

335. S. C. JOHNSON AND SON, INC., ADMINISTRATION BUILD-ING, 1936–1939. EXTERIOR CORNER.   336. CEILING DETAIL.

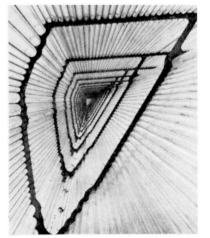

337. VIEW INSIDE BANDS OF GLASS TUBING.
338. VIEW THROUGH INTERIOR WALL OF GLASS TUBES.

The tubing is used internally for translucent walls.

339. HERBERT F. JOHNSON HOUSE, WIND POINT, NORTH OF RACINE, WIS. 1937.

This, according to Wright, is "the last of the Prairie houses". The plan is "zoned", with the living quarters in the center, the masters' rooms in one wing, the children's in another, the service in a third and the guests and garages in a fourth. Much is made of the shallow ravines of the prairie site, so that the wings of the house ride the grassed slopes as if they were floating on waves, lifted by the lightness of the projecting balconies.

340. PLAN.

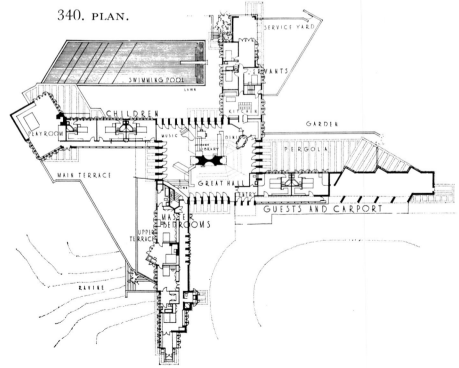

The spiral stair rising to an observatory, the tall chimney and the balconies make the most of the very high space of the central unit of the house, from which the four specialized arms of the plan project in all directions.

341.

HERBERT F. JOHNSON HOUSE, WIND POINT, NORTH OF RACINE, WIS. 1937. LIVING ROOM.

342.

The various functions of the main living space are separated by differences of level and low screens and built-in units of furniture, beneath the clerestoreyed roof, around the central chimney.

343. HERBERT JACOBS HOUSE, 441 TOEPFER ST., WEST-
MORLAND, NEAR MADISON, WIS. 1937.   PLAN. 344.

The Usonian house type appeared first in the Hoult
project of 1936. The executed Jacobs house of 1937 is
practically identical. The house rests on a concrete
floor slab with the heating pipes below. The walls are
of broad boards and sunk redwood battens inside and
out with a core of plywood. The roofs are of crossed
two-by-fours. The brick-walled kitchen and bathroom
rise above the rest of the roof for ventilation. The L-
shaped plan partially encloses the garden on which
both living room and bedrooms open through ranges
of french doors.

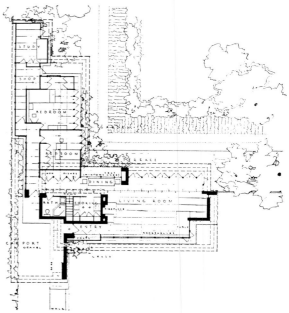

345. HERBERT JACOBS HOUSE, 441 TOEPFER ST., WESTMORLAND, NEAR MADISON, WIS. 1937.
The Rosenbaum house is a larger, more perfect version of the Jacobs house.
346. STANLEY ROSENBAUM HOUSE, RIVERVIEW DR., FLORENCE, ALA. 1939.

347. PAUL R. HANNA HOUSE, 737 CORONADO ST., PALO ALTO, CAL. 1937.   348. COURT SIDE.

349. PAUL R. HANNA HOUSE, 737 CORONADO ST., PALO ALTO, CAL. 1937. LIVING ROOM.

350. DINING ROOM.   351. PLAN.

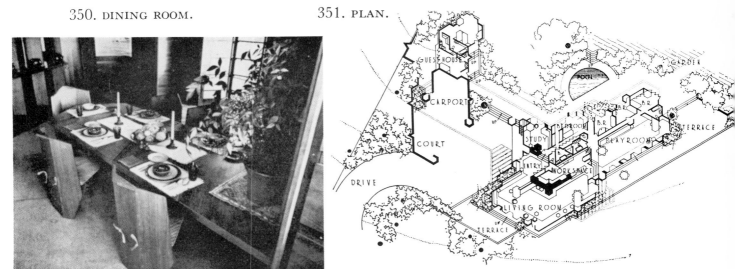

352. TALIESIN WEST, MARICOPA MESA, PARADISE VALLEY,
NEAR PHOENIX, ARIZONA. 1938–   .   353. PLAN.

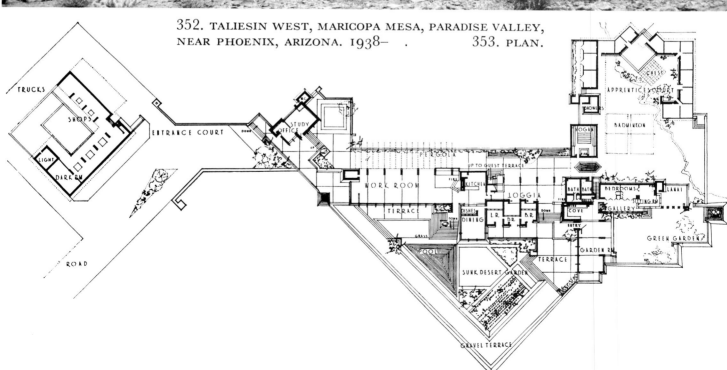

355. TALIESIN WEST, MARICOPA MESA, PARADISE VALLEY, NEAR PHOENIX, ARIZONA. 1938– .
TERRACE.

Above the massive canted base of rough blocks of red desert stone set in concrete, the superstructure is light and tent-like, chiefly canvas screens and wooden louvers held by timber trusses. The rich desert flora forms the chief decoration.

356.   ENTRANCE.

357. TALIESIN WEST, MARICOPA MESA, PARADISE VALLEY, NEAR PHOENIX, ARIZONA. 1938– .
ENTRANCE FROM THE POOL.

The deck chair helps to give the human scale of this remarkable structure. The canvas screens between the wooden trusses can be swung open like those at the entrance to let the air through.

TALIESIN WEST, MARICOPA MESA, PARADISE VALLEY, NEAR PHOENIX, ARIZONA. 1938– .

358. GENERAL LIVING ROOM.

The structure of the trusses over the masonry piers and the lighting effect of the canvas screens can be clearly seen here.

359. MR. WRIGHT'S FIREPLACE.

The variety of the interiors is surprising in this desert camp. The more extended outer portions are light and tent-like above the solid foundation walls. The inner core of the structure is, on the contrary, heavy and cavelike. The monumental scale of the fireplace, the richness of the Oriental works of art, the bold fabrics and the desert flora combine in an interior harmony as fine as that of the Taliesin living room in Wisconsin.

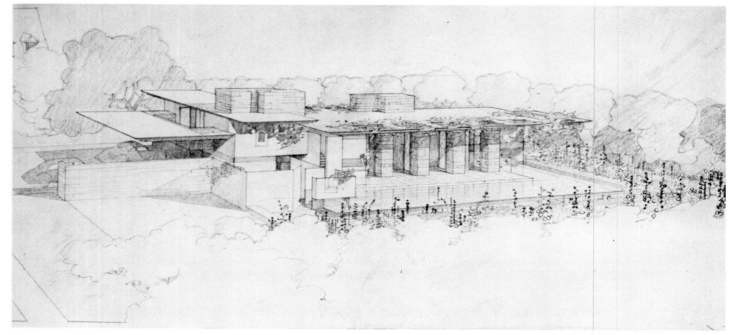

360. PROJECT: *Life* "HOUSE FOR A FAMILY OF $5000–$6000 INCOME." 1938.

361. PLANS.

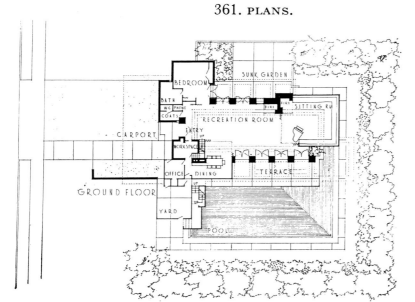

The *Life* house is considerably larger than the Usonian type and makes more use of masonry. The executed Schwartz house follows the *Life* project very closely. The interior is however typical of the interiors of the later thirties, both in large and small houses, in its finished use of structural wood and of fine exposed brick work.

362. BERNARD SCHWARTZ HOUSE, STILL BEND, TWO RIVERS, WIS. 1939.   363. LIVING ROOM.

364. PROJECT: RALPH JESTER (MARTIN J. PENCE) HOUSE, PALOS VERDES, CAL. (HILO, HAWAII). 1938 (1940). MODEL EXHIBITED AT MUSEUM OF MODERN ART, NEW YORK, 1940. 365.

Entirely different from the other houses of the late thirties is this project for a house of plywood. As plywood is strongest when curved, each room is nearly a complete circle of the appropriate size opening on a central covered space. The piers are of rough stone boldly contrasted with the smooth, grained surfaces of the plywood. Such a pattern of curves is wholly new in Wright's architecture and suggests all sorts of possibilities for the future.

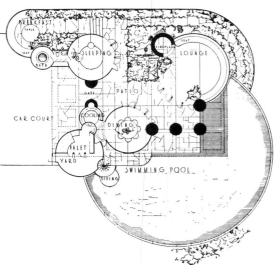

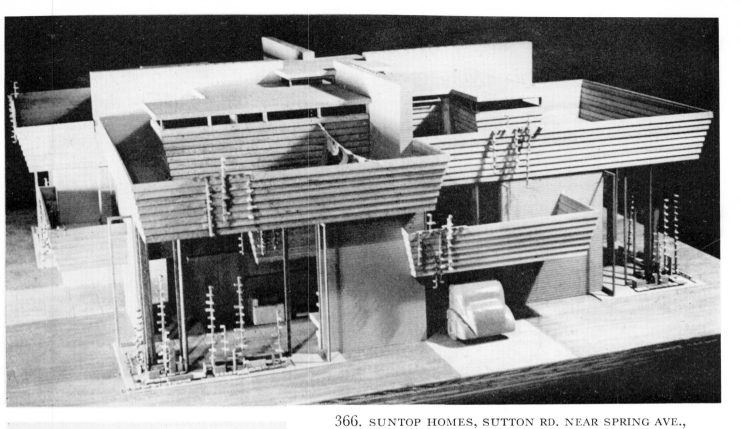

366. SUNTOP HOMES, SUTTON RD. NEAR SPRING AVE.,
ARDMORE, PENNA. 1939. MODEL EXHIBITED AT
MUSEUM OF MODERN ART, NEW YORK, 1940.

367. PLANS,
SECTION.
368. GEN-
ERAL PER-
SPECTIVE.

Only one of
the pro-
jected four
units was
built.

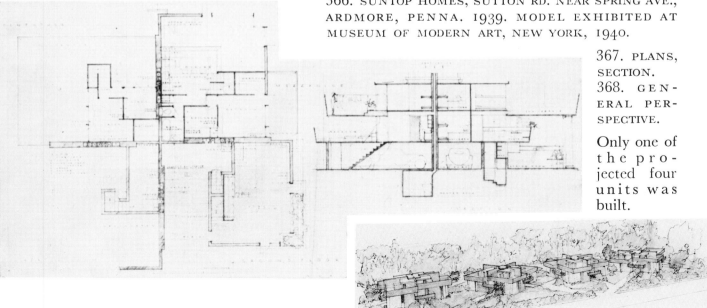

369.

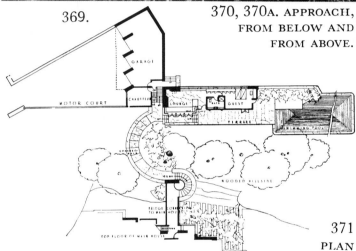

370, 370A. APPROACH, FROM BELOW AND FROM ABOVE.

371 PLAN

EDGAR J. KAUFMANN GUEST HOUSE, BEAR RUN, PENNA. 1939.

Of the same concrete and local stone, the Kaufmann guest house is much quieter than the big house below. But its severity is dramatized by the curved and stepped slab roof of the approach.

372. EDGAR J. KAUF-
MANN GUEST
HOUSE, BEAR RUN,
PENNA. 1939.
POOL AND TERRACE.

The hovering pierced
slab, the convenient
morning bath pool,
and the effective
contrast of rough
ashlar masonry and
sand - rendered ce-
ment are happy fea-
tures of this house.

373. ENTRANCE.

374. PROJECT: GROUP OF SEVEN USONIAN HOUSES, OKEMOS, MICH. 1939. MODEL EXHIBITED AT MUSEUM OF MODERN ART, 1940.

375. KATHERINE WINKLER AND ALMA GOETSCH HOUSE, HULETT RD., OKEMOS, MICH. 1939. PLAN.

Only the Winkler-Goetsch house has been executed.

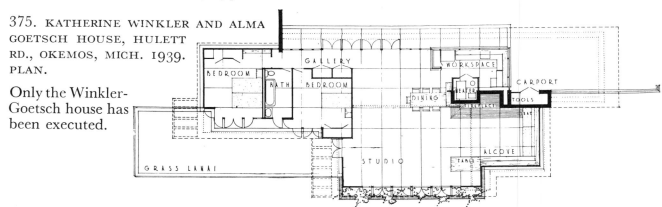

KATHERINE WINKLER AND ALMA GOETSCH HOUSE, HULETT RD., OKEMOS, MICH. 1939.

376.   FRONT VIEW.

377.   REAR VIEW.

This is perhaps the best Usonian house in plan and in elegance of finish. The walls are of redwood inside and out; the ceiling of plywood. Unfortunately the final furnishings had not been installed when the photographs were taken. The partial seclusion of the "workspace" and the area in front of the fireplace from the main living room sweeping from the french doors of the front to the rear is most subtly handled.

378.   INTERIOR.

379. GEORGE D. STURGES HOUSE, 449 SKYWAY
RD., BRENTWOOD HEIGHTS, CAL. 1939.

380. PLAN AND SECTION.

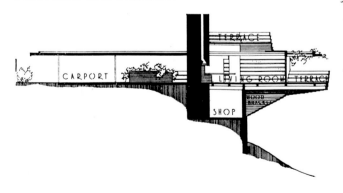

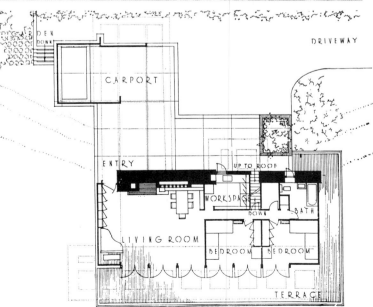

381. STANLEY ROSENBAUM HOUSE, RIVERVIEW DR., FLORENCE, ALA. 1939.   382. LIVING ROOM.   383.

DETAIL
OF
CORNER.

384. SIDNEY BAZETT HOUSE, 101 RESERVOIR RD., HILLSBOROUGH, CAL. [1940].

A California house based, like the Hanna house, on 60°-30° angles but smaller and simpler. The sloping ceiling of the living room effectively enhances the sense of height and direction.

385.
DINING ROOM.

386. SIDNEY BAZETT HOUSE, IOI RESERVOIR RD., HILLSBOROUGH, CAL. [1940].

View from below.

387. LIVING ROOM. The dramatic site on the hill slope is well utilized with an enclosed terrace above between the wings and an open porch toward the view.

388. LLOYD LEWIS
HOUSE, LITTLE ST.
MARY'S RD., LIBERTY-
VILLE, ILL. 1940.

389.   PLANS.
Raised above the damp
river edge, the Lewis
house makes interest-
ing use of varying lev-
els in an effectively one-
storey house with open
ground storey entrance
loggia below the living
room.

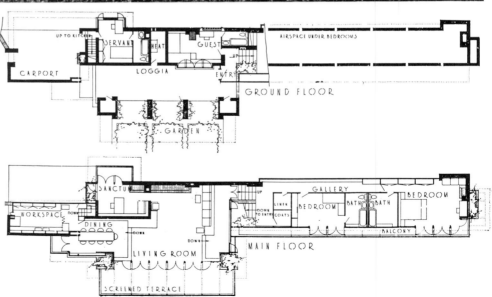

390. BEDROOM WING. The Lewis living room has the handsomest and most harmonious furnishing of any of Wright's later houses in tones of dull brick pink and somewhat yellowed green against the brick and the beautiful cabinet-work of the light wood sheathing. The living room opens on a screened terrace raised up among the trees.

391. LIVING ROOM. LLOYD LEWIS HOUSE, LITTLE ST. MARY'S RD., LIBERTY-VILLE, ILL. 1940.

392. ROSE PAUSON HOUSE, ORANGE RD., PHOENIX, ARIZONA. 1940.

The Pauson house rises on a desert knoll among the cacti against the dark red of Camelback Mountain in the grounds of the Arizona Biltmore Hotel. The base is of blocks of dark red stone set in concrete.

393.

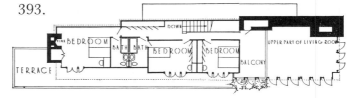

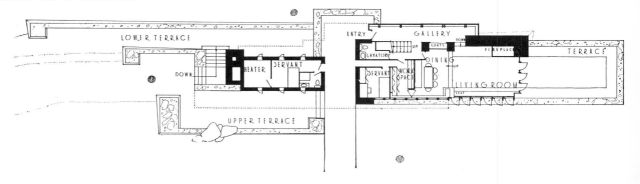

394. ROSE PAUSON
HOUSE, ORANGE RD.,
PHOENIX, ARIZONA.
1940. LIVING ROOM.

The superstructure of the house is of wood like the Usonian houses, the canted parapets of lapped siding skilfully related to the batter of the masonry elements. The tall living room opens on a high terrace toward the chief view through french doors while the other sides of the house are solid to shut out heat and wind and lighted only by slots cut in the sheathing boards. The interior has curtains especially woven by Henning-Rees. Large saguaros have been planted and stone terraces added to the rear since these pictures were taken.

395. VIEW OF LIVING
ROOM TERRACE AND
ENTRANCE FRONT OF
HOUSE.

396. JOHN C. PEW HOUSE, 3650
MENDOTA DR., SHOREWOOD HILLS,
NEAR MADISON, WIS. 1940.

397.
FIREPLACE.

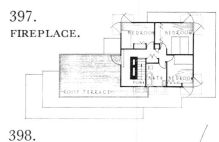

398.
PLANS.

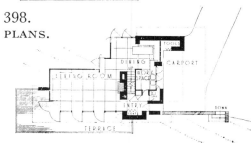

399. PASSAGE.

There is much similarity naturally in the interiors of the houses of the last few years and these two views of the Manson house, which is particularly appropriately furnished, can well stand as typical of many others. The brick and wood of the structural walls form the interior finish. Although the rooms flow together in plan there are always secluded corners, usually a private study as well as the large living-room-dining-room space.

400. STUDY FIREPLACE.

CHARLES L. MANSON HOUSE, 1224 HIGHLAND BLVD., WAUSAU, WIS. 1940.

401. CLARENCE W. SONDERN HOUSE, 3600 BELLEVIEW AVE., KANSAS CITY, MO. 1940.   402. BEDROOM.

A typical Usonian house, unfortunately photographed before the planting was completed. The bedroom illustrates well the character of the sleeping accommodations in these small houses, relatively restricted but well-lit and ventilated and with built-in hanging space and inconspicuous bed frames. The bathrooms are similarly finished but are not large enough to be photographed. Indeed the finish is the same throughout the houses.

403. THEODORE BAIRD HOUSE, SHAYS ST., AMHERST, MASS. 1940.

404. GREGOR AFFLECK HOUSE, BLOOMFIELD HILLS, MICH. IN CONSTRUCTION, 1941. MODEL EXHIBITED AT MUSEUM OF MODERN ART, NEW YORK, 1940.

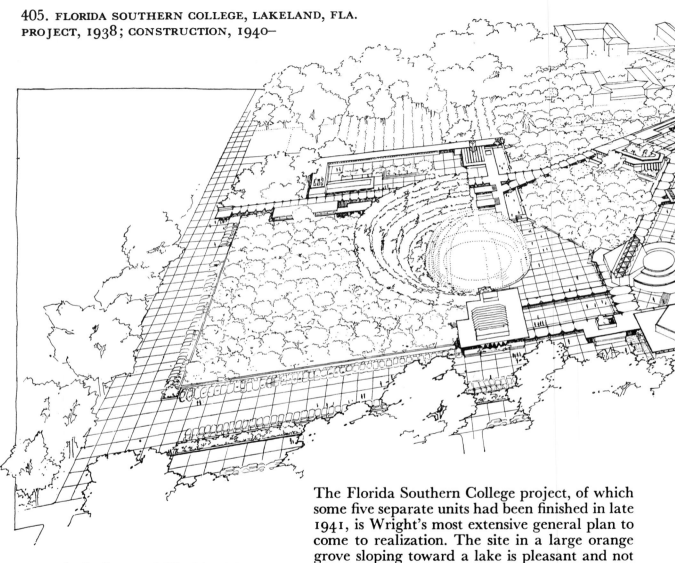

405. FLORIDA SOUTHERN COLLEGE, LAKELAND, FLA.
PROJECT, 1938; CONSTRUCTION, 1940—

The Florida Southern College project, of which some five separate units had been finished in late 1941, is Wright's most extensive general plan to come to realization. The site in a large orange grove sloping toward a lake is pleasant and not untypical of central Florida. The existing orange grove and additional hanging plants and flowers growing out of the buildings should provide the shade and the variety suited to the needs and the possibilities of the climate.

The ample provision for parking and the direct approach to the Theater are conveniences all colleges need today and very few have. Open paved terraces are effectively set before the chief buildings and around the edge.

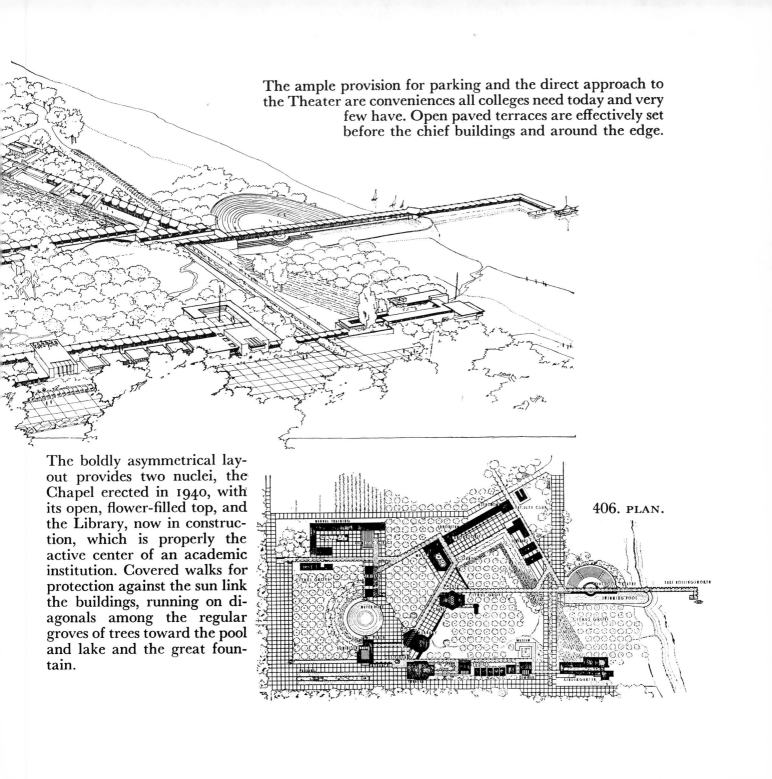

The boldly asymmetrical layout provides two nuclei, the Chapel erected in 1940, with its open, flower-filled top, and the Library, now in construction, which is properly the active center of an academic institution. Covered walks for protection against the sun link the buildings, running on diagonals among the regular groves of trees toward the pool and lake and the great fountain.

406. PLAN.

407. ANN PFEIFFER CHAPEL, FLORIDA
SOUTHERN COLLEGE, LAKELAND, FLA. 1940.

408. PLAN AND
SECTION.

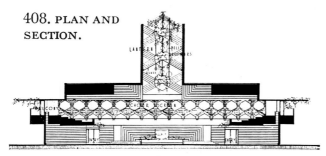

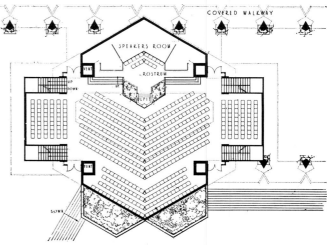

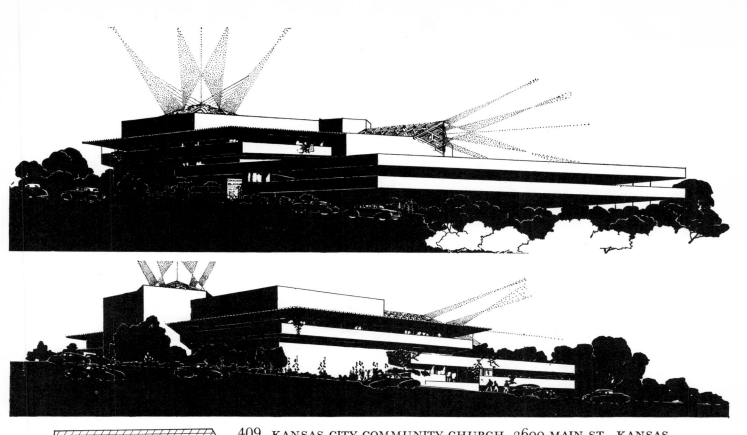

409. KANSAS CITY COMMUNITY CHURCH, 3600 MAIN ST., KANSAS CITY, MO. IN CONSTRUCTION, 1941. PERSPECTIVES.

The drawings of the Kansas City Church, now nearing completion, display the dramatic effect produced by the cantilevered parking terraces. Presumably when it is completed it will also have a refinement and precision of finish comparable to that of the Ann Pfeiffer Chapel in Florida on the opposite page.

410. PLAN AND SECTION.

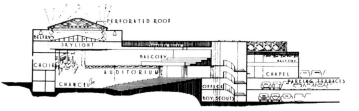

411. PROJECT: CRYSTAL HEIGHTS HOTEL, SHOPS AND THEATER, CONNECTICUT AND FLORIDA AVES., WASHINGTON, D. C. 1940. BIRD'S-EYE VIEW.

The Crystal Heights project is so tremendous that no available general plans make it as intelligible as the bird's-eye view and the general perspective on this page and the next. At the angle of Connecticut and Florida Avenues is a moving picture theater, flanked on either side by tiers of terraces on which shops are arranged. Above is a tremendous parking area, such as is badly needed in all parts of Washington. Extending out onto this terrace on the Connecticut Avenue side are the great public rooms of the hotel. Behind this the towers of the apartment-hotel are arranged in a comma-like cluster. Within their curve is a park area filled with trees. Here at last is urbanism at the proper scale for the twentieth century and an important suggestion for relieving the incredible congestion of present-day Washington.

412. PROJECT: CRYSTAL HEIGHTS HOTEL, SHOPS AND THEATER, CONNECTICUT AND FLORIDA AVES., WASHINGTON, D. C. 1940. GENERAL PERSPECTIVE.

413. PLAN OF TYPICAL HOTEL FLOOR.

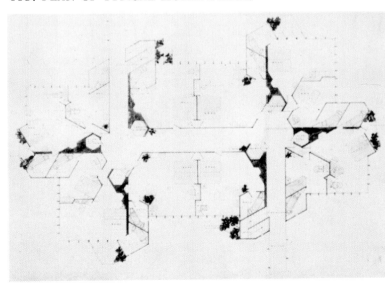

The interlocking hotel suites are the culmination of Wright's polygonal tower planning that began with St. Mark's Tower in 1929. The construction is also of that type, with the floors cantilevered out from a triangular group of interior supports, so that the exterior walls can be all of glass. Elevators and service facilities are at the core, and extraordinarily enough, the core also provides flues for fireplaces in all the larger rooms. The tremendous scale makes detail a matter of irrelevance, but one can imagine a finish comparable to that of the executed Florida Southern College buildings.

Index

Index

References to the Chronological List of Executed Work and Projects, pp. 107-130, are by date (bracketed dates indicate sequence in the Chronological List of items entered there without dates); figure numbers are italicized; sub-entries are cross-references and the word *See* should be understood before them; Wright's houses and house projects are entered under the names of the clients wherever possible.